Dreiser-Mencken
LETTERS

Edited by Thomas P. Riggio

University of Pennsylvania Press · Philadelphia

upp

Dreiser-Mencken LETTERS

The Correspondence of Theodore Dreiser & H. L. Mencken 1907–1945

VOLUME ONE

*Library of Congress Cataloging-in-Publication Data
Dreiser, Theodore, 1871–1945.
    Dreiser-Mencken letters.
    Includes index.
    1. Dreiser, Theodore, 1871–1945—Correspondence.
2. Mencken, H. L. (Henry Louis), 1880–1956—
Correspondence. 3. Authors, American—20th century—
Correspondence. I. Mencken, H. L. (Henry Louis),
1880–1956. II. Riggio, Thomas P. III. Title.
PS3507.R55Z485 1986   810'.9'0052 [B]   85-22506
ISBN 0-8122-8008-3 (set : alk. paper)*

Printed in the United States of America

Designed by Adrianne Onderdonk Dudden

For Milla

Contents

VOLUME ONE

Illustrations ix
Preface xi
Editorial Note xv
Acknowledgments xxi

1

A Receptive Mood (1907–1910)

1

2

I Want to Blaze Out with Some Dreiser Stuff (1911–1914)

55

3

The Country Is in a State of Moral Mania (1915–1918)

175

VOLUME TWO

4
And Now I Sometimes Wonder What More (1919–1923)

321

5
In Brief, Go to Hell! (1924–1926)

505

6
Just a Realist Contemplating Things Realistically (1934–1945)

555

Appendix 1: The Mencken Letters to Helen Dreiser (1945–1949)
721

Appendix 2: Reviews and Reminiscences (1911–1948)
737

Appendix 3: Annotated List of Omitted Letters (1907–1945)
813

Index of Names and Subjects
825

Index of Works by Dreiser and Mencken
839

Illustrations

VOLUME ONE

The young Mencken (ca. 1908)   15

Dreiser and Sara White Dreiser   30

Mencken and George Jean Nathan   49

Dreiser letter: 24 February 1911   61

Mencken the Smart Set *editor*   121

Mencken letter: 2 December 1914   167

Mencken in his Hollins Street study   189

Dreiser caricature with message to Mencken   215

Dreiser in his study   249

Estelle Bloom Kubitz   292

Marion Bloom   294

VOLUME TWO

Helen Richardson   361

Mencken in the backyard at 1524 Hollins Street   461

Mencken at home in Hollins Street   553

Mencken celebrates the end of Prohibition   567

Sara Haardt Mencken   588

Mencken to Dreiser: "Souvenir of the Confederacy"   599

Dreiser viewing portrait with painter Boris Chaliapin   647

Mencken sitting for a portrait with Nikol Shattenstein   648

Dreiser surrounded by nature   661

Mencken surrounded by Nietzsche, Ibsen, and Shakespeare   663

Manuscripts and bust of Dreiser on their way to the University of Pennsylvania   672

Dreiser with S. S. McClure, Willa Cather, and Paul Robeson at the American Academy ceremony, 1944   711

Dreiser: In memoriam   724

Preface

Since the University of Pennsylvania sent me photostats of my letters to you I have arranged them in their places among your letters to me, and have been through the whole series. It is full of interesting stuff and will no doubt edify posterity.—HLM to TD, 23 February 1943

Theodore Dreiser (1871–1945) and H. L. Mencken (1880–1956) began writing to each other in 1907. Their friendship lasted nearly four decades, and the best record of it—the more than 1,200 letters they left—is one of the major exchanges in American literature. When they met for the first time in the spring of 1908, a hackney might still have brought Mencken to Dreiser's editorial office in lower Manhattan, while Dreiser's final Christmas message to Mencken in 1945 alludes to the nuclear bombs that had been dropped on Hiroshima only months before. The issues and events that engaged their considerable energies—including the cause of literary realism, the politics of nativism, "puritanism," two world wars, Prohibition, the struggle against censorship, postwar modernism, and the turmoil of the Great Depression—give their letters historical as well as biographical and literary value.

The two men came to each other with little in common beyond a commitment to writing as a way of life. Partly because of the poor reception of *Sister Carrie* in 1900, Dreiser had put aside fiction, and after 1904 he worked mainly as an editor. But by 1908 he was eager to return to his writing desk. The young newsman Dreiser encountered that year was unknown outside Baltimore, but he was ambitious, talented, and eager to gain a national reputation. Within a decade, they both had succeeded in making large literary reputations for themselves. Many in the generation that came of age just before World War I could agree with F. Scott Fitzgerald who said, in 1918, that "Mencken and Dreiser were the greatest living writers in America." Dreiser became that generation's novelist and Mencken its critic, and they were indelibly linked in the public mind. Their dominance lasted into the twenties and was publicized through Mencken's editorship of two of the most influential popular magazines of the teens and twenties—*Smart Set* and *The American Mercury*.

Mencken knew, almost by instinct, that cultural fable was a by-product of criticism, and Dreiser, who had a gift for self-dramatization, proved a good match for his friend's mythmaking. Together they battled the "puritans," the Comstocks, the "lady critics," the professors, and the "Anglo-Saxons." The legendary cast they gave their early enterprises obscured a good deal of what went on behind the scenes. Legends, we know, have a way of blurring the details of personal experience, even as they put in focus the intangible core of historical event. The mass of letters the two men sent each other is a reminder of how social conditions may affect private relations as well as public postures. Though they differed greatly in personality and style, they also shared much, particularly a joy in the adversary roles they cultivated as national rebels. They defined themselves aggressively against the American grain and made a name together as intellectual bad boys, ready always to take on the prevailing literary, moral, or political gospel of the day.

At first, Dreiser helped place his younger protégé in posts that would win him a wide audience; and then Mencken, the increasingly powerful critic, hitched his star to Dreiser and realism, and became adviser cum editor cum tactician in a campaign to win the novelist an intelligent reading. As Mencken later wrote Burton Rascoe, in defense of his critical practice: "next to [Robert I.] Carter, I learned most from Percival Pollard—particularly the value, to a critic, of concentrating on a few men. Pollard used Ambrose Bierce; I used Dreiser." In turn, as the letters show, Mencken provided Dreiser with a context and a vocabulary to define his practice. In the early years, the context was determined by the conservative reaction to the naturalism of Dreiser's fiction, and, after 1914, this was complicated by the domestic politics of World War I. Though we do not think of Dreiser and Mencken as writers marked by the war, they were touched by it, perhaps in more enduring ways than Hemingway or E. E. Cummings or Dos Passos. As German-Americans, their perspective on the conflict reinforced their sense of themselves as outsiders fiercely at odds with the pieties of most Americans. So embattled, they took naturally to martial language, which gave them the terms to express their ideas about American life, as well as a way of describing the rocky course of their friendship. They left a legacy as battlers in causes that now seem remote, but in the process they significantly altered the style and tone of cultural discourse.

Their battles with each other give a human dimension, and even poignancy, to the larger drama. To some extent, the intensity of their relationship can be explained by Tocqueville's comment, found in his *Recollections*, that "shared hatreds are almost always the basis for friendship." As long as they had yet to make names for themselves or could recognize a threat to their mutual principles, they came together, drank beer and caroused, planned strategy, worked hard for each other, and masked their hurts with the comic routines that make the letters so readable. Their differences emerged when the common enemies were routed and they had to face each other one on one. Then the hidden sources of their responses (to the avant-garde, religious experience, sexuality, the nature of crime and punishment, editorial policies) came to the fore, and, never tolerant of other points of view, they found their prejudices to be as strong as the ties that held them. What caused them pain, however, serves us well, for if they had been more alike and less conflicted, their exchange would have revealed less about the times they lived through.

While I have conceived this book as a contribution to the libraries that scholars require, my hope is that these letters will be a delight for readers, all kinds of readers. Collections of this kind can be tiresome (and this one has its low points too), but after working with the correspondence for more than two years, I feel as confident as when I began that it contains a story as dramatic as that of a good work of literature. The drama is, of course, partly a product of the roles the two men assumed with each other. They enjoyed, above all, the parts of consummate professionals and literary tough-guys. This is especially true of Mencken, who was a coruscatingly brilliant letter writer—and funny even when serious. And while Dreiser is at his best in moments of outrage or tenderness, he responded to Mencken's high spirits with a winning humor of his own.

The introductions are designed to provide the necessary historical and personal background to the various periods and to the stages of the friendship. Some attempt has been made to trace the connections between the course of the correspondence and that of the public writing, and, wherever the letters allow, to correct or supplement the biographical assumptions about the two men. In this, I have tried to let the tale tell itself, though I am only too aware of how my own prejudices have shaped the evidence. My only defense is a belief that my subjects would have approved of the method, if not the meaning. In any case, if the reader arrives at the end of these pages with a better understanding of what by turns moved, depressed, angered, and inspired these two formidable figures, the book will have served its purpose.

Manchester, Connecticut   *Thomas P. Riggio*
July 1985

Editorial Note

The letters in this book represent the entire known correspondence between Dreiser and Mencken. By letter is meant any communication, whether handwritten, typed, or telegraphed, including postcards, telegrams, and even a few messages written on music programs and on joke items, like the dust jacket of a best-selling novel. The total count of letters is 1,204, of which 238 have been published in indispensable collections: by Carl Bode in his *The New Mencken Letters* (1977); by Robert H. Elias in his comprehensive three volumes, *Letters of Theodore Dreiser* (1959); and by Guy J. Forgue in his *Letters of H. L. Mencken* (1961). In addition, Carl Bode has published two Mencken letters to Dreiser in John Dorsey's *On Mencken* (1980); and another appears in Huntington Cairns's *H. L. Mencken: The American Scene* (1965).

This book was planned as an edition of the complete correspondence. In preparing the letters, however, it became clear that a compromise was in order. Of the total exchange between the two men, 168 letters have not been printed in full. These are letters that either repeat the contents of other letters or are trivial notes of invitation to dinner, confirmation of a scheduled meeting, and the like—all of which would simply take up space and detract from the readability and general high quality of the correspondence. To be sure, a number of such letters are included to provide continuity and a sense of the day-to-day routine of Dreiser's and Mencken's habits as correspondents. Those who desire further knowledge of the excluded letters can turn to Appendix 3, which lists the letters chronologically, locates their manuscripts, and briefly describes their contents. The substance of these letters is also referred to in the notes, whenever the need arises. Copies of the letters have been deposited in the Rare

Book Collection of the Van Pelt Library at the University of Pennsylvania and at the Enoch Pratt Free Library in Baltimore and may be examined on request.

The letters are presented chronologically by year, month, and (with few exceptions) day. The following abbreviations describe the nature of the document:

C   Typed Copy
H   Holograph Letter
Pc   Postcard
T   Typed Letter
Tel   Telegram

Any document of an unorthodox nature is identified in a note. Since 98 percent of Mencken's letters are typed, *H* is used only to identify his handwritten letters, and *T* not at all. Almost the same percentage of Dreiser's letters are handwritten, so the *T* is used only to identify his typed letters, and *H* not at all.

The following abbreviations identify the source of the document:

EPL   Enoch Pratt Free Library (Baltimore)
LIU   Lilly Library, Indiana University (Bloomington)
NYP   New York Public Library
UPL   University of Pennsylvania (Van Pelt Library)

Although most of the correspondence has survived, internal evidence indicates that some letters are lost. Small and large hiatuses are discussed in the introductions to each section. Letters are printed in full with no bracketed emendations or interpolations. Past editors of the letters of Dreiser and of Mencken have normalized punctuation and corrected mistakes in spelling. This was reasonable, since they were dealing with letters sent to hundreds of people—and not trying to capture the flow and flavor of a single long and complex exchange. For this edition, the guiding principle for holograph and typed letters has been that they be printed as they were received. The chief exception to this rule comes in the positioning of the place of origin, the date, and the complimentary close, all of which have been regularized. The reasons for the rule are, first, to preserve the private character of the documents, and, second, to provide the reader with a feel for the idiosyncracies of expression maintained by Dreiser and Mencken. The principle seems especially appropriate for this collection, since at times their lapses become themselves the subject of letters, as one autodidact comments on the word usage or oddities of form of the other.

Readers will not experience any difficulty with this format. Mencken typed quickly but carefully, usually on magazine letterhead or his personal halfsheet stationery with the familiar Hollins Street address. On his part, Dreiser was more careful in writing to Mencken than to other people. Furthermore, they tend to be consistent in their peculiarities, so that they establish norms of their own that the reader quickly begins to recognize and even anticipate. For example, Dreiser's misspellings include the constant reversal of the correct positions of *i*'s and *e*'s; and he regularly omits the apostrophe and the question mark, as well as the period when it occurs at the end of the page. (For the sake of clarity, I have provided three spaces between each sentence that ends without punctuation and the sentence that follows.) And no problem of clarity arises from Mencken's habit of capitalizing the seasons or his occasional Briticisms or his placing commas and periods outside quotation marks.

Errors of fact or dating are corrected in the notes. Typographical errors are retained, except in the cases where a secretary's hand made them, as in the business letters Dreiser sent from his *Delineator* office in 1907–10 or those letters copied by Mencken's secretary for which the originals are lost. The few cases where words are not legible, as well as the location of all marginalia, also have been explained in the notes. In the instances where words were inserted above lines, they have been included in the text without comment. Illegible cancellations and slips of the pen have been omitted, but legible cancellations that may tell us something about the writer's intention are included as they appear in the letter. Both men underlined words in their letters; in addition, they underlined parts of the letters they received, usually to highlight the points they wanted to respond to. Only the former underlinings are retained. Since Mencken typed, the underlinings he made in his letters are easy to distinguish from Dreiser's. The underlinings in Dreiser's letters present more problems, but, in the majority of cases, differences of ink make the identification easy.

Any editor of the Dreiser and Mencken letters owes a debt to three individuals. First, to Mencken himself who, with his near obsessive need for ordered records and his passion for literary history, convinced Dreiser to exchange and copy letters that were placed, before their deaths, at the University of Pennsylvania and the New York Public Library. Consequently, the bulk of the letters is now to be found with the Dreiser and Mencken papers at these institutions, with a few scattered letters in the Lilly Library at Indiana University and the Enoch Pratt Free Library in Baltimore. Mencken examined the letters that were sent to the University of Pennsylvania and the New York Free Library and gave them their first rough ordering. The second person to give order to the letters was Rosalind C. Lohrfinck, Mencken's secretary of many years. Mencken requested of Mrs. Lohrfinck that she make copies, from the mound of letters she had in shorthand, with special attention to his letters to authors and the responses he received from them. As a result of her years of labor, we have for the period 1934–45 copies of eleven letters for which the originals have been lost. The texts of these are printed here as Mrs. Lohrfinck transcribed them, simply with the date on the right side and the salutation on the left. The word "copy" typed at the top of the page has been eliminated, and any such letter is identified by the abbreviation *C* in the space that describes the nature of the document. In addition, the customary ending that Mrs. Lohrfinck placed on these letters—"Sincerely yours, (Signed) H. L. Mencken"—has been retained.

Almost as large a debt is owed to Robert H. Elias, Dreiser's first biographer and the first editor of his letters. His notes on the dating of Dreiser's letters are invaluable, and even where I came to different conclusions, his work offered a good starting point. Because many of the manuscript letters are without envelopes, and envelopes that have survived cannot always be assigned to a particular letter, I have rarely relied on postmarks as an indication of the date or place of writing. Luckily, internal evidence or a response to a particular letter makes it possible to date most letters with a good degree of accuracy. For all but a handful of undated letters, I have supplied approximate dates, which are placed in brackets where the date would normally appear. Whenever possible, such letters are dated either "before" or "after" a corresponding letter.

The letters are arranged in six sections that reflect what I take to be important biographical and historical divisions, and also stages in the development of the friendship. The notes are used to identify references in the letters to people, events, and documents that the reader might find obscure. With few exceptions, names in notes to each section are identified the first time they occur in that section. The index will help the reader locate these identifications, as well as a few names that do not require notes. The following abbreviations are used in the notes to identify frequently cited source books:

Bode, *Letters*:	Carl Bode, *The New Mencken Letters* (New York, 1977)
Elias, *Letters*:	Robert H. Elias, *Letters of Theodore Dreiser*, 3 vols. (Philadelphia, 1959)
Forgue, *Letters*:	Guy J. Forgue, *Letters of H. L. Mencken* (New York, 1961)

Salzman: Jack Salzman, *Theodore Dreiser: The Critical Reception* (New York, 1972)

Swanberg, *Dreiser*:   W. A. Swanberg, *Dreiser* (New York, 1965)

Appendix 1 contains a number of Mencken's letters to Helen Dreiser, written after Dreiser's death. In important ways, these letters to the novelist's widow both continue and clarify the dialogue Mencken had had with Dreiser. They also reveal an emotional side of his response to Dreiser that he rarely showed when Dreiser was alive. Of the seventeen letters to Helen Dreiser printed here, three have been published previously by Guy Forge in *Letters of H. L. Mencken*.

Since the relationship between Dreiser and Mencken was established in the public domain as well as in private interchanges, I have collected a number of documents in Appendix 2 that are essential for understanding the interaction of the two men. The most important of these are Mencken's reviews of Dreiser's books and some of his key essays on the novelist. As these pieces are often the subject of discussion—and the causes of silences—in the letters, the reader may want to consult them to get a clearer idea of the issues involved. It is not an overstatement to say that they were a determining factor in a relation that was as much a literary alliance as a friendship. Together with the letters, they offer a remarkably full index to the turbulent nature and course of that extraordinary alliance.

                                                            T.P.R.

Acknowledgments

My first debt is to the Trustees of the University of Pennsylvania for permission to publish the Dreiser letters and to the Trustees of the Enoch Pratt Free Library for permission to publish the Mencken letters. I am pleased to add that the publication of these letters would not have been possible without the able administration, cooperation, and generous support of Richard De Gennaro, Director of Libraries at the University of Pennsylvania, and Averil J. Kadis, Director of Public Relations at the Enoch Pratt Free Library in Baltimore.

The New York Public Library made possible the publication of a reliable text by allowing me to have and use photographic copies of its holdings, particularly Dreiser's letters to Mencken; copies of Mencken's letters for which the originals have been lost; and the correspondence between Mencken and Estelle Bloom Kubitz. The Lilly Library, Indiana University, also provided copies of the letters of Dreiser and Mencken in its possession. The Enoch Pratt Free Library, the Los Angeles Public Library, the New York Public Library, and the University of Pennsylvania Library made available the photographs that are reproduced in this work; and Dr. Vera Dreiser, Dreiser's niece, kindly granted permission to use the photograph of Dreiser and his first wife, Sara White Dreiser.

Daniel Traister, Curator of Special Collections, and Kathleen Reed, Assistant Curator, at the University of Pennsylvania Library, gave liberally of their own time, put the resources of the Special Collections at my disposal, and took more interest in this project than required by their respective offices. I would also like to thank Neil Jordahl of the Enoch Pratt Free Library for his kind assistance during my trips to Baltimore. Robert D. Vrecenak of the University of Connecticut Library made my work easier by providing me with books and microfilm from libraries across the country.

William T. Moynihan, Head of the English Department at the University of Connecticut, gave me the time I needed when I most needed it.

A grant from the National Endowment for the Humanities freed me from teaching duties for the spring and fall semesters of 1984. Without this support, these volumes would have taken much longer to complete. I would also like to thank the University of Connecticut Research Foundation, and especially Hugh Clark and Thomas Giolas, for providing substantial aid for travel expenses and fees in connection with this book.

A number of volumes, already published, have been extremely helpful in the editing of these letters. There are too many to list here, but of the editors and authors of these volumes, the following deserve special notice: Carl Bode, editor of *The New Mencken Letters* (1971) and author of *Mencken* (1969); Robert H. Elias, editor of *Letters of Theodore Dreiser* (1959) and author of *Theodore Dreiser: Apostle of Nature* (1949); Guy J. Forgue, editor of *Letters of H. L. Mencken* (1961); W. A. Swanberg, author of *Dreiser* (1965); Betty Adler, for *The Mencken Bibliography* (1961); and Donald Pizer, Richard E. Dowell, and Frederick E. Rusch, for *Theodore Dreiser: A Primary and Secondary Bibliography* (1975). Without the work of these and other scholars, this would have been a far poorer book.

Portions of the introductions were first published as "Dreiser and Mencken: In the Literary Trenches," *The American Scholar* 54 (Spring 1985), and are reprinted here with the permission of *The American Scholar*.

Robert H. Elias supported this project from the beginning, and always took time to respond to my many queries.

Vincent Fitzpatrick generously shared with me his knowledge of the Mencken Collection at the Enoch Pratt, helped solve many bibliographical problems, read portions of the manuscript, took time from his busy schedule to show me around Mencken's Baltimore, and offered an exchange of ideas that proved valuable at every stage of the study.

Ted Nostwich read sections of the manuscript. His editorial skills and knowledge of the period in which Dreiser and Mencken lived saved me from more embarrassments than I would like to think about.

Kenneth S. Lynn's enthusiastic support of my work helped me keep at it.

Ross Miller and Miles Orvell were willing to listen to my ideas—and to contribute a few of their own.

Pat Tobias did more than prepare a faithful transcription of the manuscript. She learned to read Dreiser's handwriting, offered valuable suggestions about editing the text and the notes, caught my errors of fact and form, and worked long and difficult hours to make this a better book.

Ingalill H. Hjelm was the best of editors and provided good counsel, good humor, and an unfailing confidence in the publication of these letters. Lee Ann Draud carefully and skillfully edited the manuscript, prepared the index, and offered suggestions that greatly improved the book.

A very special note of gratitude is owed Neda M. Westlake. Before her retirement in 1984 as Curator of the Rare Book Collection of the University of Pennsylvania Library, she provided the initial support for this project, helped arrange for its publication, and contributed to the first stages of research. After her retirement, she read the entire manuscript, gave freely of her knowledge of Dreiser and Mencken, and, most of all, offered a constant source of encouragement.

To Anna and Tommy: my thanks are offered for the time this book took from your own lives, while without complaint you allowed me the luxury of burying myself for long hours in my study or in libraries far from home.

My final and deepest thanks are expressed in the dedication.

1

A Receptive Mood
(1907–1910)

"If you want to come to Baltimore I'll put you up in the Cathedral, and introduce you to all the brewers."
—HLM to TD, October 1909

"What I want to know now is whether you are in a receptive mood."
—TD to HLM, 21 March 1910

Sometime in March or early April of 1908, when Theodore Dreiser was thirty-seven and H. L. Mencken ten years his junior, the two men met for the first time in Dreiser's *Delineator* office on Spring and McDougal streets in Manhattan. Already something of a prodigy in newspaper circles, Mencken had come to the attention of Dreiser who, as managing editor of Butterick Publications, was trying to enlist new talent for the three women's fashion magazines under his control. Though on the payroll of the Baltimore *Sun*, Mencken had begun freelancing for Dreiser as early as August 1907. Dreiser had been pleased with the younger man's contributions which, he later recalled, "bristled with gay phraseology and a largely suppressed though still peeping mirth." Sporting yellow shoes and a gaudy tie, Mencken marched into the editor's office to discuss a series of articles on infant care that he had agreed to ghostwrite for a prominent Baltimore physician. In 1925, when Dreiser wrote of this encounter, he rendered it as a rare case of "instantaneous friendship," stimulated by a comic shock of recognition.

More than anything else he reminded me of a spoiled and petted and possibly over-financed brewer's or wholesale grocer's son who was out for a lark. With the sang-froid of a Caesar or a Napoleon he made himself comfortable in a large and impressive chair which was designed primarily to reduce the over-confidence of the average beginner. And from that particular and unintended vantage point he beamed on me with the confidence of a smirking fox about to devour a chicken. So I was the editor of the Butterick Publications. He had been told about me. However, in spite of Sister Carrie, I doubt if he had ever heard of me before this. After studying him in this almost arch-episcopal setting which the chair provided, I began to laugh. "Well, well," I said, "if it isn't Anheuser's own brightest boy out to see the town." (see Appendix 2, pp. 738–40)

That early spring meeting began a friendship between two men who, at the time, had little in common beyond their large ambitions and a marked disdain for the intellectual timidity of American writing. The "brewer's son" knew more than he let on. He knew that the senior editor in New York could provide him with a larger audience than he had in Baltimore. He knew that Dreiser, an officer in the B. W. Dodge Company, could help him place the more serious work he was planning: books on German philosophy and European drama. He also knew that a certain amount of deference was due the author of *Sister Carrie*, a novel he in fact had read in 1900 and one, he felt, that showed genius.

The two men met at what proved to be turning points in their careers. While they worked Grub Street successfully, editing and writing articles and books on everything from pediatrics and women's suffrage to humorous pieces for the "Man's Page," they had their sights on a wider and more sophisticated readership. Eager to move beyond his early achievements on Baltimore's *Herald* and the *Sunpapers*, Mencken had already published a book on Shaw and was working on *The Philosophy of Friedrich Nietzsche* (1908). Dreiser, on his long rebound from what he was coming to consider the "suppression" of his first novel, was anxiously seeking acceptance from the conservative critics who supervised American literary fashion. Following his long nervous breakdown at the turn of the century, he had turned in 1904 to the first of a string of editorial jobs he would hold in the next six years. In those years he also continued turning out stories, poems, and essays, shrewdly managed a new edition of *Sister Carrie* in 1907, and waited for an occasion to complete his second novel, *Jennie Gerhardt* (1911).

The first years of their correspondence show few signs of future promise. The kind of journeywork Mencken and Dreiser record in these letters might have occupied any editor and journalist. Yet theirs was a common sort of apprenticeship for aspiring writers, especially in the quiet years before Greenwich Village, the little magazines and the little theaters offered other outlets for such talents. In 1909, Lincoln Steffens and Walter Lippmann were on the Butterick payroll, and, along with Mencken, Dreiser brought to the *Delineator's* pages Ludwig Lewisohn, Jack London, David Graham Phillips, and Gustavus Myers. Elsewhere, Robert Frost was practicing his craft in between farm chores; in the Midwest Sherwood Anderson and Edgar Lee Masters were writing stories and poems after business hours; and Willa Cather was Dreiser's female counterpart at *McClure's*. If a special fate seems to have brought Mencken and Dreiser together over the hackwork of the popular monthlies, it is only because we can now appreciate the significance of their early years together.

The letters of 1907–10 serve as an introduction to the time of Mencken's and Dreiser's greatest influence—from 1911 to the mid-1920s—when they were among the most visible figures on the American literary scene. The temptation, given their later bouts of estrangement, is to read these letters as the beginning of a friendship of convenience. To some extent, of course, it was. Mencken was dependent upon the good graces of Dreiser's editorial position; and Dreiser, under the pressure of monthly deadlines, turned to the energetic newsman for quick copy and, before long, for editorial assistance as well. These transactions, however, soon took them beyond a limited professional exchange. They discovered in each other ready sounding boards for something more than the usual banter and shoptalk of the marketplace. They quickly began what came natural to them: the endless debates over social and philosophical matters, conducted in the heady, earnest manner of bright autodidacts. They relished such contact, so much so that by December 1909, Mencken inscribed his book on Nietzsche "To Theodore Dreiser:-In memory of furious disputations on sorcery & the art of letters."

From the beginning, they showed sharp differences in temperament and style. It is also true, however, that in important ways they offered mirror images to each other. While Dreiser's sketch of their first meeting emphasizes Mencken's comic façade, he knew, certainly by 1925, that beneath the comic mask and the quick wit Mencken took the world as seriously as he did.

Outside my window, in the street, a man labors in the rain with pick and shovel, and his reward is merely a roof for to-night and to-morrow's three meals. Contemplating the difference between his luck and mine, I cannot fail to wonder at the eternal meaninglessness of life. I wonder thus and pity his lot. . . .

The feeling behind this Dreiserian meditation, written by Mencken in 1910,[1] was offset by an equally strong sense of disdain for the underdogs of the world. But the passage points to something basic in Mencken's sensibility that would make him a spokesman for writers like Hardy, Conrad, Zola—and Dreiser who, in America, came closest to his idea of how the novelist should go about his business. Mencken later would echo these lines in his earliest praise of *Jennie Gerhardt*, and it is tempting to imagine Dreiser pondering his friend's words as he tried to bring to life again his second novel, a book that embodies the lesson of Mencken's passage.

The chemistry of their mutual response is not hard to understand.

They came to each other with the intellectual biases of their generation. Following the Darwinian hypothesis, they embraced a mechanistic view of life. As younger men, they had been drawn to the same masters, particularly Thomas Huxley, Herbert Spencer, and the biological naturalists. Though they had read these writers differently, they shared a view conditioned by late nineteenth-century determinism. This perspective led them to question traditional ideals of character and destiny. Even at this stage, there are hints of their reaction to the social orthodoxy of the period, especially the reform programs that characterized the Progressive movement after 1900. With good reason, Mencken soon began envisioning Dreiser as a companion in "the German camp of violent unbelievers." And the two German-Americans shared, from the outset, a reaction to nativist and antiurban pieties that later, particularly after World War I began, would give focus to their wide range of aesthetic, social, and political interests.

But in this period the note of rebellion is muted. Both the editor and the critic had to make a living, and as they did not yet dominate the literary marketplace, they submitted to its demands, sharing in what they would later label the buffooneries of the American scene. Dreiser, in particular, avoided the tone of the outsider that he would later adopt. The letters provide the fullest picture on record of Dreiser as editor: correcting copy, formulating policy, creating new departments, and, on the side, running a monthly called the *Bohemian*. He used his influence to promote Mencken, seeking publishers for the younger man's books, printing his work in the journals he controlled, and helping him to find other publishing outlets. In the spring of 1909, he offered him an editorial post at Butterick, which Mencken turned down, as he did all jobs calling for an address outside Baltimore. When Dreiser heard that *Smart Set* needed a book reviewer, he recommended his young protégé, and, as Mencken later quipped, "Dreiser got me my job . . . and so made a literary critic of me." In his first full-time post as a critic, the magazine's new man began boosting the one-book novelist who, with the exception of a few devotees, was unknown to the reading public. Dreiser's recommendation, in fact, catapulted Mencken into a position that later would leave its mark on the novelist's career and, more generally, on American journalism.

It was toward the close of this period that the relationship became less businesslike. Besides depending on Mencken's editorial judgments, Dreiser sought and received moral support and, increasingly, an after-hours companion—a rare male intimate who managed by 1910 to crack the icy façade of the Butterick editor-in-chief to the point of being addressed as "Dear darling, Mencken." Mencken became a regular dinner guest at the Dreisers' New York apartment, and he invited Dreiser to spend the holidays in Baltimore. For the first time since his friendship with Arthur Henry, Dreiser had someone to turn to in times of crisis. In the fall of 1910, when Dreiser's infatuation with Thelma Cudlipp, the eighteen-year-old daughter of a woman close to his boss, cost him his job at Butterick, it was to Mencken that he confided his sorrows, like a middle-aged Werther, in one-line jottings on office memo sheets: "I have discovered that this is a very sad world"; "I am very lonely. Is there no hope."

Much of the more personal interchange of these years is missing; the early letters mainly detail the practical trivia of ephemeral magazine work. Unfortunately, the extant correspondence for this period is sadly incomplete. It contains only one item from Mencken (16 October 1908) for the period of eighteen months after Dreiser's first letter of 23 August 1907. The gap is due in part to the disappearance of the *Delineator* records, since Mencken surely addressed Dreiser at his editor's desk. When the relationship became more personal, after 1908, Dreiser began saving letters in his private files.

From what remains, however, we can surmise that by 1909 the two men had begun prodding each other to undertake work of a more serious nature. They also began to exchange philosophical positions based on their views of science and religion. By early November 1909, the letters reveal intellectual differences that would strain their relations over the years. From the beginning, Mencken proved more rationalistic and more consistently agnostic. Though they claimed the same intellectual mentors, their education led them in different directions. Mencken became the skeptic, the champion of the superman and the natural aristocrat who looked in vain for democratic heroes; Dreiser became the seeker after the ineffable, the chronicler of the victim who yearned for heroes to worship. For Mencken Nietzsche was a liberator, for Dreiser he was "Schopenhauer confused and warmed over."

Typical of their early "furious disputations" is Dreiser's response to an editorial Mencken had sent him on "The Decay of the Churches": "And isn't seeking knowledge (scientific) a form of prayer. Aren't scientists and philosophers at bottom truly reverential and don't they wish (pray) ardently for more knowledge . . . the truth is men are not less religious—they are religious in a different way—and that's a fact." Mencken's reply set the tone for future debates: "In all honesty, I can't follow you. The scientific impulse seems to me to be the very opposite of the religious impulse. When a man seeks knowledge he is trying to gain a means of fighting his own way in the world, but when he prays he confesses that he is unable to do so. The essential thing about prayer is that it assumes that the moods of the gods are *not* fixed and invariable. If they were, it would be silly to ask the gods to change them. This idea, I think, explains the decay of religion." Even here, at the outset, Mencken proved clearer headed, with a grasp of facts and logic Dreiser often lacked or ignored. The absence of these qualities in Dreiser, it is true, made him more open to positions not his own, partly because he was never as sure as Mencken of his position. His pluralism would later deeply offend Mencken, who could never understand the novelist's tolerance for visionaries, mystics, and political radicals; and Mencken's unremitting materialism puzzled Dreiser to the end. At this early stage, however, philosophy took a back seat to the practical business of making names for themselves.

Notes

1. *Men versus the Man: A Correspondence between Robert Rives La Monte, Socialist, and H. L. Mencken, Individualist* (New York: Holt, 1910), 247.

The Correspondence (1907–1910)

THE DELINEATOR
New York

August 23, 1907

Dear Mr. Mencken:

Mr. George Bronson Howard,[1] of your city, has suggested to me that you were just the person to get out a popular edition of a German Philosopher or Dramatist which could be sold to schools and colleges and to the general reading public. He thought that a condensed and popular edition of Schopenhauer would be very much in your line.[2]

This is a proposition which interests me greatly. It is something which it seems would be of great interest to the public at large. I would like to know whether you are in a position to undertake a scheme of this kind, and whether you have a theory as to how the matter could be worked out. If you have, I should be more than pleased to hear from you.[3]

Very truly yours,
Theodore Dreiser

1. George Bronson Howard (1884–1922), journalist, novelist, playwright.
2. This would be a fair assumption since, in addition to his growing reputation as a newsman and editor, Mencken had already published *George Bernard Shaw: His Plays* (1905) and was at work on *The Philosophy of Nietzsche* (1908). Dreiser, having recently become editorial director of B. W. Dodge & Co., was on the lookout for marketable manuscripts from promising new authors. Mencken never undertook the Schopenhauer edition.

3. With the exception of one letter of 16 October 1908, all of Mencken's letters to Dreiser in 1907 and 1908 have disappeared.

[NYP-T]

THE DELINEATOR
New York

Sept. 16, 1907

My dear Mr. Mencken:

The B. W. Dodge Company is very much interested in the idea of producing some philosophical work in popular form.[1] They do not feel that they have any plans definite enough to justify them in asking you to come to New York and talking it over with them, but they express the opinion that if you ever were here they could probably get a clearer insight into the whole proposition and do something about it.

In the meantime, they wanted me to see if you could not make a definite suggestion, yourself——some subject which could be easily carried out and the nature of which they could understand clearly by a letter. If you can make such a proposition, it would be most cordially received.

Very sincerely,
Theodore Dreiser
EDITOR

1. On 9 September 1907, Ben Dodge wrote Dreiser saying the company had no plans to publish a book on German philosophy or the drama. [UPL] In fact, the idea was Dreiser's and he was promoting Mencken as a person to do such a book.

[NYP-T]

THE DELINEATOR
New York

Sept. 24, 1907

My dear Mr. Mencken:

I have read "THE SLAUGHTER OF THE INNOCENTS" with considerable interest.[1] Can you tell me what you think it would be worth? It is much too long as it stands, and would have to be cut to about four thousand to five thousand words. However, that can be done without much trouble in this office if we can agree on terms. Would $100 be satisfactory?

And, by the way, do you work on these articles with Dr. Leonard Keene Hirshberg? If so, you might get together with him and work out an article to be entitled "IF MY BABY HAD PNEUMONIA," and "IF MY BABY HAD DIPHTHERIA." He ought to be able to give sound advice on such subjects——that is, advice which would be of great interest to mothers.[2] He writes well, and I am sure that I could use the material if you could put it together.

Very sincerely,
Theodore Dreiser
EDITOR

1. "The Slaughter of the Innocents," an article on the dangers of certain child-care methods, was published under the name of Dr. Leonard K. Hirshberg, a Baltimore physician: *Delineator* 72 (May 1909), 681, 713–14.
2. Mencken and Hirshberg collaborated on the type of baby-care articles that Dreiser suggests here. Hirshberg supplied Mencken with the facts for the two medical articles that appeared in the February and August 1908 issues of the *Delineator*. In October 1908, Hirshberg and Mencken started a series of six articles on the care and feeding of infants. Mencken did most of the writing, and the articles were collected in a book, which appeared under Hirshberg's name as *What You Ought to Know about Your Baby* (New York, 1910).

[NYP-T]

THE DELINEATOR
New York

October 12, 1907

Mr. H. L. Macon,[1]
1524 Holland Street,
Baltimore, Md.
My dear Mr. Macon:

I have had this article on "THE SLAUGHTER OF THE INNOCENTS," by Leonard Keene Hirshberg, M.D., cut in this office by Mrs. Denison, but it is still much too long.

I fancy that you have very good editing ability; and I want to know if I can send you this manuscript and have you cut it down to about 4200 words, and get into it all the important stuff. It is beautifully written, but it is simply so long that I cannot possibly save anything but the essential facts, and somebody who knows this medical game ought to cut it down to a reasonable length.

Very truly yours,
Theodore Dreiser
EDITOR

1. This may have been a typist's error, but clearly Dreiser and Mencken were not on intimate terms at this point.

[NYP-T]

THE DELINEATOR
London – Paris – New York

Oct. 19, 1907

My dear Mr. Mencken:

I am sending you herewith the article on "THE SLAUGHTER OF THE INNOCENTS," and at the same time the article on "WHEN THE BABY HAS DIPHTHERIA," which is satisfactory, but needs to be altered slightly in its point of view.

In regard to "SLAUGHTER OF THE INNOCENTS," as I told you, it wants to come down to about 4500 words. Mrs. Denison, of this office, has made a stagger at cutting it, but I am afraid it is not going to be suitable unless someone else takes a hand at it. Portions of it ought to be condensed in less space and it ought to be more or less re-written and cut.

Now, in regard to "WHEN THE BABY HAS DIPHTHERIA" I want to say that this is a fine article; I like this man and his ideas, and I wish he would make me some suggestions. The only trouble with this is that it, instead of talking at the mother, talks about diphtheria; it ought to be a direct statement. Thus, on page 8, it reads:

"Unluckily, there still lingers in the United States a superstitious dread of antitoxin."

Instead of saying this in this way, it ought to be about as follows: "You probably know a great deal about doctoring your children and some one has told you that antitoxin is a deadly poison or a filthy drug. It is nothing of the sort; if you are a wise mother you will listen closely to the wonderful facts in connection with this discovery."

That is, the doctor wants to talk to the mothers, but not any of this material wants to be sacrificed. It is all good. There ought to be a little introduction addressed to the mothers——sort of waking her up to the nature of the topic and then I am satisfied that it will be just right.

Let him write the "Pneumonia" article in the same way, and shove it along. Does he think that he ought to have $125.00 for this paper? I should say that $100.00 was a corking good sum, considering the length of it.

Now, what about the suggestions which you were going to make? Are you going to come up here some day? If you do, I want you to be sure to come in and talk to me as I think that I can put up a proposition of some kind that will be to our mutual advantage, as your letters and your attitude suit me exactly.

Very sincerely,
Theodore Dreiser
EDITOR

THE DELINEATOR
New York

December 11th, 1907.

My dear Mr. Mencken:—

I am sending you herewith an article entitled "What Science has done for the Child", which I would like to have you read and have Dr. Hirshberg read and tell me whether it is all right.[1] Although crudely done, in a way it has a lot of very excellent material if the same is true.

If you think that it is all right I should like to buy it. Let me have your united opinion at once, and oblige,

Very sincerely yours,
Theodore Dreiser
EDITOR

---

1. No response from Mencken exists, but it probably was negative since the *Delineator* never published the article.

THE DELINEATOR
New York

December 14, 1907.

My dear Mr. Mencken:

I am very much obliged to you for your prompt examination of the "Child Science" story, and the very thorough criticism which resulted. There will be other things from time to time in this connection, and when it amounts to a half dozen I shall pay you something for editorial services.

With best wishes,

Very sincerely yours,
Theodore Dreiser
Editor.

THE DELINEATOR
New York
Theodore Dreiser, Editor

March 9, 1908.

My dear Mr. Mencken:

Be sure, when you come to New York, to come in and see me. I have something I want to talk to you about.[1]

Very truly yours,
Theodore Dreiser
Editor.

1. This letter is the prelude to the first meeting of the two men, which Dreiser later recalled as taking place "sometime during the spring or summer of 1908" (see "Henry L. Mencken and Myself," Appendix 2, pp. 738–40).

THE DELINEATOR
New York
Theodore Dreiser, Editor

New York, April 24, 1908.

Dear Sir:

I hear that you are once more back in the wilds of Baltimore. I want to know if you will object to the use of your name as associate and contributor on the Literary Supplement along with such men as Ludwig Lewisohn, Joseph H. Coates, Charles Hanson Towne, Peter B. McCord, Arthur Henry, Gustavus Myers and some others.[1] It would be used on the editorial writing paper only. If so kindly let me know.

Very truly yours,
Theodore Dreiser
Editor.

1. Though Mencken declined the offer, Dreiser was adding a distinguished group of writers to the Butterick list: Ludwig Lewisohn (1883–1955), author, editor, teacher; Joseph H. Coates, editor, publisher, author; Charles Hanson Towne (1877–1949), poet, editor, actor; Peter B. McCord, illustrator; Arthur Henry (1867–1934), editor, author; Gustavus Myers (1872–1942), socialist, historian.

The young Mencken (ca. 1908) (Enoch Pratt Free Library)

[NYP-T]

THE DELINEATOR
New York
Theodore Dreiser, Editor

New York, June 17, 1908.

My dear Mr. Mencken:

The plan which you outline is very good, but you do not tell me whether we can use these in the pamphlet form which I suggested.[1] Neither did you say whether the price was satisfactory, but I presume, since you outlined the list, that it is. I suppose the low ebb of the literary life down in Baltimore has something to do with this.

Very truly yours,
Theodore Dreiser
Editor.

N.B.

I read an editorial from the Baltimore Sun, copied in the Evening Sun here, on Bachelors, which sounded so much like you that I cut it out and have been handing it around to some of my bachelor friends. I should like to know if you are guilty of this editorial or not.

1. Dreiser wanted to collect the articles on the care and feeding of infants into a pamphlet "to give away to mothers who write in and ask for them" (Dreiser to Dr. Leonard K. Hirshberg, 6 June 1908 [UPL]). That pamphlet became *What You Ought to Know about Your Baby* (1910).

[NYP-T]

THE DELINEATOR
London – Paris – New York
Theodore Dreiser, Editor

New York, July 16, 1908.

My dear Mencken:

I have at last had an opportunity to get Mr. George W. Wilder's[1] opinion on this first article in the Child series, and am now in a position to tell you what he thinks. This is his idea, and I am trying to give you just what he wants.

He claims that while this first article is very charmingly written, and I agree with him, that it does not really get down to the brass tacks of the proposition. Take the matter of crying, which you will find noted on page three. Mr. Wilder, being the proud father of four children and being very much interested in the child as a problem, insists that you do not really tell all about crying. You say "It cries when it is hungry and when it is uncomfortable, and the young mother will quickly grow familiar with its normal voice, and so learn to detect variations. If it cries unusually long, or in a strange manner, the doctor is the best person to determine what is the matter." He thinks that this information ought to be greatly broadened, and that the various kinds of crying should be indicated and the mother urged to understand just what each form means. He says, for instance, that the average child crys 20 minutes a day for exercise and nothing else. He also feels that in an article of this kind it is not wise to throw the whole burden on the doctor, and say that if the baby cries unusually long or anything else that the doctor is the best person to handle the matter. He thinks that there ought to be sufficient advice here to put the mother wise to a great many things without a doctor. Take the matter of where you say that the young wife ought not to take the advice of the grandmothers and the women of the neighborhood. This he feels ought to be elaborated, and in this way the things which the average grandmother and the women of the neighborhood advise should be listed and the folly of them made perfectly plain. For instance, he thinks that they might advise that the baby be rocked in the cradle, and according to him this is all wrong; also that it should be soothed with a nipple, and according to him there is a whole list of microbic ills that flow from such an error. He also maintains that there should be no tickling, and that the mother should not make a slave of herself waiting on the child, but clothe it in some comfortable manner and let it fight out its own troubles; also that there are various ways in which the child should be laid down during the first few months, and that it should not always be kept on its back or on its side, but that these positions should be varied. He claims that the shape of the head can be affected by the manner in which the child is allowed to lie during these early stages. Then there is the matter of children walking. Various efforts, according to him, are made to make the child walk early, and devices are furnished for the same purpose. These devices should be enumerated and their value discounted.

Now, I would not want to say all these things to Hirshberg for fear he would not take it very kindly, but I want to put you wise to just what is needed in this series. The idea is that the mother should be put wise to what the doctor knows about all these things; that he should not tell her to call in the doctor, but show her what the doctor himself would do, and what she really ought to do in a large number of cases. There is a book by Dr. Emmett Holt entitled <u>The</u> <u>Care</u> <u>and</u> <u>Feeding</u> <u>of</u> <u>Children</u> which covers all these things in a more or less itemized manner.[2] You might get

this, and then between you and Hirshberg revise your story, although it is
a thousand to one that Hirshberg is already familiar with this book and
knows what it contains. However, the point that I aim to make in connection with the book is that it contains the kind of detailed information
which ought to be put in these articles. Now if I have not bored you too
much on this one branch of the problem, I would like to have you give me
a revise on it, and oblige,

> Yours,
> Theodore Dreiser
> Editor.

N.B. With the increased rigor of the excise law, and the variable state of
the literary element plays a job of this kind, I fear for your reason, but if
things get very bad come over to New York, and I will take you to a place
where they sell horses necks as long as my arm.

P.S. By same mail I send you Emmet Holt book.[3]

1. George W. Wilder, president of the Butterick Publishing Company.
2. Luther Emmett Holt's *The Care and Feeding of Children* (New York, 1894) went
through fifteen editions and was reissued in 1943 by L. Emmett Holt, Jr.
3. The postscript is handwritten.

[NYP-T]

THE DELINEATOR
New York
Theodore Dreiser, Editor

New York, September 2, 1908.

My dear Mr. Mencken:

I am very much pleased by your very interesting letter in connection
with current plays.[1] I hope to act on that in the near future.

I am enclosing herewith your second article which you want to revise.

> Very sincerely yours,
> Theodore Dreiser
> Editor.

1. Mencken had written Dreiser to test whether the Dodge Company might be
interested in an edition of contemporary plays. Dreiser later wrote Mencken that "the
plays did not look profitable" to the firm. (17 November 1908 [NYP])

THE DELINEATOR
New York
Theodore Dreiser, Editor

New York, September 4, 1908.

My dear Mr. Mencken:

I enclose a letter which I was about to send off to Cardinal Gibbons.[1] I was wondering if instead of my sending this you could not go out and get the answer to this question. Any number of words will be satisfactory to me from ten to five hundred, according to his mood. The chances are that in any case he would not care for the money I would be willing to pay. So if you could get it for me I would gladly send you $25.

Won't you attend to this promptly, and if you think you can't get it you might mail this letter—for which I enclose an envelope.

Very sincerely yours,
Theodore Dreiser
Editor.

1. Cardinal James Gibbons (1834–1921), religious leader, author, memoirist. Mencken was unable to oblige Dreiser, since the cardinal was not in Baltimore at the time. Cardinal Gibbons had written an article, "The Evil of Divorce," for the July 1907 *Delineator*.

THE DELINEATOR
New York
Theodore Dreiser, Editor

New York, September 8, 1908.

My dear Mr. Mencken:

I am sorry about Cardinal Gibbons. Someone told me he was home. I am obliged to learn that "His Eminence" is correct.[1] I always thought it was, but it went out that way because of a dispute.

The second medical article was all right. Send it back when you are through with it.

Very sincerely yours,
Theodore Dreiser
Editor.

1. Obviously Mencken, in his response, had begun his lifelong practice of editing Dreiser's letters.

H. L. Mencken
1524 Hollins St.
Baltimore

Baltimore, October 16th. [1908]
My dear Mr. Dreiser:-
I am forwarding your letter to Hirshberg and shall see him tonight or tomorrow. He is eager to write a book of this sort, I know, but whether we can manage it remains to be seen. Nothing is more difficult to put into understandable English.
My socialist friend has begun to write his plea for socialism, and as soon as I get time I shall answer his first argument.[1]
More anon.

Sincerely yours,
H. L. Mencken

1. Mencken is referring to Robert Rives La Monte, a wealthy socialist who worked for the Baltimore *News* and was an associate editor of the *International Socialist Review*. The interchange with Mencken was published as *Men versus the Man: A Correspondence between Robert Rives La Monte, Socialist, and H. L. Mencken, Individualist* (New York, 1910).

THE DELINEATOR
London – Paris – New York
Theodore Dreiser, Editor

New York, Dec. 10, 1908.
My dear Mencken:
According to my list you have already covered "The New Born Baby, and its first few months" in your first article; "The Nursing Baby" in the second article; "The Food of the Growing Baby, and the bottle fed Baby" in the third article. Now according to the original plan you proposed to deal with the subjects in this order:
1. The baby at birth: its weight, habits, etc., and how to care for it. Some common fallacies. How to detect abnormalities.
2. The care of a very young infant. Teething. Sleep, crying, feeding, drinking, etc. Cautions regarding medicines. Dressing.
3. The formation of habits in the child. The dawn of intelligence. Exercise, airing, etc.
4. Natural methods of feeding the infant. Artificial foods.

5. The year-old baby and its care.
6. The second summer and afterward.
If you have done all this already perhaps we had better let up on the series.

> Very sincerely yours,
> Theodore Dreiser
> Editor.

[NYP-T]

THE DELINEATOR
London — Paris — New York
Theodore Dreiser, Editor

New York, January 30, 1909.
My dear Mencken:
    I have a letter from Leon C. Prince asking whether we would consider a book on American Political Institutions treated from the Historical and Critical point of view.[1] He wants me to outline my ideas as to the scope and purpose of the work, the treatment of the theme and the class of readers we want to reach. Since you talked to me perhaps you can give me such an outline that I can send him. I will appreciate this.
    I also have received an order from the Wilshire Book Company, 200 William Street, New York, for 1,000 copies of the Mencken-La Monte debate on Socialism. When will that book be finished?[2]

> Very sincerely yours,
> Theodore Dreiser

1. Leon C. Prince (1876–1937), educator, minister, lawyer, authority on international law.
2. Mencken finished his portion of the book in October 1909.

[NYP-T]

THE DELINEATOR
London — Paris — New York
Theodore Dreiser, Editor

New York, March 4, 1909.
My dear Mencken:
    Couldn't you and Hirshberg get up between you a corking good article on "What Science Has Done For the Sick", with a full account of all the

improvements, as compared with previous conditions?[1] I wish you would think this over and let me know. I think you could make a good thing of it.

Very sincerely yours,
Theodore Dreiser
Editor.

1. Mencken and Hirshberg did not collaborate on *Delineator* articles after this date. In September 1910, Hirshberg began "The Mother's Bureau" section, which answered inquiries on matters of child care, but there is no evidence that Mencken had any part in this.

[UPL]

H. L. Mencken
1524 Hollins St.
Baltimore.

Baltimore, March 7th. [1909]

My dear Dreiser:-

Thanks for your letter of the 4th. I take it that you want an article dealing especially with improvements in nursing. For instance, fever patients are now given all the water they want, whereas a few years back they were compelled to go dry. Again, it is now possible to allay the pain in many diseases which were formerly accompanied by agonies. If this is your idea, I shall ask Hirshberg to get material together at once.

I am afraid I must beg off on the Rural Life stuff.[1] I went to Washington Tuesday, but could find no one in authority, on account of the Inauguration.[2] It may seem foolish, but it is a fact that I won't have time to return next week. Happenings at the Sun office have kept me sweating, I have been in indifferent health, and La Monte is howling for copy for the Socialist book. This evening Hirshberg is to employ his saw upon a small part of my anatomy, and I suppose that a certain soreness will ensue.[3]

All in all, I find that I have too many irons in the fire. To get more time for the work I want to do, I must withdraw some of them. I am getting along toward thirty and it is time for me to be planning for the future. Specifically, I want to write a couple of books for you within the next few years. Specifically again, I want to write a play that now encumbers and tortures my system.[4] You will understand what a stew I am in.

Incidently, I have happened upon two foreign books that may interest Dodge & Co. The first is Nietzsche's autobiography, "Ecce Homo", which was recently issued by Friedrich Richter in Leipzig in a limited edition of 1250 copies. (I had to pay $6.70 for mine). The book is a semi-insane rhapsody, but I rather think it would sell. I have had no communication with the publisher and so don't know if the English translation rights are still open. I rather think they are. I wouldn't care to make the translation myself, because my German is full of scars and knot-holes, but I could get a slave, I believe, to translate it word for word, and then tease it up. The book, of course, would need a good introduction, and some explanatory notes.

II. The posthumous letters and papers of Ibsen are about to be issued in three volumes by the Hegel firm of Copenhagen, and I have already applied for the American rights. The three volumes, by judicious editing, could be brought down to one. I have a first class Danish translator on my staff and would be glad to undertake the work. So far, I have got no response from Hegel, and the whole thing, of course, is heavy with ifs and buts.[5]

If these things interest you, I'll go into them more carefully.

Sincerely yours,
H. L. Mencken

1. On 19 February 1909, Dreiser had asked Mencken to write an article on the Rural Life Commission's report for the Department of Agriculture.
2. The inauguration of William Howard Taft.
3. Mencken had his uvula removed.
4. Mencken would think of writing books "for" Dreiser, because of Dreiser's connection with the Dodge firm. The play may be what turned into *The Artist* later in the year (see Mencken to Dreiser, 15 September 1909).
5. After some consideration, Dodge decided against the Nietzsche and Ibsen proposals.

[NYP-T]

THE DELINEATOR
London – Paris – New York
Theodore Dreiser, Editor

New York, March 10, 1909.

My dear Mencken:

All right, call off the Rural Life Commission job.

If you get hold of the Ibsen letters and papers for goodness sake let me know. We ought to be able to do something with them. I am conferring with the other members in regard to the Ecce Homo.

Now in regard to "What Science Has Done For The Sick", I don't think that the improvements are entirely in the matter of nursing. Details of operations have been simplified greatly; sanitation and hygiene play such a big part in the construction of a big hospital and the arrangement of the present-day sick room; they are wiser and saner about their use of narcotics. It seems to me that an article which would show how far we have come from the old sloppy methods of the past would be most valuable. I wish if you think you have time to do it that you would outline it.

> Very sincerely yours,
> Theodore Dreiser
> Editor.

Ecce Homo[1]

1. Dreiser wrote in the title of Nietzsche's autobiography at the foot of the letter, apparently as a note to himself.

[NYP-T]

THE DELINEATOR
London – Paris – New York
Theodore Dreiser, Editor

New York, April 17, 1909.

My dear Mencken:

The articles would be much more significant if they were signed, provided the minister or the physician or the lawyer could talk as freely over his signature as not. If the articles would be much stronger without a signature, it might be worth considering that way.[1] What do you think?

I am interested in the Sketches of American Cities series. I wish, though, that you would do this for me. I wish you would do the one on Baltimore and let me see it, and then let me decide on the series. If it is good, and I can't take it, I will take measures to have the matter put before the right people at several of the different publications, Collier's, Everybody's, Harper's, etc., where I am rather strong. I may be able to do you a good service that way.

I am sorry that the literary life is in such a pathetic state. In your article about Baltimore you might tell of the tragic state of Poe's tomb, but in illustrating the article we should undoubtedly have to leave out the dogs.[2]

> Very sincerely yours,
> Theodore Dreiser
> Editor.

1. In a letter of 10 April 1909, Dreiser had suggested to Mencken a series of articles under the general heading of "A Woman as Seen by Others," each written by a different person (lawyer, doctor, pastor, etc.).

2. This may be a reference to Mencken's mock-irreverent stories about dogs urinating on Poe's tomb—a practice Mencken engaged in himself with friends after long beery evenings.

[NYP]

THE DELINEATOR
New York
Theodore Dreiser, Editor

April 25th '09

My Dear Mencken:
　Would you consider an editorial position on the Delineator at $50.00 per. Let me know by return mail.

> Yours Sincerely,
> Theodore Dreiser

[NYP-T]

THE DELINEATOR
London – Paris – New York
Theodore Dreiser, Editor

New York, April 27, 1909.

My dear Mencken:
　I wish you would tell me how this thing could be made into an interesting page for The Delineator.[1] I swear it has got me on the fence, and I don't know just exactly what to do about it. It ought to make a fascinating page of some kind, but perhaps it ought to be re-arranged. Will you give me the benefit of your advice?
　With best wishes, I am,

> Very sincerely yours,
> Theodore Dreiser
> Editor.

1. Mencken did not keep the piece Dreiser sent with this letter.

[NYP-T]

THE DELINEATOR
London – Paris – New York
Theodore Dreiser, Editor

New York, June 8, 1909.

My dear Mencken:

If you are going to come to New York as quickly as Hirshberg suggests you may I want you to come up to the house and take dinner with me by all means.

Very sincerely yours,
Theodore Dreiser

[NYP]

439 West 123rd Street

July 11th '09

My Dear Mencken:

As a side issue I have secured control of The Bohemian and am going to revise it vastly.[1] You belong by nature and ability. Won't you come across with something real snappy. I am going to make it a live one and <u>talk</u> plain. Now I'm not going to give up the Del or the control of the Butterick Publications but I'm going to have some fun with this. Write me someday about it at this address—my home.

Yours with the best wishes
& good will
Theodore Dreiser

1. Dreiser paid $1,000 for the magazine and took it over after the August number had been published. The monthly lasted for four months under Dreiser's management.

[UPL-H]

THE SUN
Baltimore

[after 11 July 1909]

My dear Dreiser:-

Fine! I am with you with both feet. Someday, when you get the time, let me know what sort of stuff you want, and I'll make a try at it. Short stories are a bit beyond me: I have retired from that department. But anything else I'll be glad to tackle. It's good of you to think of me.

How are you going to manage all of your enterprises? You will be working 26 or 27 hours a day.

The best of good wishes!

Truly,

H. L. Mencken

[NYP-T]

THE DELINEATOR
London — Paris — New York
Theodore Dreiser, Editor

New York, August 3, 1909.

My dear Mencken:

In my December number I am running a symposium,—"My Principles Of Giving." So far I have statements from Nathan Straus, John H. Converse, Evangeline Booth, John M. Glenn, who has charge of the distribution of the Russell Sage Foundation, and Booker T. Washington.[1] Is there any one in Baltimore whose name would be worth while for me in this connection whom you could land for anywhere from one hundred to three or four hundred words? If so there are twenty-five bones in it. Let me have the suggested names before you make any efforts to get the material so that I can see whether they are satisfactory. Will you let me hear from you?

Very sincerely yours,

Theodore Dreiser

Editor.

1. Dreiser's idea was to publish statements from some of the better-known philanthropists of the day.

[UPL]

H. L. Mencken
1524 Hollins St.
Baltimore.

Baltimore, August 5th. [1909]

My dear Dreiser:-

We had only one professional philanthropist in Baltimore—John M. Glenn—and New York gobbled him a few years ago. At present there is not a single big spender here. Bernard N. Baker, who made millions out of the International Mercantile Marine, is devoting some money to "the moral education of youth", whatever that may be, but his efforts are not serious, save to himself. Baltimore has no big money-burners.

I wish you would let me know what sort of paper you want to make the Bohemian. I am eager to get busy, but I scarcely know what to suggest. I retired from the short story turf three years ago, and have since written nothing in that line save a novelette (not a novelette, really, but long short story) of about 15,000 words. It would make a good $1 book, a la Brian Hooker's[1] "The Right Man", if properly illustrated. It is an attempt to write a comedy in a serious manner. There are but three characters: a bride and groom and the bridegroom's vanquished rival. The rival butts in on the honeymoon journey and raises hell. Altogether a story that pleases me more, perhaps, than it will please anyone else. But if B. W. Dodge care to see it, I will risk the postage with the nonchalance of a Rockefeller.

Hirshberg tells me he is at work on an article on hypnotism. About that and other things I hope to see you within a few weeks. Certainly I shall get to New York before Sept. 1st. Are you to be found on Sunday afternoons? A good time to talk things over.

Sincerely,
H. L. Mencken

1. Brian Hooker (1880–1946), songwriter, opera librettist, novelist.

[NYP]

439 W. 123rd St.
N.Y.C.

Aug 8th '09

My Dear Mencken
Yours of the 1st & 8th[1] before me and before explaining I want you promise not to write anything appertaining to the Bohemian to me care of the Delineator but address it instead either to me here at my apartment, (439 W. 123rd) or c/o The Editor of the Bohemian, 40 W. 33rd Street, (but don't put my name on the outside of the envelope) who will see that it reaches me. And by the way this applies to Hirschberg when you see him. Please tell him.

And now in relation to the Bohemian. I told young Krog (Fritz Krog)[2] who is in charge to write you and explain the policy but evidently he hasn't done it. I want to make it the broadest, most genial little publication in the field when I get it properly underway. I don't want any tainted fiction or cheap sex-struck articles but I do want a big catholic point of view, a sense of humor, grim or gay, and an apt realistic perception of things as they are. You could write for the Bohemian. You could write

1. Editorials for the Department to be entitled <u>At</u> <u>the</u> <u>Sign</u> <u>of</u> <u>the</u> <u>Lead</u> <u>Pencil</u> which will lead the magazine and which will contain certain broad interesting shots at current conditions from any point of view so long as it is clever. <u>And</u> your editorials are clever.

2. You could contribute to the <u>Bohemiana</u> department skits of any and all sorts, verse, humorous character sketches, playlets (farces I mean) and anything which will get a real smile out of anybody.

3. You can write essays about clever uptodate things from pickles to railway presidents as long as they are clever, and

4. Of course we are an open market for stories short and long, and

5. for articles on any and every concievable subject so long as they are interesting.

I want some good interviews with big people, some clever take offs on current political conditions, some truthful interesting pictures of current day society, and jabs and skits of all sorts. I want bright stuff. I want humor and above all I want knowledge of life <u>as</u> <u>it</u> <u>is</u> broad, simple, good natured. Are you any wiser?

Please come over some Saturday and stay over Sunday with me. I will cancel all engagements on receipt of your letter & we will talk things out.

Yours with best wishes
Dreiser

1. Mencken wrote Dreiser on the 1st and the 5th of August.
2. Fritz Krog, writer and editor who served as the nominal editor of the *Bohemian*.

H. L. Mencken
1524 Hollins St.
Baltimore.

[before 9 August 1909]

My dear Dreiser:-

Here is an essay that may serve to arouse the virtuous.[1] Others will follow anon. At the moment, I am worked to death at the office.

I called on Rider and Dodge and explained the Ibsen matter. Rider apparently thinks the chance of profit small; I have a letter from him practically declining the series.[2] Privately, I am not very eager to go on: my time is much occupied as it is. Luce,[3] meanwhile, will get out one volume

Dreiser and Sara White Dreiser (Courtesy of Vera Dreiser)

a year, thus scaring off possible competitors, and later on, when 5 or 6 volumes are ready, it will be easier to sell the whole series to some one able to handle it properly.

My best regards to Mrs. Dreiser. You must bring her down to Baltimore some day soon.

Truly,
H. L. Mencken

Possible Editorials
A Plea For a Hell
On Whiskers
Actors—are They Human?
The American Wedding
Jews and Their Ways
The Literary Life
Mothers-in-Law
American Music.
Eating as an Art
A Defense of Alcohol
American Newspapers
Revivals
The Tropics

   1. Mencken wrote "A Plea for Profanity," which Dreiser converted into an editorial entitled "In Defense of Profanity," *Bohemian* 17(November 1909), 567–68.
   2. Fremont Rider, who worked under Dreiser at Butterick (and also sub rosa at Dodge and the *Bohemian*) wrote Mencken on 31 August to say that Dodge decided against the Ibsen book. [UPL]
   3. The Boston firm that published Mencken's Ibsen volumes.

[NYP]

439 West 123rd Street

Aug. 9th '09

My Dear Mencken

"A Plea For Profanity" is all to the good. It will make a better editorial than essay. It is short enough. And your list is fine. Do them all. I wish I could have one or two more in time for November which means by the 15th. "A Plea For a Hell" would be out of sight. Mrs. Dreiser is very much pleased because of your invitation. She wants to come sometime & I would like to. You are persona grata at this commissary department. You can always eat free here. And Mrs. Dreiser says so.

> Yours with best wishes
> Dreiser

Don't bother about Rider. I haven't had a chance to take the matter up.

[UPL]

H. L. Mencken
1524 Hollins St.
Baltimore.

Baltimore, August 10th. [1909]

My dear Dreiser:-

Your letter puts the white light where it belongs, and God willing, I shall try to enter one of the five doors. I shall see Hirshberg tomorrow and tell him about your address. Will you be in New York Sunday August 29th? I am coming over in the morning, and if you have nothing else to do, there will be a good chance for a palaver.

> Sincerely,
> H. L. Mencken

[NYP]

439 W. 123rd St.
N.Y.C.

Aug 13th 09

My Dear Mencken:

For heaven sake come across with two or three or four clever editorials wont you for our "At the Sign of the Lead Pencil" & oblige yours[1]

> Dreiser

Will $10.00 be fair?

1. With the October issue, Dreiser began running the unsigned essays in "At the Sign of the Lead Pencil." In this department, he published eight pieces by Mencken (see Mencken to Dreiser, 17 December 1909). Seven of these have been identified: in October, "The Baldheaded Man," "E Pluribus Unum," "The Fine Art of Conjugal Bliss," "The Slap-Stick Burlesque"; in November, "In Defense of Profanity"; in December, "The Gastronomic Value of the Knife," "The Psychology of Kissing."

[NYP-T]

THE DELINEATOR
London – Paris – New York
Theodore Dreiser, Editor

New York, August 19, 1909.

My dear Mencken:

I think the last editorial on Bald Headed Men is delightful, and is the best thing of that kind I have read in a long time. I wish you would write four more.

Very sincerely yours,
Theodore Dreiser

[UPL]

H. L. Mencken
1524 Hollins St.
Baltimore.

Baltimore, Aug. 20th. [1909]

My dear Dreiser:-

Thanks for your note. I am glad that the two editorials pleased you. After we talk it over, no doubt, I shall be able to keep nearer form. I am coming to New York, by the way, Sunday a week—that is, Aug. 29th. I have an engagement with my Boston publisher,[1] who is coming down to meet me, at 2 o'clock; but this business will be over by 7 or 8 P.M. Can't we have a little palaver in the evening?

Within is the 9000-word story.[2] If it won't do, hold the ms., and I'll pick it up when I see you.

More editorials will follow from day to day.

Sincerely,
H. L. Mencken

1. The publisher Luce who had issued his Shaw and Nietzsche books.
2. Mencken had proposed a 9,500-word short story, and on 18 August Dreiser wrote asking him to send it. After this, there is no record of it.

[NYP]
Aug 27, 1909

My Dear Mencken:

When you come over Sunday you dine with us. Don't fail. Dinner at seven. We will wait. I meant to write you last Monday. This is a duplicate of a card sent to your house.

Dreiser

[UPL]

H. L. Mencken
1524 Hollins St.
Baltimore.

Baltimore, Sept. 15th. [1909]

My dear Dreiser:-

As soon as I get my November Smart Set article off my hands, I'll get to work in earnest. Last night I began a one-act play of a new sort. It has 1642 characters, and yet not one of them utters a word.[1] I'll send it to you when it is finished.

Yours,
H. L. Mencken

1. "The Artist—A Drama without Words" is a farce in which the speeches of the characters—a pianist and his audience—are presented as unspoken meditations (see *Bohemian* 17(December 1909), 805–8; republished in *Smart Set* 49 (August 1916), 79–84, and in *A Book of Burlesques* (1916).

[UPL-H]

H. L. Mencken
1524 Hollins St.
Baltimore.

[after 20 September 1909]

My dear Dreiser:-

My sincere congratulations on the Bohemian. It has begun to show that "different" quality: it is, in looks and contents, a decidedly attractive magazine. So far, I have yet to read some of the stuff, but all that I have tackled is excellent. You wrote "The Man on the Sidewalk"—a corking editorial.[1] "The Matter of Spiritualism" arouses my unholy horror.[2] I wish

you would read an article on the editorial page of last Sunday's N.Y. Sun—
and then tackle some of the late treatises on biology—le Dantec's "The
Nature @ Origin of Life",[3] for example. I think they would land you in
the German camp of violent unbelievers. The notion that the soul is im-
mortal seems to me utterly gratuitous and abhorrent. But enough!

I am having a one-act play copied—and more editorials will follow
soon. I'm sorry I could get in no more before the 20th. It was a physical
impossibility.

Truly,
H. L. Mencken

1. "The Man on the Sidewalk," 17(October), 422–23.
2. "In the Matter of Spiritualism," 17(October), 424–25.
3. F. A. Le Dantec's *The Nature and Origin of Life* (New York, 1906).

[NYP]

439 W. 123

Sept. 25 '09

My Dear Mencken:
The Artist is ok. It is very clever. What would be about right for that?
Yours With Great Affection
Theodore Dreiser

[UPL-H]

THE SUN
Baltimore

[after 25 September 1909]

My dear Dreiser:-
God knows. I have never sold a play. Playwrights, I hear, get a lot of
money. Therefore, about $1000. would seem natural. If the rules forbid,
give me whatever would be due for a short-story of the same length.

I'm very glad that it pleased you. I want to do another play a bit later
on. Scene: the Globe Theater, on the Bankside. Date: July 16, 1601—the
first night of "Hamlet". Characters: Shakespeare, Henslowe, Heminge @
Condell. The action takes place in the <u>box-office</u> of the theater during the
count-up. I have been soaking myself in Elizabethan stage lore.

By the way, Ford's play was a gem. I shall mention it in my edition of "Hedda Gabler."[1] It is better than any of F. Anstry's[2] burlesques of Ibsen— far better.

More editorials anon.

Truly yours,
H. L. Mencken

1. Mencken was working on a transcript of *Hedda Gabler* in 1909, but it was never published, probably because of the poor sales that year of his editions of *A Doll's House* and *Little Eyolf*.
2. F. Anstrey, pseudonym of Thomas Anstrey Guthrie, author.

[NYP-Tel]

The Western Union Telegraph Company

New York Oct. 15th [1909]

H. L. Mencken
   Need 3 funny editorials Bad. Can I get them Monday?
Theodore Dreiser

[NYP]

439 West 123rd Street

Oct. 18th 09

My Dear Mencken:
   The three received. Bachelors & Progress has the other two skinned. American Music comes next. Psychology of Kissing last. There all good. A thousand thanks. If I come over to Balt. will you put me up for the night.
Theodore Dreiser

[UPL-H]

H. L. Mencken
1524 Hollins St.
Baltimore.

[after 18 October 1909]

My dear Dreiser:-
   If you come to Baltimore I'll put you up in the Cathedral, and introduce you to all the brewers. When are you coming? Make it soon!
Yours,
H. L. Mencken

THE SUN
Baltimore

Saturday night [30 October 1909]

My dear Dreiser:-

Here is one—@ two more come tomorrow. I have just finished the book that was worrying me,[1] @ hereafter I'll have more time. Do you think well of the "sermon to preachers"?

My apologies again for my delays. They have been unwilling, I assure you.

To Mrs. Dreiser my best regards.

Yours,
Mencken

1. *Men versus the Man: A Correspondence between Robert Rives La Monte, Socialist, and H. L. Mencken, Individualist* (New York, 1910).

439 W. 123rd St.
N.Y.C.

Nov. 2nd '09

My Dear Mencken:

"The Decay of the Churches" is fine but in my judgement it is only partly right. You ask "Why should they (men) by their acts give countenance to the theory that their fate is determined by the arbitrary moods of the Gods." They shouldn't. But how about the fixed rules. And isn't seeking knowledge (scientific) a form of prayer. Aren't scientists & philosophers at bottom truly reverential and don't they wish (pray) ardently for more knowledge. If you would but add a few lines to this effect in this last paragraph I would say yes—splendid.[1] It's a fine thing as it is but the truth is men are not less religious—they are religious in a different way—and that's a fact.

Theodore Dreiser

I want Suite A—parlor floor, in the brewery

1. Dreiser never published "The Decay of the Churches," because he abandoned the magazine after the December issue.

H. L. Mencken
1524 Hollins St.
Baltimore.

November 3rd. [1909]

My dear Dreiser:-

I have no copy of the editorial on the decay of the churches, and so can't fix it up until I get back the copy I sent in. If you will do it, I'd much prefer to have you add the qualification you mention. You know exactly what you mean to convey. I am in your hands.

In all honesty, I can't follow you. The scientific impulse seems to me to be the very opposite of the religious impulse. When a man seeks knowledge he is trying to gain means of fighting his own way in the world, but when he prays he confesses that he is unable to do so. The essential thing about prayer is that it assumes that the moods of the gods are <u>not</u> fixed and invariable. If they were, it would be silly to ask the gods to change them. This idea, I think, explains the decay of religion.

The feeling of abasement, of incapacity, is inseparable from the religious impulse, but against that feeling all exact knowledge makes war. The efficient man does not cry out "Save me, O God". On the contrary, he makes diligent efforts to save himself. But suppose he fails? Doesn't he throw himself, in the end, on the mercy of the gods? Not at all. He accepts his fate with philosophy, bouyed up by the consciousness that he has done his best. Irreligion, in a word, teaches men to die with dignity, just as it teaches them how to live with dignity.

But all this is only my personal view of life, and I freely confess that I may be wrong. Therefore, I shall be glad to see you put something of your view into the editorial.

A few other things, before I forget. If the Sun is on the Bohemian's exchange list, will you please cut it off. Sending the magazine can do no good, and if any of my stuff is recognized there may be a kick. No. 2: Has any conclusion been reached regarding the Ibsens?[1] No. 3: I'd like to have "Abaft the Funnel" to review in the S.S. jointly with "Actions and Reactions".[2] No. 4: How are you? No. 5: Suite A is being made ready for you.

Sincerely,
H. L. Mencken

1. Mencken was still trying to get Dreiser to interest Dodge in publishing the Ibsen papers.
2. Rudyard Kipling's *Abaft the Funnel* (1909) and *Actions and Reactions* (1909).

[NYP]

439 W. 123rd St.
N.Y.C.

N.Y. Nov. 7th 09

My Dear Mencken:

This editorial business is too long to argue out by mail. I am coming over to your town Thanksgiving Eve. Does that invitation hold good?

By the way I want to thank you for mentioning W. H. Wright.[1] I will get right after him if you give me his address. You said Los Angeles Times but I judge he is here in the East now.

In regard to the Sun—we will cut it off the list. Will also see that you get a copy of "Abaft the Funnel". In regard to Ibsen I'm for it and I will get favorable action on this this coming week.

Yours
Dreiser

1. Willard Huntington Wright (1888–1939), author, editor, journalist. At this time Wright was literary editor of the *Los Angeles Times*. He edited *Smart Set* in 1913, and later, as S. S. Van Dine, he wrote the popular Philo Vance detective stories.

[UPL-H]

THE SUN
Baltimore

[after 7 November 1909]

My dear Dreiser:-

Good for you. Let me know exactly when you will arrive and how long you can stay. The breweries have been notified and extra bartenders are being recruited. Why not stay over Thanksgiving Day?

W. H. Wright's address is the Astoria Hotel, Los Angeles. He is on his way there now.

Yours
H. L. Mencken

Hirshberg is having a demon rum party Thanksgiving night. Stay over for it.

[NYP]

THE DELINEATOR
New York
Theodore Dreiser, Editor

Nov. 11th '09

My Dear Mencken:

Wednesday evening before Thanksgiving I will be with you. Thanksgiving P.M. or Eve Mrs. Dreiser joins me & we go to Hirschbergs. Friday am. we go to Atlantic City. You see how I accept your invitation to go to Hirschbergs. I go. I want to talk things in general Wednesday Eve & Thursday Am.

Yours

Dreiser

Ich Kann sauffen bis ich verblatz[1]

1. I can drink until I collapse. This is written at the top of the page, above the address. Below this and to the left of the address, Dreiser drew the figure of a man with a glass raised to his mouth in drinking position.

[UPL]

THE SUN
Baltimore

November 15th. [1909]

My dear Dreiser:-

Let me know the exact hour of your arrival Wednesday and I'll have the guard of honor at the station. The program arranged by the citizens' committee is as follows:

Wednesday evening: Dinner at Childs' and a burlesque show afterward.

Thursday morning: Conference on the state of literature.

Noon: Lunch at Dennett's.

Afternoon: Sociological investigations.

Dinner: You and Mrs. Dreiser at my residenz.

Evening: Beer and Meyerbeer at Hirshberg's. Demonstration by several local Eusapia Paladinos.[1]

If this program wins your O.K/ we shall proceed.

Yours

HLM.

1. Eusapia Palladino was a famous Italian medium.

[NYP-T]

THE DELINEATOR
London – Paris – New York
Theodore Dreiser, Editor

New York, November 23, 1909.

My dear Mencken:

I figure that my train reaches Baltimore at 5:15 at the Union Station, but I will call you up. There is one defect in your programme,—there should have been at least 150 saloon-keepers as a marching club.

Very sincerely yours,
Dreiser

[NYP-T]

THE DELINEATOR
London – Paris – New York
Theodore Dreiser, Editor

New York, December 6, 1909.

Dear Mencken:

I have received "The Philosophy of Friedrich Nietzsche", by one H. L. Mencken, and the book of poems from the press of Thomas B. Mosher, both duly inscribed.[1] I have read the inscriptions in both cases, and the introduction and bibliography in the case of Mr. Nietzsche. If the outline of Mr. Nietzsche's philosophy in the introduction is correct, he and myself are hale fellows well met.

I have just discovered a noble beer hall modeled after one which was in the brewer's own village in a far part of Germany. The next time you come to New York I am going to march you straight to it, and pour four gallons of real German beer down your throat.

Yours,
Dreiser

1. Dreiser is referring to Mencken's book on Nietzsche and to Lizette Woodworth Reese's *A Wayside Lute* (1909). In the Nietzsche book, Mencken wrote "To Theodore Dreiser:- In memory of furious disputations on sorcery @ the art of letters." In the Reese book he wrote simply "To Theodore Dreiser: From H. L. M."

THE DELINEATOR
New York
Theodore Dreiser, Editor

Dec. 16th '09

My Dear Mencken:

It has finally been decided to close the Bohemian out and I am trying to figure out tonight exactly how much they owe you. "The Artist" was $50.⁰⁰ and there were 5? or 6? editorials used and not paid for. How was it. I have one here on Religion which was never used & which I will return unless the book comes to life. I stand back of the sum due you. If I can't get it out of Smith[1] shortly I will mail you check.

Come over Christmas. I am deep in Nietche but I can't say I greatly admire him. He seems to Schopenhauer confused and warmed over

Dreiser

1. William Neil Smith, president of the Bohemian Publishing Co.

H. L. Mencken
1524 Hollins St.
Baltimore.

Baltimore, December 17th. [1909]

My dear Dreiser:-

It's too bad about the Bohemian, but such is the fortune of war. My own account stands as follows: I had four editorials in the October number and one in the November, for which I received a $50. check. In the December number I have four editorials and "The Artist", which makes the balance due to me $90.[1] If there is any other copy from me in the office, please have it sent to me. I can use it here.

You are to mail me no checks whatever. Unless the proper angels come down with the money, you have my receipt for the $90. I took my chance and it seems to me unfair that you should be responsible. If the plutocrats, of course, produce the cash, I take my share, or my proportionate share.

What are your plans about the semi-monthly?[2] I am eager to see it under way and have a lot of ideas that may be of use.

My best regards to Mrs. Dreiser. I wish I could get to New York during the holidays, but I can't. Meanwhile, good wishes for 1910.

Yours,

H. L. Mencken

1. Later this day Mencken sent off a brief note saying he had miscounted and had three, not four, editorials in the December number. [UPL]

2. Dreiser was considering the possibility of beginning a new weekly magazine, but he never did so.

[UPL]

H. L. Mencken
1524 Hollins St.
Baltimore.

Baltimore, Feb. 6th. [1910]

My dear Dreiser:-

First: How are you, anyhow?

Second: If you have the copy of an editorial called "The Decay of the Churches", heave it back. If it is lost, say no more!

Third: Are you making plans for that weekly you mentioned?

Fourth: Lamonte has sold "Men vs. the Man" to Holt. When it comes out, God only knows. It has been set up.

Fifth: The prospects for excellent bock beer down here could be no better.

Sixth: Hirshberg has had his bald head grained by a house painter.

Seventh: Sincerely yours,

Mencken

[UPL-H]

THE SUN
Baltimore

[before 12 February 1910]

Dear Dreiser:-

What is up? Are you thinking of starting that weekly? If so, I am with you with both feet. I may see you soon.

Yours,
Mencken

[NYP-T]

THE DELINEATOR
London – Paris – New York
Theodore Dreiser, Editor

New York, February 12, 1910.

My dear Mencken:

I have been intending for a long time to answer your kind letter, but a great many difficulties have made it inadvisable. I have been hoping all the time that I could adjust the matter of the $80.00 with some of the others who were interested, but I find there is nothing doing in that line; so I am enclosing my personal check, which I want you to accept. I haven't looked yet, but I am satisfied that I have the editorial on The Decay of the Churches, and will see that you get it back. The Weekly is very much in abeyance, but you can never tell how things will come forth.

Hirshberg came up here and walked all over the corns of Carrington,[1] and since then I have been doing my best to assuage Carrington. But I suppose it will work out all right in the long run.

Regards to both of you.

Sincerely,
Dreiser

1. Hereward Carrington, author who published under the pseudonym of Hubert Lavington.

[UPL-H]

THE SUN
Baltimore

[after 12 February 1910]

My dear Dreiser:-

Not on your life! We took our chances together and lost. Your loss was much larger than mine. I refuse to let you run a literary insurance company. If the weekly doesn't start soon, I shall start a quarterly. Seriously!

Hirshberg, like all Jews, is too damned bumptious. If I had known you proposed sending him to Carrington, I should have warned you to beware. The thing needed tact, which no Yiddisher ever had.

Let Eusapia be accursed![1] Munsterberg[2] has knocked her out.

My regards to Mrs. Dreiser.

Truly
H. L. Mencken

1. Another reference to Eusapia Palladino, the Italian medium. Dreiser had published in the *Delineator* three articles on Palladino, written by Fremont Rider; and Hereward Carrington wrote *Eusapia Palladino and Her Phenomenon* (New York, 1909).
2. Hugo Munsterberg (1863–1916), German-born professor of psychology.

[NYP]

439 W. 123rd St.
N.Y.C.

Feb. 20th 1910

My Dear Mencken:

I would feel much better if I could arrange it this way—my check to go to you for $50.00 for "the artist" because you let me have that on request & because its too good to be robbed of in this manner. And I feel a sense of responsibility beyond your kind feelings. The editorial[1] goes back under separate cover

By the way the childrens agent of the National Home Finding Society of Baltimore sent me three photos of three different children who bear a suspicious resemblance to a certain editorial writer who shall be nameless for the present. However I am looking up the facts. If it should prove, as I surmise that he is the guilty party, I propose to have him arrested. This unrestricted traffic in copulation must cease. I give fair warning.

And as for Hirshberg, well the more I think of him the more I am sure he is punished enough   He has to live with himself.

More regidity to your epigaster.

Dreiser

1. "The Decay of the Churches."

[NYP-T]

THE DELINEATOR
London – Paris – New York
Theodore Dreiser, Editor

March 21, 1910.

My dear Mencken:

I have a plan for a department in The Delineator which makes room for a number of contributions of from 250 to 300 words in length, for which I am willing to pay ten cents a word. It is going to be called "The

Man's Page", and it is going to be in a way a take-off of the Women's Page in the average daily paper, only it is going to be written entirely for men. The contributions want to have a basis of serious advice with just a slight undertone of josh. By that I mean they can be fairly funny, but they oughtn't to be rank nonsense: they ought to contain some bits of wisdom by which a man might profit. I propose to burlesque the names of such well known writers as Dorothy Dix, Ella Wheeler Wilcox, Mabel Herbert Urner, and have the contributions signed by such noble souls as Elihu Wilcox Wheeler, Dirithy Dox, Dan Rittenhouse, Able Herbert Werner, and others of that sort. I propose to assign certain subjects such as "The Etiquette of the Purse", "How to Keep a Wife's Love", "Coming Styles for Men", "Taking Off the Extra Pound of Flesh", "Economical Recipes for Careful Husbands", "The Hair That Is Left In Your Brush", "When Her Relations Come", and things of that sort which I am going to ask the black horse cavalry of humor to discourse upon. You and Eugene Wood and Paul West and Franklin P. Adams and Wallace Irwin and Gelett Burgess and Oliver Herford will all be given assignments if you will take them so long as the department lasts.[1]

What I want to know now is whether you are in a receptive mood. Aside from the subjects which I have indicated there are going to be some standard departments such as, "Fashions For Men", "Before Your Mirror", "Answers to Etiquette Letters by Dan Rittenhouse", "The Cozy Corner" which will be devoted to booming the circulation of the magazine, "Easy Confidence With Uncle Tallweed", a monthly poem, such as "To a Deserted Husband," "To a Husband Whose Policy has Expired" and things of that sort, and a series of "Interviews with a Henpecked Husband."

I should like your opinion if you are interested as to which one of these things you would like to undertake, and after notifying me I want you to wait long enough for me to notify you in regard to the general assignment, as I want to harmonize the various humorists so as to place the assignments as much as possible in line with each individual's particular taste. If you have any counter suggestion which you will make and which you think you could do better let me have the same by return mail. 250 to 300 words won't be much work and I suppose you could make use of the $25. or $30.

With the season's good wishes, I am,

Yours,
Dreiser

1. Dreiser did get all the writers he mentions here to contribute to "The Man's Magazine Page." Under his own name, Mencken contributed "How to Put On a Collar," 76 (July 1910), 80, and "The Legal Liabilities of the Best Man," 76 (August 1910), 152.

THE DELINEATOR
London – Paris – New York
Theodore Dreiser, Editor

New York, March 25, 1910.

My dear Mencken:

Your letter gives me great joy.[1] On my first table of contents of the Man's Page I have you scheduled for "How To Keep A Wife's Love", but I will waive that in favor of "The Duties of a Best Man" or "How To Put On A Collar Two Sizes Too Small." I think you might also send this way "Choosing a Barber", which if it is as good as it sounds will be promptly paid for.

I wish to announce that if I didn't hear definitely in regard to the $50.00 check that the $80.00 check will come your way and this time there will be no return. Accursed be all editorial writers.

Yours,
Dreiser

1. This letter has disappeared.

H. L. Mencken
1524 Hollins St.
Baltimore.

Baltimore, March 27th [1910]

My dear Dreiser:-

I shall fall to the task in a few days. Unluckily, we are just preparing to launch a new evening paper and much of the work is on my neck. When do you want copy?

As for the Bohemian, I forbid you to mention it again, on pain of the bastinado. If you actually owed me any money, I would take it without a murmur, and even harass you with catchpolls if you showed any hesitation in coming down, but I'll be hanged if I can see how you are personally responsible for the debts of the Bohemian. I was well aware of the risk and took it, breaking about even.

Meanwhile, it is a pleasure to report that the crab season promises to be excellent. Why not drop down? Hirshberg will not pester you. His effrontery growing painful, I have recently given him a rough settler.

Sincerely,
H. L. Mencken

THE DELINEATOR
London – Paris – New York
Theodore Dreiser, Editor

New York, April 6, 1910.

My dear Mencken:

I got Charles Battell Loomis[1] to do "How To Keep A Wife's Love", and it turned out very satisfactory. I will take all five suggestions you made if you will only please get on the job and do one or two of them now. "Sure Tests For Cigars", "Choosing a Barber", "The Duties of a Best Man", "How to Put On a Collar Two Sizes Too Small": any or all of these will be welcome at this stage of the game. Forward.

Sincerely,
Dreiser

1. Charles Battell Loomis (1861–1911), poet, humorist.

THE DELINEATOR
London – Paris – New York
Theodore Dreiser, Editor

New York, April 27, 1910.

Dear, darling Mencken:

"How To Put On A Collar Two Sizes Too Small" helps me greatly. It looks like 300 words and a check for ten cents a word follows.

Fairest of thy sex, dream again.

Sincerely,
Theodore Dreiser

THE DELINEATOR
London – Paris – New York
Theodore Dreiser, Editor

New York, May 19, 1910

My dear Mencken:

"Thoughts on Whiskers" is a little too solemn. It is funny in a way, but is not light enough in its texture. Can't you loosen up? You can become a

Mencken and George Jean Nathan (Enoch Pratt Free Library)

little too deep in your citations and phraseology, you know. As Hamlet said, "Something too much of this." [1]

But let me see more, and others.

> Very sincerely yours,
> Theodore Dreiser
> Editor.

1. *Hamlet*, III, ii.

THE DELINEATOR
London – Paris – New York
Theodore Dreiser, Editor

New York, July 28, 1910

My dear Mencken:

Mrs. Dreiser was quite bad, but is better and it looks as though she will be all right in the course of ten days or two weeks. [1]

I think it is a crime that you haven't sent me "Choosing a Barber." The few things you did do for me were, in my judgment, the most comical of any.

Hell to your soul!

> Yours,
> Theo. D.
> Editor

1. Sara White Dreiser had been sick with rheumatic fever.

THE DELINEATOR
London – Paris – New York
Theodore Dreiser, Editor

New York, August 27, 1910

My dear Mencken:

I am sorry to hear that they have got you down on your back. These doctors are all scoundrels and when they get hold of a humorist it is pathetic what they do to him, and for why should you pick Hirshberg of all

people? There are doctors here in New York who will kill you readily
for nothing.

What is it Epicticus said about making a swell corpse out of a live
man?[1]

Yours for health,
Theodore Dreiser

1. Dreiser means Epictetus, the Greek Stoic philosopher.

THE DELINEATOR
London — Paris — New York
Theodore Dreiser, Editor

Aug. 30th 1910.

My dear Mr. Mencken:

The Delineator likes from time to time a good humorous special of
about 4,000 words which will relate to some interesting subject and not be
too far removed from the members of the average family to have it miss
their perception or sense of propriety. Sometimes I am able to make suitable suggestions, but the best I can do in this instance is to give you a list
of the type of articles we have purchased in times past.

Americans Abroad   By Harrison Rhodes

With Our College Boys and Girls at Commencement   By Walter P.
Eaton

The Hard Work of a Foreign Tour   By M. Landon Reed

The Funny Side of Indian Home Life   By F. G. Moorehead

On Shopping Abroad   By Virginia Frame

Childhood's Happy Hour   By Eugene Wood

It is perfectly obvious that a great many articles that are treated seriously can be treated humorously, and it is just such subjects which I would
like to consider. As I say, I have no subjects in mind at this moment, but I
would take it as a favor if you would try and think of something for me and
make a suggestion.

The articles enclosed will give you a slant on the method. I would be
very much pleased if together we could work out something which would
be just right.

Very sincerely yours,
Theodore Dreiser
Editor.

THE DELINEATOR
London – Paris – New York
Theodore Dreiser, Editor

Oct. 1, 1910.

My dear Mr. Mencken:

This is to tell you that my connection with the Delineator ceases October 15th, 1910.[1]

I will tell you about it when I see you.

Very sincerely yours,
Theodore Dreiser

1. Because of the scandal attached to his rather platonic affair with Thelma Cudlipp, the eighteen-year-old daughter of an assistant editor at Butterick, Dreiser had been forced to leave his post.

PARK AVENUE HOTEL
New York

Oct. 11th 1910

My Dear Mencken:

Nothing's up save a big row. It's all over now though & I am considering several good things. My conscience hurts me a little though for first-off I should finish my book.[1] And I may. If you come over—439 W. 123rd St.

Yours
Dreiser

1. *Jennie Gerhardt.*

OFFICE MEMO
Editorial Department

[October 1910]

Dear Mencken

Ten cents a word & I am very lonely. Is there no hope.

A Gloomy Editor.
Dreiser

OFFICE MEMO
Editorial Department

[October 1910]

I have just discovered that this is a very sad world.

2

*I Want to Blaze Out with
Some Dreiser Stuff
(1911–1914)*

"I expect to try out this book game for about four or five books after which unless I am enjoying a good income from them I will quit."
—TD to HLM, 24 February 1911

"I want to blaze out with some Dreiser stuff."
—HLM to TD, 11 August 1914

When Dreiser left Butterick, he went back to his writer's desk, never again to earn his living from any other source. A decade later he would write Mencken that "except for your valiant and unwearied and even murderous assaults and onslaughts in my behalf I should be little further than in 1910." 1910 was a turning point. For Dreiser the next five years saw a phenomenal burst of creative energy that included the completion of four large novels (*Jennie Gerhardt, The "Genius," The Financier,* and *The Titan*), an autobiography (later published as *Dawn*), a travel book (*A Traveler at Forty*), as well as plays, poetry, stories, and miscellaneous essays.

More than friendship accounts for Mencken's response to this body of writing. As the *Smart Set*'s critic-in-residence, he had been lamenting the sad state of contemporary American fiction. Before he read the manuscript of *Jennie Gerhardt* (the story of a "fallen" German-American girl who, by the way, had the same last name as the second wife of Mencken's grandfather), he could hold out only David Graham Phillips as worthy of serious notice. *Jennie Gerhardt* offered both men a second surprise of recognition, but this time Mencken dropped the comic mask. After a first reading he wrote Dreiser that the book "comes upon me with great force. It touches my own experience of life in a hundred places; it preaches (or perhaps I had better say exhibits) a philosophy of life that seems to be sound; altogether I get a powerful effect of reality, stark and unashamed. It is drab and gloomy, but so is the struggle for existence. It is without humor, but so are the jests of the great comedian who shoots at our heels and makes us do our grotesque dancing." With this, the bright humorist with literary pretensions became for Dreiser a critic whose underlying seriousness matched his own.

Their exchange, in fact, took a somewhat unexpected turn. When they first met, no one could have predicted that Mencken would become a power in literary circles or that he would be the key agent in establishing Dreiser's career. But by 1911 his lively book reviews were winning him an attentive audience. With Dreiser's fiction he was able, for the first time, to elaborate an argument for a native writer around the principles he had adapted from his study of the European realists. The fact that Dreiser's work embodied his aesthetic ideals reinforced the friendship. Both men brought with them out of the 1890s a similar belief in the function and purpose of fiction. They had absorbed nineteenth-century European writers—especially realists like Balzac, Ibsen, Shaw, Tolstoy, and Hardy—and combined them in a peculiar synthesis with native interpreters of the American scene like the urban columnists George Ade and Eugene Field. And in the background were larger figures like Poe, Whitman, and Twain, whom they idealized as victims of American puritanism.

In these years, Mencken read all Dreiser's books in manuscript, and his letters in response show how quickly Dreiser had become for him something more than the senior editor who had written a rare first novel. These letters—on *Jennie Gerhardt* (23 April 1911), *The Financier* (6 October 1912), *A Traveler at Forty* (16 November 1913), and *The Titan* (23 March 1914)—constitute a *classicus locus* of literary realism as Mencken and Dreiser presented it in the mid-teens. In them Mencken defined realism as it reached its modern apogee in naturalism. His excitement—what thirty years later Dreiser would call his "Jennie Gerhardt spasm"—stems partly from the opportunity Dreiser presented him to elaborate his critical premises on a living American novelist. In the process, he provided Dreiser with a vocabulary to define his practice as a writer. It is a vocabulary that evolved out of a shared dedication to realism—to its mimetic bias, its mission of "honesty in art," its goal of portraying the human struggle within the environment, its emphasis on "the slow unfolding of character," and its nationalism yoked to its high purpose as a "searching criticism of life." These letters were the raw material for Mencken's reviews of Dreiser—essays that instilled in his readers the idea that realism and naturalism need not exclude a sense of human dignity or high artistic standards.

Mencken and Dreiser were very conscious of working out a philosophically tougher version of realism than that fashioned by earlier pioneers like Howells and Hamlin Garland. They were kept conscious of this by what Mencken referred to as the "lady critics," for whom modern realism was something best reserved for decadent Europeans. Within a decade, their example effectively closed debate on the subject. Their practice, which combined naturalism with a broad aesthetic sensibility, anticipated writers of the twenties. While both the critic and the novelist generally remained impervious to formal innovation, they reshaped traditional forms to include characters and events prohibited by the conservative norms of their day. Both in its philosophy and in its challenge to the social and moral orthodoxies of the time, Dreiser's and Mencken's writing came to represent the transition from Howellsian realism to postwar modernism in America.

Mencken encouraged Dreiser to think of himself as the banner carrier in the struggle for realism in America, a message the critic began to spread across the country in 1911. Moreover, the treatment Dreiser's work received at the hands of hostile reviewers and timid publishers encouraged Mencken in his thinking about the alienation of the artist in America. In these years, he elaborated on this idea, as he wrote for each of Dreiser's books a series of reviews that reached different audiences. In the case of *Jennie Gerhardt*, for example, he wrote a *Smart Set* review, and another for the Christmas book section of the *Los Angeles Times*, and yet another for his "Free Lance" column in the Baltimore *Sun*. In addition, he put together a pamphlet that Harper used in its advertisement. He also wrote to writers he knew, conveying the same message he sent the novelist Harry Leon Wilson: "keep your eye on [Dreiser]. He has lately finished a new novel, 'Jennie Gerhardt,' in which he tells the story of 'Sister Carrie' again, but with vastly better workmanship. Dreiser and I are old friends and so he sent me the ms. Believe me, the story is an astonishing piece of work. . . . The lady critics will denounce it—as 'The Bookman' denounced 'Jude The Obscure.' God, what a country." [1] He enlisted the aid of his friends on the New York journals, and critics like Floyd Dell in Chicago and Willard H. Wright in Los Angeles followed his lead. "It looks to me from the drift of things as though your stand on Jennie would either make or break you," wrote Dreiser, judging correctly that Mencken's campaign was uniting them in the public mind. At this point their relationship turned, in effect, from a good friendship into something closer to a literary alliance.

Dreiser found in Mencken an enthusiastic supporter, a friend who believed in his star and who was willing to champion him in respectable literary circles. The decade of the teens saw Mencken guiding Dreiser's career in much the same spirit that the novelist had earlier advanced his. Despite such support, Dreiser's books sold poorly. Always insecure about his talents, Dreiser needed not only promotion but sympathetic understanding—and, most of all, a good editor. Mencken met these needs tirelessly. In reviews, he expanded on what he had said in his letters to

Dreiser. There were reservations in both—especially about Dreiser's habit of piling up "irrelevant detail" and his careless phrasing—but Mencken always ended on an upbeat. He praised the novelist as America's only great modernist, the peer of Conrad and the major Russians. In America, Dreiser alone used the novel the way Mencken supposed it should be used: his fiction pictured a harsh world in which people were moved like pieces on a chessboard. Of *Jennie Gerhardt* he wrote, "It has no more moral than a string quartet or the first book of Euclid," and he exulted in "the profound unmorality" of *The Titan*, which he read as "a great Nietzschean document." Mencken advertised Dreiser—and, of course, himself—as a homegrown *immoraliste* at a time when his readers were learning about such things in new editions of Nietzsche, Ibsen, Shaw, and Gide.

As Mencken's comments suggest, he early on cast Dreiser in his own image. Even before the outbreak of the war in Europe, the friendship was cemented by a shared sense of social identity. Conservative critics quickly—and correctly—branded them as part of the newer forces breaking with the dominant Anglo-American tradition. Their letters took on the air of strategy papers aimed at winning over a hostile publishing establishment and marshaling an offensive against what both referred to as American puritanism. At the time, Mencken was beginning to take on the "moralists" and vice crusaders in his "Free Lance" column, and to formulate his criticism of national mores in essays like his 1913 "American" series for *Smart Set*. The ideas he developed in these pieces became part of his defense of Dreiser. By 1914, the two men had developed a sense of common cause that often overflowed into the charged rhetoric of their personal exchange. "The philistines," Dreiser wrote in that year, "will never run us out as long as life do last. Given health and strength we can shake the American Jericho to its fourth substory." In effect, their private dialogue became the mine out of which they began forging a public image of themselves as blood brothers in the fight for literary freedom. Dreiser supplied the text—the "suppression" of *Sister Carrie*, the subsequent nervous breakdown, the decade of silence imposed upon him by agents of repression, the manuscripts bowdlerized by puritanical publishers, the hack work necessary to survive as a writer—and Mencken supplied the theory of a culture bent on destroying its true artists.

Much of this was less radical than it appears in hindsight. By the midteens, attacks against cultural orthodoxy had won over a large enough audience to pay its own way, whether in the national journals or the proliferating little magazines and theaters or the groups beginning to think Greenwich Village a nice place to visit. Mencken alienated many but he amused more, and the whole enterprise was carried on in great high spirits. He crusaded cheerfully for his friend, edited his prose, saw him through regular bouts of self-doubt, and muted his reservations about the writer who, he recalled after Dreiser's death, "came into the world with an incurable antipathy to the *mot juste*" and "an insatiable appetite for the obviously not true." They traded reviews, consulted the Ouija board for tips on how to confound the censors, and discussed, in the flush of excitement that marked this period, the possibility of a Nobel Prize. In their correspondence, Mencken's comic routines moved Dreiser to humor of his own, a bit heavier-handed but humor nonetheless. The two became familiar figures on the town, hunting up beer gardens, consuming sizable portions of bratwurst and sauerbraten, and (after Dreiser separated from his wife, Sara White Dreiser) meeting together with women friends. Above all, they relished the battle of books. They enjoyed a shared sense of purpose that few writers knew—the more staid Howells-Twain friendship and the high-minded Hawthorne-Melville exchange are notable exceptions—in a literary landscape that discouraged such bonds.

The revolt against literary orthodoxy included a telling paradox: the greatest living American novelist, Mencken argued, was so by virtue of his break with an impoverished native tradition. His fiction was "so European in its method, its point of view, its almost reverential seriousness, that one can scarcely imagine an American writing it." [2] This was the basis of his case for the novelist, and it helps explain a good deal of the intensity behind their response to each other. For in initiating the critical cliché of Dreiser as a presence with no cultural roots in America, Mencken linked his friend's achievement to what he sensed were the wellsprings of his own creative energy. The critic and the novelist shared, above all, a pervasive ambivalence about their public roles, an intense conflict between their large professional ambitions and their postures as gadflies to a society from whose native traditions they seemed, by birth and temperament, to be alienated.

In these years both men made their first trips abroad, and their time in Europe sharpened their feelings of cultural separateness. In the summer of 1914 two events, one affecting the world community and the other more limited, put other demands on the friendship. First, there was the war in Europe. Mencken wrote Dreiser, "God's benison upon the Kaiser. He will lick 'em all"—a sentiment shared by the novelist and one that would leave a permanent mark on their professional lives. In addition, Mencken and George Jean Nathan began their famous tenure as the editors of *Smart Set*. This move altered the critic-author relation Mencken and Dreiser had established, injecting into it a new element of practicality. Editorial demands intruded themselves upon Mencken's criticism, and, as he now had to publish—and pay for—what he read, he became less willing to shade his prejudices. Dreiser's growing desire to

608 Riverside Drive

Feb. 24th 1911

My dear Mencken:

The truth will out. I have just finished one book — Jennie Gerhardt — and am half through with another. I expect to try out this book game for about four or five books after which unless I am enjoying a good income from them I will quit. There is going to be a dandy lobster

Dreiser letter: 24 February 1911
(Rare Books and Manuscripts Division, New York Public Library)

win a new audience for his experimental work—plays of the "super-natural," prose poems, philosophical essays—met with resistance from Mencken, who wanted the Dreiser of *Jennie Gerhardt* and *The Titan* for his magazine. At this time, however, both men could draw on reserves of good will, and their differences ended in compromise.

Notes

1. Mencken to Wilson, 4 September 1911, in Forgue, *Letters*, 17.
2. Mencken, "A Novel of the First Rank," *Smart Set* 35 (November 1911), 154.

The Correspondence
(1911–1914)

H. L. Mencken
1524 Hollins St.
Baltimore.

[before 24 February 1911]

Dear Dreiser:–
   Where the devil are you? And what are you doing? I hear from the Jews
that you have written two or three novels, but experience has taught me to
put no faith in the Yiddish.

Yours,
M

608 Riverside Drive

Feb. 24th 1911

My Dear Mencken:
   The truth will out. I have just finished one book—Jennie Gerhardt—
and am half through with another.[1] I expect to try out this book game for
about four or five books after which unless I am enjoying a good income
from them I will quit. There is going to be a dandy lobster blowout free to
the initiated at the studio of Messrs Amick & Cowan[2] 63 Washington Sq.
on March 8th. If you and Hirshberg[3] want to come over I will see that you

get your share of the deep sea going variety. The land species you cannot avoid.

Dreiser

1. *The "Genius."*
2. Robert Amick and Percy Cowan, painters, illustrators.
3. See Dreiser to Mencken, 24 September 1907, n.1.

[UPL]

H. L. Mencken
1524 Hollins St.
Baltimore.

Baltimore, March 3rd. [1911]

Dear Dreiser:-

Bully news! You know I am one of those who hold "Sister Carrie" in actual reverence, as one of the best novels this fair land has ever produced. What is more, I have often said so in print, in a clarion voice. What is still more, I have really meant it. So I look forward eagerly to "Jennie Gerhardt" and to her successors. Give the game a fair trial: you have got the goods, and soon or late the fact will penetrate the skulls of those who have anything within. Whether you know it or not, "Sister Carrie" has begun to soak in. Such fellows as Wright[1] in Los Angeles are enthusiastic about it, and you will see the result when your next one comes along. The money be damned. You will not grow as rich as McCutcheon and Garvice, but there's a good living in it.[2]

Unluckily, I can't attend the lobster party, but I'll have a mass said for you. Here's hoping that Mrs. Dreiser has recovered her health and that you are well. My folks send their best regards.

Yours,
H. L. M.

1. Willard Huntington Wright, at the time the literary editor of the *Los Angeles Times*.
2. George Barr McCutcheon (1866–1928) and Charles Garvice (1883–1920) were best-selling authors of the day.

608 Riverside Drive

Mch 10th 1911

My Dear Mencken:

Many thanks. I sometimes think my desire is for expression that is entirely too frank for this time—hence that I must pay the price of being unpalatable. The next book will tell. I wish I could see you oftener. Work holds me pretty close.

By the way were you familiar with David Graham Philips books and did you like them?[1] Let me know.

Th. D.

1. David Graham Phillips (1867–1911), muckraking journalist and novelist, had been fatally shot two months earlier by a madman who believed Phillips had maligned his sister in *Joshua Craig* (1909).

H. L. Mencken
1524 Hollins St.
Baltimore.

Baltimore, March 14th. [1911]

Dear Dreiser:-

As for Phillips, I am a great admirer of his later work—particularly "The Hungry Heart" and "The Husband's Story". Such stuff as "The Fashionable Adventures of Joshua Craig" seems to have been done to get the money. In the S.S. for Jan. I had an article entitled "The Leading American Novelist", in which I pointed out a few of P's merits. Unluckily, there was no space for a long and serious discussion of him. I have no doubt that you find him immensely interesting, for your own method, as shown in "Sister Carrie", suggests his. I suspect that "Sister Carrie" taught him something. Incidentally, I seize every opportunity to ram in the idea that your book must be read. In the S.S. for Dec. (p. 165) there was a note about it. Here we behold, not a yearning to please a friend, but honest admiration for an arresting work of art. I look forward eagerly to "Jennie". Meanwhile, the bock beer delights and the season of boiled hard crabs dawns.

Yours,
M

Don't answer this: stick to your work![1]

1. The postscript is handwritten.

608 Riverside Drive
N.Y.C

Mch. 18th 1911

My Dear Mencken:
   Enclosed an opinion of Jennie Gerhardt which I thought you might like to see.[1] If you had the time I would like to have you read the mss in advance & give me your opinion.

                              Th. D

1. This has not been identified.

H. L. Mencken
1524 Hollins St.
Baltimore

Baltimore, March 22nd. [1911]

Dear Dreiser:-
   I am very eager to see "Jennie Gerhardt" and shall be glad to go through the ms. and give you my opinion of it. Let it come along at your convenience. I'll make time for it. The two reviews (which I enclose herewith)[1] stir up my curiosity. Meanwhile, let me hope that you are well. Myself, I sweat under an attack of tonsilitis.

                              Yours,
                              M

1. The reviews are missing.

608 Riverside Drive
N.Y.C

April 10th 1911

My Dear Mencken:
   I am sending you under separate cover the mss of Jennie Gerhardt which I hope you will do me the favor to read & give me your opinion. I

am sending it to your house. By the by I have been intending since Mch. 23rd to write and thank you for "them kind words" of the 22nd which Hirshberg was good enough to send me.[1] Could I, by any chance get a few copies of the issue of that date. I have signed up with Harper & Bros. for this book and the next which will be done about May 1st. It is called "The Genius"[2]   Did I ever autograph you a copy of <u>Carrie</u>?[3] Seems to me I did once at your house. Oh! that pleasant Baltimore visit.

Well, beer is beer and whiskey is whiskey and God save the Irish.

Th. D.

1. Dreiser is referring to Mencken's comments in "The Novel Today," Baltimore *Sun*, 22 March 1911. Mencken advertised Dreiser as "the man of tomorrow," and he said of *Sister Carrie*, "not many books . . . have been written in this fair land of ours . . . not many are better worth reading and pondering."

2. Dreiser does not use quotation marks for "*Genius*" at this time.

3. In Mencken's library there are two inscribed copies of *Sister Carrie*: the Double-day, 1900 edition in which Dreiser wrote, "The punishment of virtue is more virtue. To the only Henry L., chief of the Vice-Crusaders"; in the Dodge, 1907 edition he wrote, "To H. L. Mencken. In honor of breweries, witches, materialism, Mark Twain and all the winds of doctrine. Let's fill up the glass."

[NYP]

608 Riverside Drive

April 17th 1911

My Dear Mencken:

Miss Simonton, a newspaper writer, novelist, etc wanted to read the book & at the last moment I let her take it.[1] It goes to you this P.M. Thanks for the clippings & the coming reading. I know you will give me a sound critical opinion. The 3rd book draws to a close.[2] Its grim, I'm sorry to state, but life-like. Spring comes on belated feet and the George Ehret Brewery is installing 9 more vats. I see the shad nets being set in the North River. Tra Lee! Tra La! Such is life on Washington Heights this A.D. <u>1911</u>

Th. D

1. On 16 April Mencken wrote to Dreiser, asking about the *Jennie Gerhardt* manuscript, which Dreiser was to have mailed on the 10th. Dreiser came to know Ida Vera Simonton when she wrote for the *Delineator*.

2. *The "Genius,"* which Dreiser finished in 1911 but did not publish until 1915.

[UPL-H]

H. L. Mencken
1524 Hollins St.
Baltimore.

April 19th [1911]

Dear Dreiser:-

The ms is here and I tackle it eagerly tonight. It should be back in a week. Eat well!

H. L. M.

[UPL]

H. L. Mencken
1524 Hollins St.
Baltimore.

Baltimore, April 23rd. [1911]

Dear Dreiser:-

When "Jennie Gerhardt" is printed it is probable that more than one reviewer will object to its length, its microscopic detail, its enormous painstaking—but rest assured that Heinrich Ludwig von Mencken will not be in that gang. I have just finished reading the ms.—every word of it, from first to last—and I put it down with a clear notion that it should remain as it stands. The story comes upon me with great force; it touches my own experience of life in a hundred places; it preaches (or perhaps I had better say exhibits) a philosophy of life that seems to me to be sound; altogether I get a powerful effect of reality, stark and unashamed. It is drab and gloomy, but so is the struggle for existence. It is without humor, but so are the jests of that great comedian who shoots at our heels and makes us do our grotesque dancing.

I needn't say that it seems to me an advance above "Sister Carrie". Its obvious superiority lies in its better form. You strained (or perhaps even broke) the back of "Sister Carrie" when you let Hurstwood lead you away from Carrie. In "Jennie Gerhardt" there is no such running amuk. The two currents of interest, of spiritual unfolding, are very deftly managed. Even when they do not actually coalesce, they are parallel and close together. Jennie is never out of Kane's life, and after their first meeting, she is never out of his. The reaction of will upon will, of character upon character, is splendidly worked out and indicated. In brief, the story hangs together; it is a complete whole; consciously or unconsciously, you have avoided the chief defect of "Sister Carrie".

It is difficult, just rising from the book, to describe the impression I bring away. That impression is of a living whole, not of a fabric that may be unravelled and examined in detail. In brief, you have painted so smoothly and yet so vigorously that I have no memory of brush strokes. But for one thing, the great naturalness of the dialogue sticks in mind. In particular, you have been extremely successful with Gerhardt. His speeches are perfect: nothing could be nearer to truth. I am well aware that certain persons are impatient of this photographic accuracy. Well, let them choose their poison. As for me, I prefer the fact to the fancy. You have tried to depict a German of a given type—a type with which I, by chance, happen to be very familiar. You have made him as thoroughly alive as Huck Finn.

These are random, disordered notes. When the time comes, I'll reduce my thoughts to order and write a formal, intelligible review.[1] At the moment I am too near the book. I rather distrust my own enthusiasm for it. Perhaps I read my own prejudices and ideas into it. My interest is always in the subjective event, seldom or never in the objective event. That is why I like "Lord Jim." Here you have got very close to the very wellsprings of action. The march of episodes is nothing: the slow unfolding of character is everything.

If anyone urges you to cut down the book bid that one be damned. And if anyone argues that it is over-gloomy call the police. Let it stand as it is. Its bald, forthright style; its scientific, unemotional piling up of detail; the incisive truthfulness of its dialogue; the stark straightforwardness of it all—these are merits that need no praise. It is at once an accurate picture of life and a searching criticism of life. And that is my definition of a good novel.

Here and there I noted minor weaknesses. For one thing, it is doubtful that Jennie would have been able to conceal from so sophisticated a man as Kane the fact that she had had a child. Childbearing leaves physical marks, and those marks commonly persist for five or six years. But there are, of course, exceptions to this rule. Not many readers, I suppose, will raise the point. Again, if I remember correctly, you speak of L. S. & M. S. "shares" as being worth $1,000 par. Don't you mean bonds? If bonds, the income would be fixed and could not fluctuate. Again you give Kane $5,000 income from $75,000 at 6 percent. A small thing—but everywhere else you are so utterly careful that small errors stick out.

A final word: The least satisfactory personage in the book is Jennie herself. Not that you do not account for her, from head to heels—but I would have preferred, had I the choice, a more typical kept woman. She is, in brief, uncompromisingly exceptional, almost unique, in several important details. Her connection with her mother and father and with the facts of her life grows, at times, very fragile. But I can well understand how her essential plausibility must have reacted upon you—how your own creation must have dragged you on. There is always Letty Pace to show Jennie's limitations. In her class she is a miracle, and yet she never quite steps out of that class.

But I go back to the effect of the book as a whole. That effect, believe me, is very powerful. I must go to Hardy and Conrad to find its like. David Phillips, I believe, might have done such a story had he lived, but the best that he actually wrote, to wit, "The Hungry Heart", goes to pieces beside "Jennie".[2] I mean this in all seriousness. You have written a novel that no other American of the time could have written, and even in England there are not six men who, with your material, could have reached so high a level of reality. My earnest congratulations. By all means let me see that third book. "Jennie" shows immense progress in craftsmanship. As a work of art it is decidedly superior to "Sister Carrie."

I'll return the ms. by express tomorrow morning. Maybe chance will throw us together soon and we'll have a session over "Jennie". At the moment I am rather too full of the story as a human document to sit down in cold blood and discourse upon its merits and defects as a work of art. I know that it is immensely good, but I have still to get my reasons reduced to fluent words.

God keep you. As for me, I lately enjoyed the first of the season's rashers of crab a la creole. With genuine Muenchener to flush the esophagus afterward.

Yours

H. L. M.

Reading this over it seems damned cold. Why I really want to say is just—"Hurrah!" You have put over a truly <u>big</u> thing.[3]

1. Mencken wrote reviews of *Jennie Gerhardt* for the November *Smart Set* 35, 153–58 (see Appendix 2, pp. 740–44); the Baltimore *Evening Sun* (27 November); the *Los Angeles Times* (10 December); and the *Los Angeles Times Magazine* (8 December).

2. Some of David Graham Phillips's novels deal with the changing attitudes toward women in this period. Had it been available at this time, Phillips's posthumously published novel, *Susan Lenox: Her Fall and Rise* (1917), might have tempted Mencken to compare it to *Sister Carrie*. *Susan Lenox* is the story of a small-town girl who is led into a number of romantic liaisons, lives for a while as a prostitute, and eventually becomes a successful, though unfulfilled, actress.

3. The postscript is handwritten.

[NYP]

600 Riverside Drive

April 28th 1911

My Dear Mencken:

It sounds too good to be true but it is a great comfort nevertheless   You & Charles B. De Camp & James Huneker[1] are as grim critically as any I know and you seem to be agreed as to the general merits of the proposition. Yours is the sanest & best analysis I have received yet. It is broader in its understanding than the others. However—will it sell? I am going to do three more books after the one I am doing or finishing now—then if there is no money in the game I going to run a weekly. I can write a book every six months I think so I won't be so long out of the editing game unless perchance I should make a living this way. Who knows.

Meanwhile its spring. Come over & lets take a three days walking tour.

Th. D.

1. Charles B. DeCamp, an editor and author who was Dreiser's assistant when he edited *Everybody's Magazine* and *Broadway Magazine*; James Gibbons Huneker (1860–1921), novelist, biographer, and critic whose literary interests and impressionistic, vigorous style influenced Mencken.

[UPL-H]

H. L. Mencken
1524 Hollins St.
Baltimore.

May 8th [1911]

Dear Dreiser:-

"The Mighty Burke"[1] pleased me a lot: I am in favor of any effort to knock out that curse of fiction, the formal plot. The short story of tomorrow will be of the pattern of Galsworthy's sketches in "A Commentary." Damn the O. Henry stuff. "Jennie Gerhardt" sticks in my mind—a fine piece of work. That it will be a best-seller I doubt, but I suspect that it will make you. I hope Heinemann[2] does it in London.

That scheme for bottling beer is interesting—but only academically. Down here we don't bottle it, but <u>drink</u> it. As well preserve roses in cans!

Yours
H. L. M.

1. "The Mighty Burke," *McClure's* 37(May 1911), 40–50. More a biographical sketch than a short story, this piece is based on Dreiser's experience as a laborer on the New York Central Railroad in 1903. It was republished as "The Mighty Rourke" in *Twelve Men* (1919).
2. Heinemann, the English publisher who issued *Sister Carrie* in 1901.

[NYP]

3609 Broadway
N.Y.C

Aug 5th 1911

My Dear H. L:

The London Academy for May 19th last (so W. J. Locke[1] writes me) had a notice of Sister Carrie putting it with the 24 best books of the World, beginning with the Bible. All the other celebrities dead this long time but yours truly. Also putting it above The Scarlet Letter here & Vanity Fair in England   Hows that? Poor old Thack[2]—Well, heres a glass of beer to you[3]

Th. D.

1. William T. Locke (1863–1930), English novelist.
2. In "Twenty Favorite Books," *Academy and Literature*, 80(27 May, 1911), 635–54, Frank Harris placed *Sister Carrie* among twenty of his favorite books, finding Dreiser's novel superior to any of Hawthorne's and better than any "realistic story" yet written in England.
3. At the left of his signature, Dreiser drew a sketch of a glass of beer.

[UPL-H]

H. L. Mencken
1524 Hollins St.
Baltimore.

June 20th [1911]

Dear Dreiser:-

I enter your new address on my archives; before long I may visit your fair city for a day.

What is the news of "Jennie Gerhardt"? That book sticketh in my mind. Is it to be published this fall?

Yours
H. L. M.

[NYP]

3609 Broadway
N.Y.C

Aug 8th 1911

My Dear H. L.:

Proofs will be ready in a few days now I fancy—I am reading them—
but I wish you would write Harpers direct. I have had several requests for
data but everytime I suggest giving out anything now they leap in the air
with loud cries and protest that I am endangering the wave of interest later
by talking too soon. Your request is so well based that they will no doubt
comply but I would like you to write direct for the good it will do. If they
dont surrender proofs in time, I will.

Yes, book three is done & being typewritten slowly. The data for book
four—The Financier—is practically gathered. I shall begin writing in
September. If Jennie doesn't sell though I wont hang on to this writing
game very long.

Th D.

[NYP]

3609 Broadway
N.Y.C

Aug 13th 1911

My Dear Mencken:

This appeared in the Chicago Eve. Post supplement. It shouldn't have,
so early, I suppose but at the time Miss Kenton came here I didn't know
Harpers felt so keenly the danger of a preliminary discussion. Since a part
of your letter is quoted & a part of Hunekers I thought you ought to
see it.[1]

Th. D.

Return this sometime at your convenience.[2]

1. On 4 August 1911, the Chicago *Evening Post* printed a column by Baldwin Macy,
which discussed in some detail the history and plot of *Jennie Gerhardt*. Dreiser's comments here suggest that he transmitted the story and some dozen letters Macy mentions having seen through Edna Kenton, a Chicago critic who was an early fan of *Sister
Carrie*. Macy quoted from Mencken's letter of 4 June 1911 [UPL]. Incidentally, Macy
gave a muted version of the "suppression" of *Sister Carrie*, showing that Dreiser's and
Mencken's campaigns to establish the story were beginning to pay off.
2. Dreiser added this in the top left-hand corner of the page.

[UPL-H]

H. L. Mencken
1524 Hollins St.
Baltimore

Aug 15th [1911]

Dear Dreiser:-

No word, as yet, from the Harpers—but there is still time to stir them up. If the worst comes to the worst I'll ask you for a few names—and write from memory.

My compliments to Huneker whenever you see him. He and William Archer,[1] two very different men, have given me more ideas than any other living critics. Tell him he simply must do a volume on the new dramatists—Synge, Galsworthy, Barber, Brieux, Gorki, Wedekind, Schnitzler, Barber, Bennett, etc. The material is at hand, or at least part of it, in his Sun articles.

Meanwhile, the blessing of S. S. Anhaüser @ Busch be upon you!

Yours
H. L. M.

1. William Archer (1856–1924), British playwright, translator, critic. Mencken used the Archer translations of Ibsen in the preparation of his editions of *A Doll's House* and *Little Eyolf*.

[UPL]

H. L. Mencken
1524 Hollins St.
Baltimore

Baltimore, August 28th. [1911]

Dear Dreiser:-

I can't get an answer out of the Harpers: I have written twice without reply. If you think it safe to run the review in the November S.S., out October 15th, will you please let me have that ms. again? If not, I'll run the notice in the December number. I don't want to jump the release date and cause a row. But if I can't make it November I must know very soon, in order to knock together other matter. Don't undertake to stir up the Harpers: just give me your own opinion.

All publishers be damned. I launch the major curse upon them. One and all—no exceptions! Which reminds me of the story of the stinking contest between an Afro-American bishop and a goat. First they brought in the goat—and the jury fainted. Then they brought in the bishop—and the goat fainted. I have sent this tale to the Ladies' Home Journal for its page of brothel humor.

> Yours,
> H. L. M.

[NYP]

3609 Broadway
N.Y.C

Aug 31—1911

Dear H. L. M.:

I phoned Dunela of Harpers[1] this A.M. & he says if you can wait until Wed. next he will surely send you proofs—page or galley. Is that too late. Let me know & I will mail you my original mss. He also says to have it appear Oct 15 would be—commercially—much better than Nov. 15th. About that I'm not so sure. However, Take your choice. Hirshberg wrote me the other day that he had proof positive that you were subsidized by me in some way. Possibly annually. My answer is its fine weather in Frisco.

But, be that as it may, God wot.

> Th. D

Still another beer for you. Looks kinda frothy, don't it?[2]

1. Dreiser means F. A. Duneka, secretary of Harper's.
2. At the left of the postscript, Dreiser drew a sketch of a glass of beer.

[UPL-H]

H. L. Mencken
1524 Hollins St.
Baltimore.

[after 31 August 1911]

Dear Dreiser:-

I trust to the good Lord @ Dunela: if the proofs don't reach me Wednesday or Thursday I'm in hell's hole. Meanwhile, that beautiful painting of a Pilsner cornucopia makes me dizzy. I'll be in N.Y. for a day or so along about Sept 15. My best thanks for the Transcript clipping. That godly paper has been kind to me more than once

> Yours
> H. L. M.

[NYP]

3609 Broadway
N.Y.C

Sept 4th 1911

Dear H. L. M.

To be sure I am sending you the original mss by express today. It is marked for cutting but it was not cut in that fashion. I had it edited all the way through, some, but there is no essential difference. If Harpers proofs should reach you in time you can see for yourself.

When you arrive, Saturday 15th come up to the house to dinner & we will go to the theatre together or anywhere else. Come out Sunday & I'll entertain you with some friends or we'll walk or go to some resort. I'd ask you to stay here <u>sure</u> but the apartment hasn't a good guest chamber. Its a beautiful view of the river & the drive & youll enjoy it. If you can't come, alright, but I hope you can.

Th.D.

By the way I am including for your inspection the dozen or so letters, outside your own, of editors & critics (literary friends of mine who read the story & wrote about it: You will be interested in some of them—particularly Hunekers & DeCamps I think.

[UPL]

H. L. Mencken
1524 Hollins St.
Baltimore.

Baltimore, September 15th. [1911]

Dear Dreiser:-

I sent in my notice of "Jennie Gerhardt" tonight: it is much under the mark I set, but a rotten cold in the head must take the blame. I got your telegram last night at 9.30 and the O'Neill letter was posted at once.[1] I am sending the ms. by express. It should reach you Monday. My best thanks for the loan of it. Have no fear about "Jennie Gerhardt". It is a novel of the first rank—the best ever done in America. The lady critics will discover that fact some time in 1913.

Yours,
H. L. M.

1. In a telegram of 14 September 1911, Dreiser asked Mencken to return an "O'Neill" letter he had sent him. [NYP] This refers to a letter from Eleanor R. O'Neill, an editor at the *Boston Transcript* who had praised *Jennie Gerhardt*.

[NYP]

3609 Broadway
N.Y.C

Sept. 18th 1911

Dear H. L. M:

Harper & Bros want me to allow them to make excerpts from the various letters written me which they propose embodying in the advs.—at least that is their present intention. Have you any objection to an excerpt from yours & how may you be officially designated? Are you editor of the Eve. Sun? I was hoping so much to see you Saturday—why didn't you come?

Th D

[UPL]

H. L. Mencken
1524 Hollins St.
Baltimore.

Baltimore, Sept. 20th [1911]

Dear Dreiser:-

Use whatever you please, but don't mention The Sun. My official title is associate editor of The Evening Sun—at this writing—but I have little to do with the book reviews of the paper. Call me critic of The Smart Set.

I am still in the mines and the chances are that it will be October 4 or 5 before I can escape. Believe me, I am sorry. I'll let you know a week before I hit N.Y. God bless all honest men.

My second reading of "Jennie Gerhardt" has increased my enthusiasm for it. Let no one convince you to the contrary: you have written the best American novel ever done, with the one exception of "Huckleberry Finn". It hangs together vastly better than "McTeague".[1] It is decidedly on a higher plane. The very faults of it are virtues—as I argue in my S. S. article. But of all that anon.

If the Harpers want my review in advance they can get a proof of it by telephoning to Norman Boyer at the S.S. It is in type by now. God bless all honest men.

Yours,
M

1. Frank Norris's *McTeague* (1899).

3609 Broadway
N.Y.C

Sept. 22nd 1911

My Dear H. L. M.
    Did you read the printed proofs of Jennie? If so did you think the telling had been improved or otherwise. I suppose the Harper Galleys have been returned. Otherwise I would like to borrow them.

Th.D

3609 Broadway
N.Y.C

Oct. 17th 1911

My Dear Mencken:
    I picked up the Smart Set today & read your notice.[1] I confess that my cheeks colored some for I'm not ready yet to believe it. However I wish you were here in order that that we might drown our philosophic woes in good pale beer.

Th. D.

    By the way, on the Jacket of the book Harpers quoted from your letter but they spell your name Menken, although the title is right.[2] I have asked them to change it on the second run.
The other book[3] is soon ready for you now.

1. The November issue (see Appendix 2, pp. 740–44).
2. The title given Mencken was Associate Editor, Baltimore *Evening Sun*.
3. *The "Genius."*

3609 Broadway
N.Y.C

Oct 20th 1911

My Dear Mencken:
    Under separate cover I am sending you an autograph copy of Jennie.[1] Will you do me the favor to read it again & see whether in your judgment you think it has been hurt or helped by the editing? Regards.

Th D

Your review has created a real stir over here.[2]

1. Dreiser's inscription reads, "My Dear Mencken: What shall I say in this first copy I have secured? Oh, yes. May your good opinion of it never change. And may you live long and prosper."
2. Dreiser placed this in the top left-hand corner of the page.

[UPL]

H. L. Mencken
1524 Hollins St.
Baltimore.

October 25th. [1911]

Dear Dreiser:-

I am sending the English edition of Moore's "Memoirs"[1] by this mail. Return it or be forever accursed.

I hope to begin reading "Jennie Gerhardt" tomorrow. Did you see what Arnold Bennett said of you in Sunday's Times?[2]

Yours,
H. L. M.

1. George Moore's *Memoirs of My Dead Life*.
2. Arnold Bennett, interviewed while in New York, was quoted in the *New York Times* of 22 October 1911 as saying that *Sister Carrie* was the one American novel he would recommend to readers.

[UPL]

H. L. Mencken
1524 Hollins St.
Baltimore.

Baltimore, October 25th. [1911]

Dear Dreiser:-

This looks very good to me.[1] It sets forth your ideas, as I understand them, very clearly, and beside it is well written. I wish you would look through Nietzsche—say, "The Genealogy of Morals" and "The Antichrist". Fairly good English translations are published by Macmillan. You'd get a lot of pleasure out of both books.

Yours,
M

1. On 24 October Dreiser wrote Mencken that he had given a "youth" his "philosophy in some concrete form." He sent a copy of the statement, which has not survived, to Mencken.

[NYP]

3609 Broadway
N.Y.C

Oct. 25th 1911

My Dear Mencken:
The Kansas City Journal of Sunday, October 22—1911 gives Jennie a big send off in the news columns.[1] And it contains this line—"And no less a critic than Mencken says in a current magazine" etc. etc. Can you get the paper there or shall I send for a copy for you.

Th. D

1. Anon., "Dreiser's New Novel Reaches Friends Here," Kansas City [Mo.] *Journal*, 22 October 1911, second section, 1B.

[UPL]

H. L. Mencken
1524 Hollins St.
Baltimore.

Baltimore, October 27th. [1911]

Dear Dreiser:-
That Post fellow doesn't worry me. He takes a hack at me every now and then. Some day, when the mood strikes me, I am going to tear off his hide—and without anesthetics, you may be sure. He is, I believe, not the same man who reviews novels, so you are not apt to be involved. Let us pray.

Sincerely,
M

P.S.—I am getting the K.C. Journal. God all help all poor sailors, with the winter coming on.

[NYP]

3609 Broadway
N.Y.C

[ca. 1 November 1911]

My Dear H. L. M:
It looks to me from the drift of things as though your stand on Jennie would either make or break you—judging as an outsider. They are tying you up pretty close to it.

Th. D.

[NYP]

3609 Broadway
N.Y.C

Nov. 6th 1911

My Dear Mencken:

Has the book been advertised in any Baltimore paper as yet? Let me know.

Th.D.

I see by the reviews that you are certainly the bell-weather this trip.

[UPL]

H. L. Mencken
1524 Hollins St.
Baltimore.

Baltimore, November 9th. [1911]

Dear Dreiser:-

Dell's notice is a corker: it ought to sell a lot of books in Chicago. His account of the story shows a lot of discernment and good sense. Altogether it's a splendid review.[1]

On first going through "Jennie", in the printed form, the cuts irritated me a good deal, particularly in the first half, but now I incline to the opinion that not much damage has been done. As the story stands, it is superb. It will get a few lambastings, perhaps a few sneering notices, but on the whole the reviews should do it justice. In England it will make a killing.

Willard Wright has asked me to write an account of it for the Christmas number of the Los Angeles Times. I'll duplicate the stuff in the Baltimore Evening Sun, and get in other notices from time to time. George Howard[2] tells me he is going to print an article about the book in the N.Y. Telegraph. He is very enthusiastic.

Do you want the clipping returned? What news of "The Financier"?

Yours,

M

1. Floyd Dell, "A Great Novel," Chicago *Evening Post Literary Review*, 3 November 1911, 1.
2. George Bronson Howard (see Dreiser to Mencken, 23 August 1907, n.1).

[NYP]

3609 Broadway
N.Y.C

Nov. 10th 1911

Dear H. L. M.

Has any notice of Jennie appeared in Baltimore. My clipping bureau Romeike reports no, but they miss a lot. If you have seen anything give me the dates & I write the business managers. Your recommendation has not been advertised in Boston, Chicago & St. Louis.

Th D

[UPL-H]

THE SUN
Baltimore, Md.

[after 10 November 1911]

Dear Dreiser:-

So far I have seen no notice in Baltimore. My own will be printed within the next 2 weeks. J. H. Adams, editor of the Evening Sun, is enthusiastic over "Jennie".

More anon
Yours
H. LM

[EPL]

3609 Broadway
N.Y.C

Nov. 11th 1911

Dear H. L. M:

Things are moving around here in a peculiar way. I may go to Europe on the 22nd of this month for the Century Company—London, Paris, Rome & The Riviera!—hows that? I'll let you know before. Strictly between you & myself they would like me to move with my books to Union Square but theres nothing definite about that, and Grant Richards, the English publisher who is here says I have a good chance of getting the next Nobel prize for literature following Maeterlinck, if it is worked right.

He is going to organize the sentiment in England where he says I am a strong favorite, through Frank Harris, & others and he is going to get the Century Crowd to work for it here. He thought some American critic of prominence ought to make the suggestion somewhere to which he could call attention & I spoke of you. How about that? Do you think its advisable?

Concerning the Financier I have 39 Chapters done which is about one third. I think it is shaping up in a strong way, but I cant tell exactly. I can only have faith. It will be longer than Jennie or Carrie—much. When I come back, if I go I want to get together with you & show you the result.

Thanks for rereading the book   It's a relief to hear you say its all right. I wish when you mention the book in the Sun you would send me a few copies—or at least call my attention to the matter.

Hail, Mencken!
Th. D

In regard to the clippings if you can use them in any way by sending or showing keep them or if you have any other use save the waste basket. If not send them back[1]

1. Dreiser is referring to the reviews he had been sending Mencken as they came to him from his clipping bureau.

[EPL]

3609 Broadway
N.Y.C

Nov. 16th 1911

Dear H. L. M:

I am actually leaving next Wednesday on the Mauretania (hows that) for England. I am going to London, Paris & Rome & possibly to Athens & the Riviera. I wont be back before April possibly or May. My London Address will be c/o Harper & Brothers, 45 Albemarle St., London. Please note that. If you are serious about coming to Europe for goodness sake let me know. And what shall I send you for Christmas?

Th.D.

Keep the clippings. I have duplicates. And if you come accross anything interesting please mail it & oblige. Your right about the Nobel prize idea.[1]

1. Mencken's letter has disappeared.

[UPL]

H. L. Mencken
1524 Hollins St.
Baltimore.

Baltimore, November 19th. [1911]

Dear Dreiser:-

By gar, I envy you that trip! All expenses, I take it, are paid, and there will be plenty of leisure for victualing. Unless all the signs go for naught, I'll certainly be in London the last week in April. Thence to Munich for the waters. One, and possibly two old friends will be with me—gentlemen with viscera of elastic copper. We must have a round-up in Lunnon, by all means. Exact schedules later.

Meanwhile, I send clippings of whatever reviews fall under my eye. "Jennie" is perfectly safe: the book is making the best of impressions. Down here there are already half a dozen mad mullahs preaching it fanatically—and without suggestion from me.

A pleasant and profitable voyage. You need the rest. Let me have a line now and then.

Yours,
H. L. M.

P.S.—If you send me a Christmas present, I'll never speak to you again. I am a frenzied foe of Christianity in all its forms, and particularly in that one.

[EPL]

SS Mauretania

Nov. 22nd 1911

Dear H. L. M:

I'm off. Wish me luck. I value your friendship above many things.

Th. D

London Address
  c/o Harper & Brothers
  45 Albemarle St.

[UPL]

H. L. Mencken
1524 Hollins St.
Baltimore.

November 28th. [1911]

Dear Dreiser:-

Within is a cutting of a notice I printed in The Evening Sun yesterday—pretty poor stuff, but still it may have some influence on the Southern newspaper reviewers. I have rewritten the article, expanding it considerably, for the Los Angeles Times, which will print it in its Christmas book number.

By the way, if your New York apartment is still open, will you drop a line home and have my Moore book shipped back? If not, don't bother about it. I have no need of it, save to lend it occasionally. It may very well await your return.

I shall sail about April 15, and if you are still anywhere in Europe we'll certainly have a session!

Sincerely,
M

[EPL]

Big Frith
Cookham Dean
Berkshire, Eng.

Dec. 2nd 1911

Dear H. L. M.

Simply to let you know that I arrived safe & am now by degrees putting down my impressions of dear old England. I had a letter from you yesterday. When you come we meet. It can be arranged. Address as before. c/o Harper & Brothers, 45 Albemarle St. London.

Th. D

[EPL]

Hotel Capitol.
1. Regent Street
St. James Square

Dec 7th 1911

Dear H. L. M:

Thanks for the clipping. I'm rushed to death over here. Wait to read my commentary on this game. I want you to. We meet when you come.

Th. D

45 Albemarle St.—as before.

[UPL]

H. L. Mencken
1524 Hollins St.
Baltimore.

Baltimore, December 18th. [1911]

Dear Dreiser:-

I am sending by this mail a copy of the Los Angeles Times containing a review of "Jennie" and a portrait of T. D. Percival Pollard,[1] whom you probably knew, died here yesterday, after an operation for a brain tumor. His wife brought him to Baltimore for treatment about two weeks ago. He was already at the point of death. The poor woman knows very few people here and so I have been looking after her.

I am sending another copy of the Times to Mrs. Dreiser. More anon about my little German trip. Thayer of the S.S.[2] wants to pay some of the expenses.

Yours,
M

1. Percival Pollard (1869–1911), critic, playwright, novelist. Born in Germany, Pollard lived in Baltimore, and Mencken considered him an important influence on his critical writing. In a letter to Burton Rascoe in 1920, Mencken wrote "Next to [Robert I.] Carter, I learned most from Percival Pollard—particularly the value, to a critic, of concentrating on a few men. Pollard used Ambrose Bierce; I used Dreiser" (see Forgue, *Letters*, 186). Mencken helped care for Pollard in his final days.

2. John Adams Thayer, owner of *Smart Set*.

[EPL]

Hotel Capitol
London

Dec 30th 1911

Dear H. L. M:

Thanks for the Los Angeles notice. It was excellent. I should think you would be tired singing the praises of J.G. by now. Tomorrow night I leave for 4 days in Manchester & on the 13th I am going over to Paris. My London address remains as before only to save time I think you had better address me care Grant Richards, 7 Carleton Street, Regent Street, W. London.

I am glad Thayer knows a good man when he sees him.

Th. D

[EPL]

Midland Hotel
Manchester

January 1 1912

My Dear Mencken:

Just to wish you success—1912 & better yet, happiness

Theodore Dreiser

[EPL-Pc]
[before 3 January 1912]

Dear H. L. M

I have found it. The name is <u>Beer</u> <u>Lane</u> & it runs or winds for 1 block out of Lower Thames Street. There are a number of saloons there. If ever we are near it I will guide you safely through.

Th. D

[UPL-H]

H. L. Mencken
1524 Hollins St.
Baltimore.

Jan 3rd [1912]

Dear Dreiser:-

Buy me a house on Beer st—a house with a roomy cellar! Within a new evidence of fame! By the way, there is a fellow here who sends out tips on the new novels, listing the 3 best each month. "Jennie" led his Nov. list. This month, with no good <u>new</u> novels in sight, he advised his subscribers to read "Sister Carrie". Not my suggestion. Perfectly spontaneous.

Yours
M

[EPL-Pc]

London

Jan 10 1912

Your old friend philosopher guide Sir Francis Bacon lies in here. It's a pretty place.

Th D.

[EPL-Pc]
Jan. 11, 1912

Just in passing. I leave for Paris in just one hour. When I get there I'll drink your health.

Th D

[UPL]

H. L. Mencken
1524 Hollins St.
Baltimore.

Baltimore, January 15th. [1912]

Dear Dreiser:-

Within two reviews picked up by accident today, one from the Pittsburg Dispatch and one from the San Francisco Argonaut.[1] Both belong to the Punk School, though the Dispatch notice shows a certain dim understanding.

With the temperature at 3 below zero, what is a man to do? As for me, I hug the radiator and damn the weather. The one consoling fact is that I sail, God willing, April 16, and will strike you in London or Berlin or wherever it is a week later. My travelling companion, McDannald, weighs 240 pounds and has a gullet like a bass clarinet.[2] He proposes to devote himself exclusively to drinking the waters, with perhaps a few side ventures into the forcible entry of German chambermaids.

Yours,

M

1. James Edward Leslie, "Book News," Pittsburgh *Dispatch*, 14 January 1912; Anon., "The Latest Books: Jennie Gerhardt," *Argonaut* 69(30 December 1911), 449.
2. A. H. McDannald, a Baltimore *Sun* reporter and longtime friend of Mencken.

[UPL]

H. L. Mencken
1524 Hollins St.
Baltimore.

Baltimore, January 25th. [1912]

Dear Dreiser:-

Maybe you will remember a little one-act grotesque, "The Artist", which I wrote for the Bohemian. My old publisher, Luce of Boston, wants to do it as an illustrated gift book.[1] What is the status of the Bohemian's copyrights? As I understand it, they went upon the market and failed to draw a bid. Is this true? Or were they bought? If so, by whom?

By the way, who is Miss Eleanora R. O'Neill?[2] I remember that you sent me her opinion of "Jennie Gerhardt", but I don't recall that you told me anything else about her. Lately I had a letter from her, regarding "Jennie". She seems to assume that you told me about her. Tell me briefly what work she has done, that I may not affront her by my ignorance.

The American Magazine, out today, has a sketch "The Men in the Dark", bearing your name.[3] Frankly, I don't like it worth a damn. It is merely a rough note for a story, and altogether too casual and careless. However—however—I may be wrong!

Neuralgia has me by the face—and I sweat and swear. More anon.

Yours,

H. L. M.

1. Luce published *The Artist, a Drama without Words* (Boston, 1912).
2. See Mencken to Dreiser, 15 September 1911, n.1.
3. "The Man in the Dark," *American Magazine* 73(February), 465–68; repr. in *The Color of a Great City* (1923).

[EPL-Pc]
Jan 29, 1912

Dear H. L. M

Thanks for the clipping. See Paris if you can. Its a real world—individual & forceful. I've enjoyed every hour.

Th D

[UPL-H]

H. L. Mencken
1524 Hollins St.
Baltimore.

February 2nd [1912]

Dear Dreiser:-

A clipping from the Boston Transcript. The author, Braithwaite, is a colored poet.[1] I once deplored his desertion of Pullman portering—and so he holds me in great affection. What news?

I wish I could pull up stakes now, instead of in April. Work is a curse.

The first keg of 1912 bock, from Munich, is due next Saturday. Would that you were here to go down the river with us on the tug we have hired!

Yours
H. L. M.

1. William Stanley Beaumont Braithwaite (1878–1962).

[EPL-Pc]
[February 1912]

Dear. H. L. M.

What do you know about this. From Left to Right. Th.D Grant Richard & Sir Hugh Lane.[1] This was at Cafe Martin between Mentone & Monte Carlo Feb 1st last. Notice the profound atmosphere of learning reigning.

1. Sir Hugh Lane, art collector and director of the Municipal Art Gallery in Dublin. Dreiser sent a picture postcard with a picture of him and the two men.

[UPL]

H. L. Mencken
1524 Hollins St.
Baltimore.

Baltimore, February 14th. [1912]

Dear Dreiser:-

Here is something for you. This Lawrence Bureau is run by a Baltimorean named Lawrence Perin, a man of large wealth, but interested in books. He sends out a card each month for $1 a year and has a good many subscribers, particularly in New England. He accepts no review copies from publishers, and will have nothing whatever to do with them. In November, entirely without any suggestion from me, he put "Jennie" at the head of his list. In January, as you see, he recommended "Sister Carrie". I met him only lately and found him an ardent admirer of T.D. He thinks "Sister Carrie" better than "Jennie", chiefly, it appears, because he objects to certain obscure details in the high society scenes of the latter.

I hear you are to return March 15th. Can it be? I hope not. I have been looking forward to a meeting in Munich or London

The spring Bock is just around the corner. Already the kaif-keepers disinter and disinfect the stuffed goats.

Yours,
M

[EPL]

GRAND CONTINENTAL HOTEL
Rome

Feb 17th 1912

Dear Mencken:

Thanks for the clipping from the Transcript. I wish—and this is very important to me—you would try and get me a copy or better <u>two</u> of your first review of Jennie in the Smart Set last November. Do this if you can and mail them to me care of Harper & Brothers, Franklin Square, New York. I'm coming home in April—about the 15th so I wont see you over here. I have to in order to finish my book. I hoped to see you, too. By the way there is a friend of yours here at this hotel at the present time—Mrs. Paul Armstrong[1] whom I now know right well & she sends you her regards.

Life, Health, Strength.
Th. D

1. Rella Abell Armstrong, who later collaborated with Dreiser on a dramatization of *The Financier* and *The Titan*, a project that happily remains in manuscript.

[EPL-Pc]

Perugia

Feb 28th—1912

This is a wonderful place—60,000 and built up on a mountain. You would have to see it to believe it. An American to the core. Rarely a street over 12 feet wide.

Th D

[EPL-Pc]

Florence

Feb. 29th 1912

In Italy a saloon is labelled "vino e spirito". Beer is <u>bierre</u>—how's that? Still its good enough for the thing they call beer—serves it right in fact. Wait till you read the unexpurgated mss of my trip.[1] Venice March 5th.

1. Dreiser is referring to the manuscript of *A Traveler at Forty* (1913), which was edited before publication by the Century Company, mainly to cut what Dreiser later called the "woman stuff" (see Dreiser to Mencken, 18 November 1913).

[UPL-H]

H. L. Mencken
1524 Hollins St.
Baltimore.

March 6th [1912]

Dear Dreiser:—

Boyer is sending 2 copies of the Nov. S.S. to the Harpers. It's too bad that you must come home so soon—but the book first! I sail on April 16th for Bremen. Within a clipping you may have missed.

Yours
H. L. M.

[EPL-Pc]
March 25, 1912

H. L. M.

I struck my father's birth place yesterday and found real German beer to say nothing of a quaint old village which is 900 years old. The only Dreisers I can find are in the local graveyard.

[EPL-Pc]
[after 25 March 1912]

Dear H. L. M.

A German scene which really isn't German, but English. I had a note from you enclosing Dells review   Thanks. When you go to Munich send me a card now & then & it is understood that you read the mss of the Financier for me, isn't it? I need your opinion.

Th. D.

[EPL-Pc]
April 7, 1912

Amsterdam is a northern Venice—actually full of canals. A steamboat is a "stoom boots" & a telephone a "teleflom." It's amusing & beautiful. No critics, no books, no nothing. Just spring.

Th D.

[UPL-H]

On Board the R.M.S. "LACONIA"

April 17 [1912]

Dear Dreiser:-

Despite its damnable tricks, life could be worse. We have had smooth seas all the way from N.Y., @ hence I have waded into 5 or 6 meals a day. One of the ports of call is your old stamping ground, Monte Carlo. I'll probably risk $2.25; pray for me!

Yours
M

[UPL-Pc]

Munich

April 27, 1912

I come up for air and to ask where art thou? Weather here is perfect. Ditto the beer. Ditto the May wine. Ditto the gals. Did we cross on the Atlantic?

H. L. M.

[EPL]

Saint Paul Hotel
New York

May 26, 1912.

Dear H. L. M.

I have no address but I send this care your home & suppose it will reach you sometime. Am living (after tomorrow) at 605 W. 111th St. N.Y.C though Harper & Bros. will reach me. Phone 4740 Morning. When you come back look me up. I have had two postals relating to beer and women only. Scandilious! Am hard at work on The Financier which is to be brought out in 3 volumes—Vol 1—August 1912—Vol 2. Mch. 1913—Vol 3—August 1913.[1] After that heaven knows what. The Century Company may (probably will) bring out my travel book in the spring.[2] How are you? I hope well. If you go to London, call on Grant Richards, 7 Carleton Street, Regent Street, who will treat you nobly. Merely say you are Mencken & that I told you to come. Love to all. (all meaning all the breweries)

Th. D

1. Dreiser's "Trilogy of Desire" fell short of this ambitious schedule: *The Financier* (1912), *The Titan* (1914), *The Stoic* (1947).
2. *A Traveler at Forty* was published on 25 November 1913.

[UPL]

H. L. Mencken
1524 Hollins St.
Baltimore.

Baltimore, June 2nd. [1912]

Dear Dreiser:-

Can it be that we crossed on the ocean? I sailed by the Krp. Wilhelm April 16 and got back by the Baltic yesterday. On arriving home I found my young brother[1] in hospital with pneumonia—a serious business. So more anon.

Yours,
H. L. M.

1. August Mencken (1889–1967).

[NYP]

605 W. 111th St
Phone 4740 Morningside

Friday, May[1] 7—1912

Dear. H. L. M:

Lord I'm glad to know your back   I thought you were still over in Munich. When are you coming over here? I wish I could talk to you. I have a whole raft of things to discuss not the least of which is the present plan of publishing this book in 3 volumes—1 volume every 6 months. If I had time I'd run over there. I may anyhow. For heaven sake keep in touch with me by mail for I'm rather lonely & I have to work like the devil.

Th. D

I hope you enjoyed your trip much.

1. Dreiser means June.

[UPL]

H. L. Mencken
1524 Hollins St.
Baltimore.

Baltimore, June 8th. [1912]

Dear Dreiser:-

Come down, by all means. Why not next Sunday? I can't put you up—my house is in a mess—but I can at least offer you a rasher of victuals. Luckily, my brother is getting on very well—but what a week of it!

Don't talk about the time. You can leave New York early Sunday morning, have five or six hours here, and still get back before midnight. Or take the night train back and have 12 hours here. I have made the reverse trip often. Certainly I want to hear all about the book—and I'm tied up here.

Yours,
Mencken

[NYP]

605 W. 111th

June 11—1912

Dear H. L. M.

Sorry about your brother—very—but if he's out of danger you ought to be smiling. I can see you with your sense of responsibility! I can't come next Sunday and not sure of the next but I may run down at that. Will give you due notice. The pen, with me, moves steadily forward.

Th. D

[UPL]

H. L. Mencken
1524 Hollins St.
Baltimore.

Thursday [19 June 1912]

Dear Dreiser:-

Come along any Sunday that's convenient. But Sunday a week (June 29th) I have to go up to Pennsylvania to see my brother.[1] New breweries are talked of here and so literature looks up. By the way, have you my copy of Moore's "Memoirs of My Dead Life"? If it's lost and packed away, say naught: I can get a copy in London. But if it happens to be laying about, send it back: I want to lend it.

Yours,
H. L. M.

1. Charles Mencken (1882–1956), who worked as an engineer in Pennsylvania.

[NYP]

3609 Broadway
N.Y.C

Aug 28th 1912

Dear H. L. M.

I am just crawling out from under 250 galleys of the Financier— the first half—and am almost all in. It is supposed to issue Oct 1 or thereabouts.¹ When I get a presentable set I will send or bring it over if you will let me. It looks to be a book of 700 pages or more unless I can cut it. Alas, alas.

Th D.

If you come over come up. Mrs. D. says you said you were coming

1. Harper & Brothers published *The Financier* on 24 October 1912.

[UPL-H]

H. L. Mencken
1524 Hollins St.
Baltimore.

Aug 30 [1912]

Dear Dreiser:-

Eureka! Let me have those proofs, by all means. And bring them down yourself. You can make a round trip on Saturday-Sunday without fatigue. I doubt that I get to N.Y. for a month.

Don't let the damnable Harpers cut the story! A curse on all such butchery.

Say when.

Yours
H. L. M.

[NYP]

3609 Broadway

Sept 14—1912

Dear H. L. M.:

I'll either send or bring over the mss of the Financier—I mean the page proofs this coming week sometime. It is something over 800 pages long—about 270,000 words. Do you suppose you can crowd it in for reading or is this asking too much? I salute you.

Th. D.

[UPL-H]

H. L. Mencken
1524 Hollins St.
Baltimore.

Sept 16th [1912]

Dear Dreiser:-
    Too long to read? Not at all! I'll be glad to do it. And to see you. I have a wedding to go to Saturday evening, but aside from that the week is yours. Why not come down Sunday morning? You can get here by noon—and have eight hours. Or better still, stay over. If you are delayed, send the proofs ahead, @ then come down to get them.
    God bless all honest men.

Yours
M

[UPL-H]

H. L. Mencken
1524 Hollins St.
Baltimore.

Sept 26 [1912]

Dear Dreiser:-
    Where are those proofs? I was hoping to get a notice into the December Smart Set?

Yours
H. L. M.

P.S. My November article has been lost in the mails. I curse.

[UPL-HPc]
Oct 3 1912

The proofs of "The Financier" are here, @ I fall to them at once. But I fear they're too late for the Nov. S.S. However———

M

[UPL]

H. L. Mencken
1524 Hollins St.
Baltimore.

Baltimore, October 6th. [1912]

Dear Dreiser:-

I have just finished "The Financier". Frankly, there are spots in it that I don't like a bit. It is not that you have laid on too much detail—I am in favor of the utmost detail—but that you have laid on irrelevant detail. Why give the speeches of the lawyers in full? Why describe so minutely the other prisoners sentenced with Cowperwood? Why describe particularly the architecture of the jail in which Cowperwood spends his five days? All of these things are well described, but they have nothing to do with the story. On the other hand, there are essential things left undescribed. For instance, Cowperwood and Aileen in their flat—their conversation, the girl's initiation, the dull days (they always come!), her probable alarms, the constant menace of the remote chance of pregnancy, perhaps a bad scare or two.

But all these things, after all, are but minor blemishes on a magnificent piece of work. You have described and accounted for and interpreted Cowperwood almost perfectly. You have made him as real as any man could be. And you have given utter reality to his environment, human and otherwise. No better picture of a political-financial camorra has ever been done. It is wholly accurate and wholly American.

Again, you have given great plausibility and interest to the affair between Frank and Aileen, from beginning to end, despite the reserve I have mentioned. It is credible that such a girl should succumb in such a way; it is credible that such a man, after marrying Lillian, should respond. Yet again, old Butler is excellently done, particularly as he appears in conflict with Aileen. These, to me, the most difficult of all the scenes, are done best of all. The reality in them is absolute. All sense of fiction is lost.

That is the feeling, indeed, that I get from the book as a whole. The very particularity of it helps. The irrelevant, in the long run, becomes, in a dim and vasty way, relevant. As you laboriously set the stage, the proscenium arch disappears, the painted trees become real trees, the actors turn into authentic men and women. And at the end, you stop upon just the right note. The big drama is ahead. We have seen only the first act.

I can't praise too much the evident painstaking of the whole thing. The story of Cowperwood's financial transactions is superbly thought out: it hangs together beautifully. And the same care shows in minor ways. The Cowperwood houses may be a bit too exhaustively described, but at any rate they are accurately described. There are no smudges here. Every line is distinct. So with the people: down to the least of them they stand out in the round.

Is the book too long? I doubt it. "Clayhanger" can't be much shorter.[1] You are trying to lay in a large landscape and to draw its people to the last dot. That requires space. The reader who once ventures into the story will not be apt to complain of its length. He may rebel at some of the chapters and even skip them, but you have kept the feeling of impending events, of drama just around the corner, strong throughout. In brief, the story is well managed. Its machinery works.

So much for first impressions. I want to go through certain parts again. By the way, how long may I keep the proofs? My December article has gone in, but my January article, out December 15, is yet to be written. Will the book come out in time for me to review it in that article? I hope so. Meanwhile, I must get together raw material for the review, and so I'd like to have the proofs for a few days more. But if the book itself is due very shortly I can wait for it.

More anon.

Yours,
M

1. *Clayhanger*, by E. A. Bennett.

[NYP]

3609 Broadway

Oct 8th 1912

My Dear H. L. M:

Owing to your letter, between the chapters which relate to Cowperwoods failure and the chapter where he is sentenced I am taking out considerable material, the speeches of course and other financial stuff. This will delay the book a little but not later than Nov. 1st, if so late. You ought to know this if you propose to say anything at present. Harpers have been very nice in letting me do this as the plates were cast. I am letting the sentence chapter stand with the negro in it.

Th. D

Would I were a brewer's son—

[UPL]

H. L. Mencken
1524 Hollins St.
Baltimore.

Baltimore, October 8th. [1912]

Dear Dreiser:-

Don't take too seriously my objections. I think you have done well to make the cuts, because the redundant matter breaks the back of the story, but that story, as a whole, is a splendid piece of work. Nothing could be finer than some parts of it, and what is more important, it hangs together. That is to say, it does not blow one way in one place and another way in another. Cowperwood is a genuine man from first to last. The fair Butler is as real as any hussy I ever met on the field of honor. And old Butler is a fit companion for old Gerhardt, for all his differences.

I'll keep the cuts in mind in writing my review, which goes into the Jan. S.S., out December 15.[1] How far have you got with the next volume? There you will be in the midst of Cowperwood's greatest adventures. I am eager to see it.

Caution for clergymen: Be ascetic, and if you can't be ascetic, then at least aseptic.

Yours,
M

1. "Again the Busy Fictioneers," *Smart Set* 39(January 1913), 153, 155–57. See Appendix 2, pp. 744–48, for Mencken's *New York Times* review of the book.

[NYP]

3609 Broadway

[after 6 October 1912]

Dear H. L. M:

Keep the page proofs I sent you as long as you choose. The book is now scheduled to appear Oct. 22nd or 3rd. I meant to write a note and say I thought it would be better if it could be cut 200 pages but I have worked under great difficulties in connection with it some of which I will narrate to you sometime. But this is important. In your review dont mention the speeches <u>because</u> <u>they</u> <u>wont</u> <u>be</u> <u>there</u> <u>when</u> <u>the</u> <u>book</u> <u>comes</u> <u>out</u>. I ordered them out today, and some of the trial stuff. I am glad you like it fairly well only I suspect your good nature is getting the better of your judge-ment   I have to thank you for direct forceful statements which have brought about this final change. You always see a thing as a whole which is a Gods blessing

Th. D

If you think of any whole chapters that could be taken out bodily, wire me.[1]

1. This appears in the right-hand corner of the letter, beside the address.

[UPL-H]

H. L. Mencken
1524 Hollins St.
Baltimore.

Oct. 24th [1912]

Dear Dreiser:-

My best thanks for your note[1]—and Mrs. Dreisers. Unluckily, I'll be so tied up with engagements that it will be impossible for me to stay overnight. But I'll get to your house promptly at 8.15 Saturday night, God willing, for a long talk. There is a man I must dine with—a matter of business. I can get away from him by 7.30.

I'm sorry I'm so rushed, but such is life.

Yours
Mencken

1. On 23 October Dreiser wrote Mencken a note inviting him to stay overnight. [NYP]

[EPL]

3609 Broadway
N.Y.C

Oct. 24—1912

Dear Mencken:

Under separate cover I am sending you the final bound copy.[1] Wish me luck. It is cut 77 pages from the proofs as you saw them—in small bits. Look it over.

Th. D.

Am expecting you Saturday. Will meet you down town if you say.

1. Dreiser's inscription on this copy reads: "To H. L. Mencken, from Dreiser, in grateful friendship."

[UPL-H]

H. L. Mencken
1524 Hollins St.
Baltimore.

Oct 30 [1912]

Dear Dreiser:-
    The proofs are going forward by this mail. I have just finished the
printed book. Fear not, beloved: you have produced a Book. And how can
I thank you for that No 1 copy?

Yours
H. L. M.

[NYP]

3609 Broadway
N.Y.C

Nov. 4—1912

Dear H. L. M:
    I thought you might want to see 3 more N.Y. opinions. Please return
these three. The book should have been cut 170 pages instead of 77.

Th D

We live and learn.

[UPL]

H. L. Mencken
1524 Hollins St.
Baltimore.

November 4th. [1912]

Dear Dreiser:-
    Don't let these notices worry you. There is a certain justice in their
complaints, true enough, but none the less the general effect of the book
is excellent, and I have the utmost confidence that the second volume will
be a knockout. You have paved the way and you have got a thorough grip
on Cowperwood. What these fools will have to understand, soon or late, is
that you are not trying to produce a thriller, but a work of art. Let them
read Conrad's "Lord Jim" or George Moore's "Sister Theresa", and it may
occur to them at last that allegro furioso is not the only tempo known to

man. But, as I have said, there is a certain truth in their charge of wordiness. Well, you will avoid that next time.

I had a telegram from the N.Y. Times Saturday asking me to do their notice.[1] I have sent it in, but it is decidedly un-Timesy in style, and so I await the issue. If they make any complaint I'll take it back and give it to Wright. My S.S. review went in today. The main thing in it, and in the Times notice, is the idea that the present book is merely an overture to the next one.

Lebe wohl.[2]

Yours,
M

1. "Dreiser's Novel: The Story of a Financier Who Loved Beauty," New York *Times Review of Books*, 10 November 1912, 654 (see Appendix 2, pp. 744–48).
2. Live well.

[UPL-H]

H. L. Mencken
1524 Hollins St.
Baltimore.

November 6th [1912]

Dear Dreiser:-

This Tribune notice[1] gets very close to the book: it is correct in both its praise @ its blame. Most of the other notices so far are obviously by fellows who have been scared off by the mere bulk of the book.

"He has imposed himself upon our current fiction"—a very fine phrase. I wish I had thought of it.

Yours
M

Let me see the later notices, will you?

1. Anon., "Fiction: 'Traction' Interests," New York *Tribune*, 2 November 1912, 11; repr. in Salzman, 97–98.

3609 Broadway
N.Y.C

Nov. 8—1912

Dear H. L. M:

Return this[1] at your leisure. I sent that stuff on Prostitution[2] to Duneka of Harpers. I want to get you connected up with the North American Review. It needs you badly. That is the best stuff on the socalled Social Evil that I have sent[3] yet. But why evil. If there weren't a lot of women who make prostitution their business there would be good many more really not suited for it who would be ripped open & thrown on the ash heap. The prostitute is as necessary as a lawyer & more so. She is the worlds sex safety valve. More power to your punch.

Th. D

1. A review of *The Financier* in the *Brooklyn Daily Eagle*, 2 November 1912.
2. See Mencken to Dreiser, 11 November 1912.
3. Dreiser means "seen."

H. L. Mencken
1524 Hollins St.
Baltimore.

Baltimore, Nov. 11th. [1912]

Dear Dreiser:-

This Eagle review is excellent—the product, I should say, of some one of very conventional mind, and yet of one intelligent enough to see your purposes. It shows an actual reading of the book.

Thanks for your doings regarding Daneka. That prostitution article was done on election day (God save the mark!) in the midst of noise and interruptions. It had the remarkable effect of making the Vice Crusaders ask (quite formally and solemnly) for quarter. Before that they had been disposed to bellow and threaten. Such is life.

My review of "The Financier" was printed in the Times of Sunday.[1] Observe two rotten typographical errors. In the last line of paragraph one it should be "artifice to art." Also, in the same paragraph, it should be "turn of phrase", and not or. But printers are all scoundrels. I wish this article could have appeared two weeks earlier, but even so, it may be in time to influence some of the reviews.

There is a fellow here in Baltimore who sends out monthly tips on the new novels, charging $1 a year for the service. He is enthusiastic about "The Financier". What is more, his opinion is worth hearing, for he seldom goes wrong about books, and beside, he has an intimate knowledge of financial operations. He told me today that the book was absolutely correct in detail.

I am in a hell of a sweat over business matters. I have a chance to make a lot of money by acting as a sort of literary attorney for a crowd of pirates. The cash is very tempting, and beside, I am in full sympathy with the pirates, but I fear I'd be horribly homesick for the newspaper business. This is under the rose. I'll decide in a week or so. Meanwhile, I am planning some new work.

The Smart Set begins to stink. Thayer has a munseyized[2] mind. His ideal is Ainslee's Magazine. Last month he cut a "damn" out of my copy. I have served notice that the next time will be the last. But there is still a chance of making him useful, of which more anon.

Yours,

M

1. See Mencken to Dreiser, 4 November 1912, n.1.
2. A reference to the editor and publisher, Frank A. Munsey, whose publications Mencken considered uninspired and conservative.

[NYP]

[11 November 1912]

Fairest Mencken:

I saw the notice in the Times yesterday. You certainly handed them a heavy mouthful. If anything will help this book here that will. The enclosed from the Transcript[1] has about the same quality as the stuff in the Eagle.

Th D.

I saw this in a ten cent restaurant
"Now I get me up to shirk
I pray to God there aint no work
And if I die before tonight
Thank God there'll be no work in sight"

1. Edwin Francis Edgett, "Theodore Dreiser," *Boston Evening Transcript*, 6 November 1912, 24.

[NYP]

3609 Broadway
N.Y.C

Nov. 12—1912

My Dear Mencken:

This notice from the Eve. Sun[1] will please you I'm sure. Return it with the others. I am wondering, in case I should prepare a codicil to that effect, if you would act as my literary executor in case of my death. I am particularly keen to have someone whose judgement I respect go over the material that is apt to be on hand in the case of a sudden demise and throw out the worthless. You are that one. You will find various things—poems, short storys, essays, a complete novel,[2] over half of a book on my labor experiences,[3] a part of another novel[4] & of course all my letters. I should want all writings turned over to you, of any kind, letter files & all, and would expect you to demand them and to examine them without inter- ference and without admitting anyone to consultation unless you felt so inclined. Thats a good deal to ask but you can say.

I am glad you are considering a good offer but please be sure it wont "bust-up" after you have severed important connections elsewhere.

Yours
Dreiser

Keep this letter[5]

1. Anon., "Theodore Dreiser's New Novel," New York *Evening Sun*, 11 November 1912, 8; repr. in Salzman, 101–4.
2. *The "Genius."*
3. *An Amateur Laborer.*
4. Possibly "The Rake," six chapters of which remain in manuscript at the Univer- sity of Pennsylvania.
5. Dreiser placed this above the salutation.

[UPL]

H. L. Mencken
1524 Hollins St.
Baltimore.

Baltimore, Nov. 12th. [1912]

My dear Dreiser:-

Of course I won't be glad to do it, but if the practical joking of our humorous Boss ever gives me a chance to write about you in the past tense, I'll consider it a high privilege to go through your manuscripts and see to other such things. I needn't thank you for this proof of confidence; I can only hope that the actual work will remain for some better fellow, long after I am safely cremated. But why let so much good stuff remain unpublished? I think a book of your essays, for example, would help to make plain what you are trying to get at in your novels, and so shut off some of the nonsense that now occasionally gets into print about you. But of all this more anon: we must talk of it some day soon and I must hear more about what you have in hand. I'm sorry a better palaver wasn't possible week before last, but Wright was very eager to meet you, and he is a fellow, I believe, whose enthusiasm will be worth something in the future. Aided by my chicanery, he has just signed a contract with Thayer of the S.S. to put some genuine intelligence into the office of that degenerate and maudlin sheet,[1] and to establish a weekly later on. But all this is still a secret. I am working constantly on this weekly scheme. We must have at least one publication in this country which will be open to ideas. The S.S., succumbing to Mark Luther,[2] is now merely a 25-cent edition of Ainslee's Magazine. Thayer, of course, has the same sort of mind, but I believe it possible, as incredible as it may seem, to lure him into the very sort of thing he fears and detests. At all events, Wright has made a long stride in that direction. The next six months may see some fun.

The Evening Sun notice is excellent, and the Transcript notice is full of unaccustomed sense. I think you need have no fears about the reception of the book, despite the plain fact that its sheer length will scare off many reviewers and some readers. Wright will do some bally-hoing out on the coast, and I am sending him some copy for use in Town Topics. But somehow I can see "The Financier" only as an overture to the next volume. I have no doubts about that next volume. You have the thing perfectly in hand: you will knock them out with it.

I have a chance to make $200 a week, but I think I'll pass it up. It means press-agenting and I don't like it. We live but once.

Yours,
M

1. Mencken helped convince John Adams Thayer, the *Smart Set* publisher, to hire Willard Huntington Wright, who became editor for one year (1913).
2. Mark Lee Luther, an associate editor at *Smart Set*, established policy for which Mencken had little regard.

[UPL]

H. L. Mencken
1524 Hollins St.
Baltimore.

Baltimore, Nov. 26th. [1912]

Dear Dreiser:-

This review is the best yet[1]—well thought out and well written. Cary describes the book justly, and, what is more difficult, accurately. This one article is worth more than all the rest appearing so far. It carries authority and conviction in every line of it. It will make readers.

Dids't note Frank Harris' praise the other day? But if you see him tell him his view of Mark Twain is wholly and damnably absurd.[2] Can it be that he is blind to "Huck Finn"?

Yours,
M

1. Lucien Cary, "A Big Novel," Chicago *Evening Post Friday Literary Review*, 22 November 1912, 1; repr. in Salzman, 109–12.
2. In an interview, Frank Harris called Dreiser, Emerson, and Frank Norris "America's great writers." He called Twain "the poorest specimen of a man of letters that I know anything about."

[NYP]

3609 Broadway
N.Y.C

Nov. 29—1912

My Dear H. L. M:

I don't know Frank Harris so I can't give him your message. If you will look on page 695 of Current Literature for December you will see yourself referred to as the distinguished Baltimore Nietchean[1] and if you will turn over to 696 you will see what they have to say of The Financier.[2]

ThD

1. In a review of P. P. Howe's *J. M. Synge, A Critical Study*, the anonymous reviewer mentions Mencken, calling him "the distinguished Baltimore Nietzchean."
2. Anon., "Literature and Art," *Current Literature* 53(December 1912), 696–97. This is a favorable review of *The Financier* in which the reviewer refers to Dreiser as "an arriving giant of American literature."

[UPL]

H. L. Mencken
1524 Hollins St.
Baltimore.

Nov. 30th. [1912]

Dear Dreiser:-

The enclosed[1] was written without any sugestion from me—by a lady at least 44 years old, and militantly virgin. The world do move. You may live to be praised by Hamilton Wright Mabie.[2]

The Current Literature stuff is just and modest praise of both of us. I like the word "distinguished". It was constantly used by Paul Wilstach, press agent for Mansfield,[3] to describe his boss. Whenever I cut it out of copy Paul would be insulted. He really believed that Mansfield was the greatest actor in history, and one of the greatest men.

By the way, don't miss looking into Albert Bigelow Paine's life of Mark Twain, an excellent piece of work.[4]

Achtungsvoll![5]
M

1. This is missing.
2. Hamilton Wright Mabie (1845–1916), author, editor, critic, whose genteel Victorian criticism was an object of Mencken's scorn.
3. Richard Mansfield (1854–1907), famous romantic actor who helped introduce Shaw and Ibsen to the American stage.
4. Paine published his three-volume biography of Twain in 1912.
5. Respectfully.

[UPL]

H. L. Mencken
1524 Hollins St.
Baltimore.

Baltimore, Dec. 10th. [1912]

Dear Dreiser:-

It is amusing to see the virtuosi of virtue on the job. Some day I am going to write an essay on the moral mind: its inability to see anything save as a moral spectacle. Naturally enough, Cowperwood's cleanly paganism was bound to disgust such snouters into man-made muck. Down here I am in constant conflict with such vermin. At the moment they propose a law making copulation a felony, with a penitentiary penalty for the first offense and castration for the second! Imagine it! Remember, I mean simple copulation, fornication—not adultery. I meet a woman of full age, propose a harmless recreation, she consents, and we co-operate. Result: both of us to the pen for a year's hard! I venture an epigram: A moralist is one who holds that every human act must be either right or wrong, and that 99 percent of them are wrong.

The reply of Dell is excellent.

Yours

M

Did I ever send you a copy of "The Artist?"[1] You are its grandpa @ must have it.[2]

1. The play, written for the December 1909 number of Dreiser's *Bohemian*, was issued in 1912 by Mencken's Boston publisher, Luce. Mencken sent a copy to Dreiser with the inscription, "To Theodore Dreiser, in admiration and affection." Alongside this he pasted in a photograph of himself and wrote beside it, "No retouching! Every wart saved.!"
2. The postscript is handwritten.

[NYP]

3609 Broadway, N.Y.C

Dec. 17th 1912

Dear H. L. M:

The enclosed I cut from the Los Angeles Times. I am retaining the picture of you for myself.[1] The review of The Financier I also read there.[2] It is as good as the others but I sympathize with your struggles   If anybody says <u>Financier</u> to you I suppose you feel like striking them down— felling them to the plain. However, send me an inscribed copy of The Artist for I rejoiced in that is one of the best things I ever published— certainly the best peice of satiric humor. More power to your German fist

Th. D

In this picture you look for all the world like the pride of the Brewery. How I love our American cross stocks.

1. Dreiser sent Willard Huntington Wright's review of *The Artist* in which Mencken is called "America's first satirist." A photograph of a somewhat dour-looking Mencken accompanies the article.
2. "'The Financier.' Powerful Novel of Modern Commerce by Theodore Dreiser," *Los Angeles Times Magazine*, 8 December 1912, Holiday Book Section, p. 6.

[UPL]

H. L. Mencken
1524 Hollins St.
Baltimore.

Baltimore, Dec. 18th. [1912]

Dear Dreiser:-

I suppose our clippings crossed. "The Artist" goes to you by this mail. In it a Rogue's Gallery picture—no retouching; every scar, wrinklet, wart and wild hair perfectly rendered. Such art is rare.

Don't think I tired of "The Financier". It was royal sport to keep the notices different, and yet alike. I am only sorry I didn't send Wright twice as much. But it was a rush order and I hadn't the time. If you didn't read his novel notices in his Christmas number, you have missed a dozen loud laughs. I lent him some of my Baltimore Sun stuff, but he greatly embellished it. He has signed a contract with Thayer and should put some life into the Smart Set, which is now merely a bad imitation of Smith's Magazine. He has a great hand for lewd wit, a style of writing that we get too little of. He tells me he didn't do "The Artist" notice, but offers no proof.

May 1913 be kind to you!

Yours,
Mencken

[NYP]

3609 Broadway
N.Y.C

Dec 23rd 1912

Fairest Mencken:

All the blessings of the season on your solid German noggin—chastity, sobriety, deep religious thought.

(Please dont strike me before I get out the door.)

Th.D.

Thanks for the book.[1]

1. Dreiser placed this in the top left-hand corner of the page, beside the address. It is a reference to *The Artist* (1912).

[UPL-H]

H. L. Mencken
1524 Hollins St.
Baltimore.

December 24th [1912]

Dear Dreiser:-

This notice is reprinted in the <u>Nation</u>.[1] He misses the point that you have <u>no</u> answer to offer, but otherwise it seems to me to be very well done. Louis Untermeyer, the poet, blew in the other day: one of your admirers.

May 1913 treat you well!

Yours
Mencken

1. Anon., "Current Fiction: The Financier," *Nation* 95(19 December 1912), 589–90; repr. in Salzman, 121–22.

[NYP]

Hotel Sherman
City Hall Square
Chicago, Ill.

Dec. 30 1912

Dear H. L. M.

I am out here now for awhile.[1] Address me c/o W. C. Lengel, Room 920 City Hall Sq. Bldg. Chicago.[2] I think I see my way to a good second volume—long perhaps, but compact & intimate. Write me anything new. Happy New Year. Before God, Chicago has the finest saloon interiors I ever saw.

Th D

1. Dreiser was in Chicago to resume research on Charles Yerkes's career for the second volume of the Cowperwood trilogy, *The Titan*.
2. At this time, William C. Lengel was editor of *Building Management Magazine* in Chicago.

[UPL-H]

H. L. Mencken
1524 Hollins St.
Baltimore.

Jan 7 '13

Dear Dreiser:-

This stuff doesn't surprise me: I was sure from the start that it would come bobbing along. The few unfavorable reviews were obviously written by gents who hadn't read the book. It's good news that Vol. II is under way: there will be the real story.

Excellent Pilsner is now on tap here. Why not travel via Baltimore on your way home, @ take a dip? Saturday night is the night: a refined assemblage of the literati and musicali.[1]

Yours
H. L. M.

1. Mencken is inviting Dreiser to one of his Saturday Night Club's evenings of music and beer.

[UPL]

H. L. Mencken
1524 Hollins St.
Baltimore.

February 5th. [1913]

Dear Dreiser:-

How are things moving? Down here we have just emerged from smallpox and now prepare for yellow fever. One of my old girls got married the other day: such things give a man pause, and make him sad. But excellent Pilsner is still on tap. When are you coming East? I note the notices: you have the game won.

Yours,
H. L. M.

[NYP]

712 Lincoln Parkway
Chicago

Feb. 8th 1913

Fairest Mencken:

Your note to hand. I am leaving Chicago Monday (Feb 10) at 5:45 P.M. over B & O and arrive in Baltimore Tuesday at the same hour. Cant we foregather. I can leave my bags at the depot and dine. There are one or two things I want to talk about. Will wire exact time later. Praise God. Eat lightly. Have no regrets. As long as the prostate holds out to burn there is hope.

Dreiser

[UPL-Tel]
Feb 11/13

WILL MEET YOU AT CAMDEN STATION AT FIVE FORTY-FIVE.
H. L. MENCKEN

[NYP]

3609 Broadway

Feb. 17–1913

My Dear H. L. M:

Enclosed is a programme of the Little Theatre.[1] I wish you would do something about this along the line you suggested—only mention it by name. Another thing—please send me at once if you can—six sets of pages containing The Free Lance Column which will indicate exactly the nature of the fight you are making so I wont have to write long explanatory letters.[2] I am going to place them where they will do real good. If you have a radical one act play—something remote from the courage of the average stage send it to me & I'll get Browne[3] to read it. He's the real thing.

Th D

1. Dreiser spent much of his spare time in Chicago with the Little Theatre Company where he met with Floyd Dell, Maurice Browne, Kirah Markham, John Cowper Powys, Sherwood Anderson, Edgar Lee Masters, and others.
2. Dreiser wants copies of Mencken's Baltimore *Evening Sun* column, "The Free Lance," in which Mencken was attacking anti-vice crusaders.
3. Maurice Browne, founder of the first Little Theater in America.

[UPL]

H. L. Mencken
1524 Hollins St.
Baltimore.

Baltimore, February 19th. [1913]

Dear Dreiser:-

Thanks for the Little Theatre stuff: I'll try to get in something about it within the week. Just what sort of Free Lance stuff do you want? Most of it is against the Puritans and has little to do with artistic endeavor. At present, it is chiefly a defense of the poor harlots, and is so controversial that it is hard to understand. That damned book, "The American"[1] is going very badly: I work like a dog—and accomplish next to nothing. So I can't tackle a play at the moment, though I have one or two ideas.

Yours,
Mencken

1. Mencken never published his book on "The American." Instead, the project resulted in a series of six articles that ran intermittently in the *Smart Set* from June 1913 to February 1914. Mencken called the introductory essay "The American" and to the others he added subtitles: "His Morals" (July 1913), "His Language" (August 1913), "His Ideas of Beauty" (September 1913), "His Freedom" (October 1913), "His New Puritanism" (February 1914).

[NYP]

3609 Broadway

[after 19 February 1913]

My Dear Mencken:

I was thinking for one thing of the column attack you once made on the anti-vice crusaders, a copy of which you sent me. Also the particular bitter paragraph you pointed out to me the night I was in Baltimore. Three or four other marked pages—paragraphs marked—would convey the significence of the whole thing. My letters will do the rest. Let me know

Th D.

The Chicago Little Theatre Co. Plays Boston March 10 and New York a day or two later.[1]

1. This is written in the top right-hand corner, beside the address.

[NYP]

3609 Broadway, N.Y.C

[after 19 February 1913]

My Dear Mencken:

This introduces Edger L. Masters of Chicago of whom I spoke and wrote. You may have a few thoughts in common.[1]

Theodore Dreiser

1. On 2 March 1913, Masters wrote Dreiser saying he "may stop off to see Mencken at Baltimore" [UPL]; and in a letter of 20 March 1913, Masters tells Dreiser that he and Mencken are exchanging letters. Apparently the letter was presented sometime in March 1913, but probably not in person. On 30 July 1915, Kirah Markham wrote Mencken inviting him to a party at Dreiser's. She said, "His friend Masters who wrote 'Spoon River' will be here and he is so anxious that you two should meet." [NYP] See Dreiser to Mencken, 6 November 1924. Also see Mencken to Dreiser, 31 October 1924, in which Mencken suggests he had only recently met Masters for the first time.

[NYP]

3609 Broadway

[after 19 February 1913]

Thanks for the clippings.[1] There is much dandy stuff therein. I'm sorry you couldn't send me several sets but—such being the case, therefore, etc. A fine day here today—very like spring. I gave Edgar L. Masters who comes to Washington in a day or two & thence on here a letter to you which in all likelihood he wont present. An able man, in sympathy with your point of view. He's a fine lawyer but a better philosopher. A papal indulgence of 90 days is hereby granted for any slight courtesy expended.

Dreiser–Pontifex Max.

1. Mencken had sent the clippings Dreiser requested from "The Free Lance" column.

[NYP]

3609 Broadway

[before 15 March 1913]

Dear Mencken:

Tis plain your words stir up the animals. I had a letter from Mr Lucas which I referred to Mr. Browne.[1] If you see any more of Lucas, as you probably will, ask him if he knows any individual in Philadelphia who might undertake a similar stunt. It would break his trip nicely from New York & possibly get him better rates. Thanks for the notice & its result.

More power to murder, lust, arson and all individual & noble deeds.

Th.D

1. Through Mencken, Dreiser had gotten the agent Lucas to schedule performances for Maurice Browne's Chicago Little Theatre Company in Baltimore.

[UPL]

H. L. Mencken
1524 Hollins St.
Baltimore.

March 15th. [1913]

Dear Dreiser:-

Just home from the inauguration.[1] I saw Lucas this morning and he tells me he is already in communication with Browne. Browne wants to do four performances, but Lucas is wisely in favor of one or two to begin with. No doubt it will be possible to squeeze them between Philadelphia and Washington. Lucas is looking into the Philadelphia matter, but wants to get Baltimore going first. He will make the engagement, if it goes through, a very fashionable affair. But a lot of work is ahead of him. There are but 200 civilized human beings in this town. I will give him newspaper help as soon as he gets under way.

Blessed are the pure in heart, for they shall leave more for the rest of us. Three days of Washington have left me sore and sleepy.

I.H.S.
H. L. M.

1. Woodrow Wilson's inauguration.

[NYP]

3609 Broadway, N.Y.C.

Mch. 23rd 1913

My Dear Mencken:

B. W. Dodge, who used to be with me in B. W. Dodge & Co. has gotten in with a fellow here by the name of Hill[1] who wants to go—or rather really is—in the publishing business but wants to go farther. Hill who is

really rich got in first with a friend of Dodges who publishes slightly (or
did) & because Hill himself had written a book, started The Morningside
Press. Dodge's friend came along & introduced Dodge to Hill & finally
Ben (Dodge) quite innocently enough succeeded his friend, or rather
made a new arrangement. Hill wants to start a new company, keep 50 per
cent of the stock, give Ben 30 or 35 per cent and—here's the proposition—me 15 or 20 per cent and a certain fixed salary for the use of my
name as "consulting Editor," no book to be published or rejected without
my consent. I am to have the privilige of naming a reader and an office
manager to co-operate with Hill & Dodge, principally Dodge who will
look after manufacturer, trade, agencies and the drumming up of books &
publicity generally.

Question: would you advise this at any price? Would or could you suggest a reader or office manager? or both. I have one or two in mind myself.
I am not expected to read mss or do any work—merely advise, keep the
personnel up to tow, see that the spirit of the house is dignified & strong.
If I touched it of course the books published would be as liberal as I
chose. What do you think? I have my novels, but here is a chance to make
one publishing house right or sufficiently liberal when necessary. Would it
be bad to have my name used as consulting editor, in your estimation.

Th. D.

Easter greetings.

1. William Stanley Hill, vice-president of Rowan Realty Company. Dodge had
written to Dreiser on 20 March 1913, presenting the terms of the proposition that Dreiser outlines in this letter. [UPL]

[UPL]

H. L. Mencken
1524 Hollins St.
Baltimore.

March 24th. [1913]

Dear Dreiser:-

The only objection I see to the scheme lies in the habits of Dodge.
Will he stick to the bench—or go roving again?[1] There is a point to be well
pondered. If he runs amuck, the whole thing falls to pieces. As for lending
your name to it, why not? You will be able to protect yourself, and you may
get a chance to do some fine work. It won't take up much of your time. I
think, however, that you had better keep your own books elsewhere until
there is some certainty of success. Also, make sure that you will have an

actual veto on bad stuff. At the moment I don't know of a likely reader, save perhaps George Nathan. I have no acquaintance whatever with publishing people, and never meet such fellows. Again, there is Leo Crane,[2] now rotting on an Indian reservation in Arizona, and crazy to escape. But he has no experience, of course.

I think it would do you good to have some such interest. You need a little variety in life. The job would not interfere with regular writing: most of the work attached to it, in fact, would be recreation for you. Beside, there would be the stimulation of really accomplishing something in the publishing field. At present the condition of affairs is hopeless. Scores of first-rate manuscripts must be going begging. Even Kennerley,[3] who has often taken chances, has been six months deciding to accept a ms. I sent to him. I think I told you about it: a truly startling piece of autobiography. There should be no difficulty about getting it away from Kennerley. Such a damned fool doesn't deserve it.

How much money has Hill got? That is, how much is he willing to put into the firm? In the past all such firms have failed for lack of capital.

Altogether, my first thoughts are in favor of the venture, always supposing Dodge is safely on the track. But if he takes to the jug again, there will be hell.

Yours,
Mencken

1. Ben W. Dodge was an alcoholic, and within a few months of this letter he went to a farm for treatment. His last letters to Dreiser, dated shortly before his death in 1916, show him working on a chicken farm in New Jersey, searching for a way back into "the book world." It remains unclear whether his drowning in the East River was a suicide or an accident resulting from a drinking spree. In light of these events, it was fortunate for Dreiser that he decided against the venture.

2. Leo Crane, a popular author whose work Dreiser published when he was editing *Broadway Magazine* and *The Delineator*.

3. Born in England, Mitchell Kennerley came to New York in 1905 to begin a career as a book and magazine publisher of progressive writers.

[NYP]

3609 Broadway—NYC

[before 18 July 1913]

Dear Mencken:

Enclosed is a one-act reading play which I hesitate to offer Smart Set yet it might be of interest.[1] Would you care to let me know whether it has any value. The second & only remaining copy (type) of the Genius was

Mencken the Smart Set *editor. Photo by Bachrach, 1913*
(Enoch Pratt Free Library)

lost in the mails. Loss $135⁰⁰. A recopying is necessary. When it is done will let you know.² Hard on at work on more Cowperwood.

Th D

1. *The Girl in the Coffin.*
2. On 9 July 1913, Mencken had written "What has become of that ms. I was to read?"

[UPL]

H. L. Mencken
1524 Hollins St.
Baltimore.

July 18th. [1913]

Dear Dreiser:-

I think the play is so good that I have rushed it to Wright, with a strong recommendation. No more about it here. I'll be in N.Y. the latter part of next week, and we can talk it over. Will you be home Thursday evening?

Yours,
M

[UPL-H]

H. L. Mencken
1524 Hollins St.
Baltimore.

Aug 1st [1913]

Dear Dreiser:-

This review (by Wright)¹ bears out what I said the other day: that you are gaining a definite place, by general acceptance, as the leading American novelist. I see you mentioned constantly, @ always with the same respect. New serious novels are no longer compared to "Silas Lapham" or to "McTeague", but to "Sister Carrie" @ "Jennie Gerhardt". I think you will note this plainly in the reviews of the new book.²

Temperature here: 105.

Yours
H. L. M.

1. Wright's essay, published in *Town Topics*, was a review of *Hager Revelly*, which made a flattering reference to Dreiser.
2. *A Traveler at Forty* (New York, 1913).

[NYP]

3609 Broadway

Aug 9th 1913

My Dear Mencken:

Thanks for the notice of Hagar Revelly.[1] Is this man all that Wright says he is? To me Wright is about a third impression of Henry L. Mencken. He is so overcome by your spirit that he even uses your language—almost verbatim and I think unconsciously. Well, every great man must have his satellites—but—Sorry I couldn't see you again. Much power to all your efforts.

Dreiser

Shortly I shall send you proofs of the travel book.

1. *Hager Revelly* (1913), by Daniel C. Goodman (see Mencken to Dreiser, 10 December 1913, n.1).

[UPL-H]

Hotel Woodstock
127–135 West 43rd Street
Times Square East
New York

[before 10 November 1913]

Dear Dreiser:-

I spent the afternoon at the Holts,[1] @ came to the conclusion that the place was not for you. You have enthusiastic admirers there, @ they would be much tickled to see you in the fold, @ eager to give you full swing, but there is the old man to consider—nearly 75, @ full of New England tradition.[2] He reads the house novels—he has notions about fiction—why risk new rows?

But I found out something that will interest you: Doran[3] is regarded as a first-class man, and as the coming leader in the field of fiction. He picked Bennett and he has lately added Birmingham, Walpole, etc. What is more, he is determined to get you,too, @ will give you the very freedom @ support you need. In brief, he looks very good, @ so my advice is that you see him. The reason he held off in the past was on a/c of antagonism to Grant Richards. At all events, talk to him. He believes in you thoroughly.

Let me know what you do. And get the travel book to me as soon as possible.

Yours
H. L. M.

1. The Holt Publishing Company.
2. Henry Holt (1840–1926).
3. George H. Doran.

[EPL]
Nov. 10—1913

My Dear Mencken:

Under separate cover, to 1524 Hollins Street, I am sending you complete page proofs of the travel book—"A Traveler at Forty." This book which will be out on the stands in 10 more days has a red cover & square gold space for title & author. It carries ten illustrations by W. L. Glackens. This copy or set has not been corrected. The finished book for instance has chapter titles which do not appear here—and rather good titles—appropriate. There are minor corrections—a paragraph here & there and of course all typographical errors removed. But from these pages just the same you get the general effect. Will mail you the first completed copy when it arrives. The proofs went by Adams Express.

Yours
Th. D.

In regard to Doran. He wants me to transfer, says he will give me full liberty this side criminal libel & will arrange for debts. I am to talk to him some more.

[UPL]

H. L. Mencken
1524 Hollins St.
Baltimore.

November 11th. [1913]

Dear Dreiser:-

The proofs are here—just too late for my January article! Such is fate! But I'll play up the book, of course, in the February number, out about January 12th.[1] Do you want the proofs back?

Yours,
M

1. "Anything But Novels," *Smart Set* 42(February 1914), 153–54; repr. in Salzman, 164–65.

[NYP]
Nov. 14—1913

Dear Mencken:

Never mind about the proofs. They are of no value. But send me your opinion which I am waiting to hear.

Yours
D

[UPL]

THE SUN
Baltimore, Md.

Sunday. [16 November 1913]

Dear Dreiser:-

No need to say that I have read the travel book with interest: some parts of it show the best writing you have done since "Jennie Gerhardt". But I wish that you had held it down to 350 or 400 pages. The whole Italian section is dragging in tempo: you have got in a lot of stuff that is unimportant, and you have put little of yourself into the rest. After all, it is nothing new to praise Rome and the hill towns: the thing has been done before. Nor is there any novelty in the story of the Borgias. The defect here, I believe, lies in the fact that there is more description than narration. You are at your best in those parts wherein narration is to the fore— for example, in the English chapters.

These English chapters I have enjoyed immensely, and particularly those telling of the incidents of your visit to Richards.[1] The Smart Set chapter on street-walkers is also excellent,[2] and so are the Paris chapters. But in the latter I note an effect of reticence. You start up affairs which come to nothing. The Riviera section is a fine piece of work—beauty seen through a personality—a soul's adventures among masterpieces. That week must have been a superb experience. I must see the Coast the next time I go to Europe.

But don't assume from the foregoing that the book has disappointed me. Far from it. You have got into it, not only a definite revelation of your personality, but also a clear statement of your philosophy. Do you know that this last is substantially identical with Joseph Conrad's? You will find his confession of faith in "A Personal Record". He stands in wonder before the meaninglessness of life. He is an agnostic in exactly the same sense that you are—that is to say, he gives it up. You put down your own ideas very clearly: they lift the whole book above the level of travel books, and make it significant and different. Without the slightest doubt it will be read eagerly by all who admire your novels. I am glad you have done it, and I hope you will follow it with that volume of essays.[3] What you want to enforce is the idea that you are not a mere story-teller, but an interpreter of the human comedy. That is precisely the difference between a bad novelist and a good one—say Chambers and Wells.[4]

What is the present state of the second volume of "The Financier"? My advice is that you bring it out as soon as possible after the travel book, to take advantage of the discussion of the latter. And let that story of the artist (When am I going to see it?) follow quickly. I believe you are injured by long intervals between books. You ought to have seven or eight volumes on the shelves, instead of only three. Once you get them there, you will be discussed more, and also read more.

I note that the sheets of the travel book need not be returned. If you don't want them yourself, let me have them. I have a lot of postcards from you, covering the whole route, and I want to bind them with the sheets, thus enriching my library with a novel work of art.[5]

Take the Doran offer, by all means. I hear only good of Doran, despite his publication of bad books by Irvin Cobb, Will Levington Comfort et al. He is more secure financially than the Harpers, and he has an incomparable finer taste in books. I think you will find him a comfortable publisher.

Two ships laden with Pilsner arrived from Bremen yesterday. After all, the world is not so bad.

Yours,

H. L. M.

1. Grant Richards, the English publisher.
2. Mencken is referring to chapter 13, which Dreiser called "Lilly: A Girl of the Streets." The piece was published earlier as "Lilly Edwards: An Episode" in *Smart Set* 50(June 1913), 81–86.
3. Dreiser had mentioned doing a volume of philosophical essays.
4. Robert W. Chambers and H. G. Wells.
5. Mencken tipped into these sheets Dreiser's postcards and letters from abroad, as well as a number of letters relating to the book. The volume is now in the Mencken Collection of the Enoch Pratt Free Library in Baltimore.

[EPL]
Nov. 18—1913

My Dear Mencken:

Thanks for the opinion. I wish now I had cut down the last half of the book more or left in a lot of woman stuff which they objected to like hell.[1]

After I am dead please take up my mss of The Financier, Titan & Travel book & restore some of the woman stuff—or suggest that it be done. I am afraid I shall have to go to Doran on a try for freedom. I want you, if you will, to read the galleys of The Titan and suggest cuts or additions or variations. Have you the time or the heart.

D

The dummy book is yours of course. Fill it with the cards & my blessing.

1. The Century Company edited out scenes—and at times whole chapters—dealing with Dreiser's encounters or impressions of women on this trip. For an example of such chapters see Thomas P. Riggio, "Europe without Baedeker: The Omitted Hanscha Jower Story—from *A Traveler at Forty,*" *Modern Fiction Studies* 23(Autumn 1977), 423–40.

[EPL]
[after 16 November 1913]

[To Mencken]
Please return. For heaven sake dont over emphasize the dullness of the Italian scene or you will have every critic in the U.S. yelping your remarks like a pack of curs. They've done it every time before & they'll do it again.

D

[UPL-H]

THE SUN
Baltimore, MD.

[before 10 December 1913]

Dear Dreiser:-
   My best thanks for the book: my library will delight my morganatic widows when I am gone! I am going through it again before reviewing it. What luck with Doran? I hope you come to terms with him.

Yours,
H. L. M.

   I send you a copy of my new Nietzsche by this mail—mainly the old stuff, but with corrections @ 2 new chapters.[1]

M.

1. The third edition of *The Philosophy of Friedrich Nietzsche* (Boston, 1913).

[NYP]
Dec 10—1913

My Dear Mencken:

Thanks for the Nietzsche (what a name to spell) book. It is so sensible & vital. You ought to make some money out of that. I am glad you have included his vital statements on principal things. It makes it a primer for beginners as well as a real summary. Has any body done as much & as well for Schopenhauer? Heres luck. I am winding up the Titan of which galley will float to you soon.

Dreiser

Please return the clippings.[1]

1. Reviews of *Traveler at Forty*.

[UPL]

THE SUN
Baltimore, Md.

Wednesday. [10 December 1913]

Dear Dreiser:-

Let me have the galley-proofs of "The Titan" by all means. I am very eager to see it. I sincerely hope you will give it to Doran instead of to the Harpers. Doran will give you more liberty and so rid you of an unbearable nuisance. I can well imagine that you had a row with the Century Company over the travel book. An air of restraint is in it. But enough good stuff remains to give it distinction, and I look for a good sale. The first half is the best, with exceptions in favor of the Mayen episode and the encounter with the pianiste at Frankfort.

I hear that Kennerley is in serious trouble over the "Hagar Revelly" business.[1] The court rules forbid him to introduce witnesses in favor of the book, nor can he put the whole book in evidence. He must plead to the passages that the pornographic Comstock has carefully singled out. What a mess!

I am working hard on the final draft of my American book, but making little progress.[2]

Rush the proofs: I have time at the moment.

Yours,
H. L. M.

1. *Hager Revelly*, a novel by Daniel C. Goodman, a St. Louis physician and social hygienist. In 1913, Mitchell Kennerley published this book about a young woman

whose naïveté leads to her seduction and finally, to avoid prostitution, to a life as her employer's mistress. Anthony Comstock, founder of the New York Society for the Suppression of Vice, secured an indictment against the book, had Kennerley arrested, and the stock and plates of the novel confiscated. Kennerley's lawyer, John Quinn, known for his defense in cases of literary censorship, argued that *Hager Revelly* reflected the values of the period's social-hygiene movement—a plea that won an acquittal for Kennerley.

2. See Mencken to Dreiser, 19 February 1913, n.1.

[UPL]

H. L. Mencken
1524 Hollins St.
Baltimore.

January 1st. [1914]

Dear Dreiser:-

My apologies for not printing a notice of the travel book in The Sun before this. I have been on the verge of the fantods as a result of physical discomforts, and almost unable to work. But my February Smart Set article is in, and the book leads it. Also, I have got a Sun review in type at last, and it is to be used Saturday.[1] A clipping will follow.

The usual poppycock about the New Year! If 1914 is any worse than 1913 I shall file a formal protest with the Devil.

Yours,
Old Dr. Mencken

1. "Dreiser in Foreign Parts," Baltimore *Evening Sun*, 3 January 1914, 3.

[EPL]
Jan 8—1914

H. L. M.

Thanks for the review.[1] Its excellent   Most interesting. Wont you send me 8 or 9 of the full pages on which it appeared. What about Wright?[2] I hear he is off and out & doing F.P.A.[3] column on The Mail. And who takes his place? A mad world, captain! It spins and spins. Do you suppose I will ever reach the place where I will make a living wage out of my books or is this all a bluff & had I better quit. I am getting ready to look for a job.

Yours—fronting the abyss

Th. D.

1. The Baltimore *Evening Sun* review of 3 January 1914.
2. Willard Huntington Wright, who became literary critic of the New York *Evening Mail* after spending one year as editor of *Smart Set*.
3. Franklin P. Adams.

[UPL-H]

H. L. Mencken
1524 Hollins St.
Baltimore.

January 11th [1914]

Dear Dreiser:-

Certainly you'll reach the place where your novels will keep you. I think it is just ahead. "The Titan", with its melodrama, ought to make both a popular and an artistic success. And once you escape from Harpers all of the books will pick up. What are the results of your meetings with Doran?[1] Let me hear about them.

I am in rotten shape physically @ mentally, but look for improvement. A hell of a world.

Yours
M

1. George H. Doran, publisher.

[NYP]

3609 Broadway, N.YC

Jan 14—1914

Dear H. L. M:

What is the trouble? Are you seriously ill? Is there anything I can undertake for you? or do? I'll even review books if necessary. Command me. It distresses me to hear you seriously complain.

D

H. L. Mencken
1524 Hollins St.
Baltimore.

January 13th. [1914]

Dear Dreiser:-

I do not know who Knopf is, but I presume he is connected in some way with Doubleday, Page & Co.,[1] who are probably disinclined, for obvious reasons, to approach you directly. Four or five months ago I had a letter from them asking me to sign an appeal to authors on behalf of Conrad. I agreed to do so and have since signed. Doubleday, Page & Co., I think, own six of the Conrad copyrights. Harpers also own six. The rest are scattered. I have no more desire to boost the Doubleday-Page business than you have,[2] but they are the only American publishers who seem to take any interest in Conrad, and so I am glad to lend a hand. Certainly, Conrad deserves all the help he can get.

"Chance", however, is rather poor stuff—for him.

Yours,
M

Anna, I wish you would consider this.[3]

1. Alfred A. Knopf was associated with the Mitchell Kennerley firm at this time.
2. Together Dreiser and Mencken had helped establish the story of Doubleday's "suppression" of *Sister Carrie.*
3. This, in Dreiser's hand, was added as a message to Anna Tatum, Dreiser's secretary at the time.

H. L. Mencken
1524 Hollins St.
Baltimore.

Baltimore, Feb. 24th [1914]

Dear Dreiser:-

I have inquired about Doran confidentially, and come to the conclusion that he is not the right man. I hear that he runs, or is running, to religious bosh, and that he is soon to start a new religious review. Also, that he has a lot of pious books on the stock. Finally, I am told that he is an unpleasant sort personally. So I think it would be unwise to tackle him. As for Huebsch,[1] I hear that he is a fine fellow, but that he has no money, and must fly very close to the ground. Have you ever thought of Duffield?[2]

Yours,

H. L. M.

1. Benjamin W. Huebsch (1876–1964), publisher.
2. Pitts Duffield (1869–1938).

[NYP]

HOTEL BRADLEY
Chicago

March 6 1914

My Dear Mencken:

How is your health?—and fortune? Since writing you last I have some slight news. Harpers, after printing a first edition of 10,000 copies of The Titan, have decided not to publish. Reason—the realism is too hard and uncompromising and their policy cannot stand it. Doran is considering at present. Result uncertain.[1] Will send you pages. It is only within 10 days that I succeeded in cleaning it up. If this were Sister Carrie I would now be in the same position I was then. You should look over Chicago carefully sometime. It is a great and entirely individual city

Th.D.

1. John Lane assumed publication of *The Titan*; and the firm used the first impression of the novel prepared by Harper's. John Lane published the book on 22 May 1914.

[UPL]

THE SUN
Baltimore, Md.

March 9th [1914]

Dear Dreiser:-

The Harpers be damned. Jump to Doran, by all means. I think he can be brought into line. Would it do any good if I wrote to him? Curiously enough, one of the Doubleday-Page men asked me three or four months ago to find out if you would consider a proposition. I told him that you would not do it so long as any other reputable publisher remained on earth. Doubleday-Page, of course, would want you to imitate Gene Stratton Porter.[1]

Can't you get me a copy of "The Titan"? I want to read it at once. I am booked to sail for Naples April 11, returning about June 1. Naples, Rome, Venice, Munich, Paris, home. Two good fellows are going along, and we'll probably have a high old time.

I am in rotten shape physically. I have had a sore tongue for nine months, and no relief in sight. So far, no sign of a tumor—but the discomfort keeps me from all save routine work.

When do you head past again?

Yours,
M

1. Gene Stratton Porter (1863–1924), best-selling novelist of sentimental tales like *Laddie* (1913).

[NYP]

HOTEL BRADLEY
Chicago

March 16, 1914

My Dear Mencken:

I am awfully sorry to hear about the troublesome tongue. No one would wish you a swifter healing than I. Your chart of the uplift to hand and I had a loud laugh where I found sociology under magic.[1] Like everything else in life the classification has some justification.

Well, a pleasant trip to you in Europe. Don't do the Riviera in summer and go to your southernmost point first which you naturally do anyhow. They say the mosquitos are bad & malarial in Venice in summer. Make them give you mosquito netting. I have various plans—books etc in mind—a new philosophic interpretation of Earthy life for one thing, but meantime I am nursing wounds made when I was under ether to remove carbuncles—the devils own. Write me when you can. Tis a painful life.

Th. D.

1. Mencken's "chart" has disappeared.

[UPL]

H. L. Mencken
1524 Hollins St.
Baltimore.

March 18th. [1914]

Dear Dreiser:-

A copy of "The Titan", unbound, has just come from Miss Tatum.¹ I'll read it tonight. You'll never see it again.

An eternal pox upon the Harpers. And Doran be damned for his flight.² God knows, this country needs that weekly I once planned. The forward-lookers are eating us up. Even the Smart Set is now as righteous as a decrepit and converted madame. The Owen Hatteras³ stuff that I used to do is now being done by some member of the Men and Religion Forward Movement.

When the carbuncles? I certainly hope they have all vanished. A painful, and often dangerous pestilence. My tongue could be worse. I sail April 11th.

Yours,
M

1. Anna P. Tatum worked closely with Dreiser on *The Titan* and handled much of his correspondence with publishers. Mencken corresponded with her at times because he could not locate Dreiser. On 16 March 1914, he wrote Tatum that "I have written to Doran, as you suggest, but not to Jones (of the John Lane Co.). This is not only because I doubt the advisability of writing to both, but because I want to see Doran take hold of Dreiser's books, if it is at all possible. He has more sense than all the rest of the American fiction publishers put together, and I hear that he is an honest man." [UPL] It was Anna Tatum who sent the unbound *Titan* to Mencken in time for him to write a review before he left for Europe. Throughout March Tatum managed the negotiations between Dreiser and his various publishers, sending them copies of the manuscript, meeting with them, and steering Dreiser away from those she considered too conservative. In addition, she regularly wired Dreiser in Chicago with words of encouragement: "Keep nerve, M[encken] wrong" (7 March 1914); "No need discouragement" (12 March 1914 [UPL]).
2. Doran decided against publishing *The Titan*.
3. Owen Hatteras was the pseudonym Mencken and Nathan used in the *Smart Set*'s "Pertinent and Impertinent" department, begun in 1912. Under this comic mask, the two lambasted middle-class morality and "puritanism" in all its forms.

[NYP]

Hotel Bradley
Chicago

March 21, 1914

My Dear Mencken:

I shall be in New York Monday, March 23—where address me—c/o
P.O. Box 39—Hamilton Grange Branch. Yours concerning receipt of page
proofs to hand. Keep it—bad as it is with my arthurial[1] blessing. My carbuncles are well [2](←drawing of man tapping on wood) providing they are
and no new ones develop. A telegram from John Lane accepts Titan if I
will, with seeming happiness. What fools these mortals be. It is spring
here. The Cafeterias clatter, the car conductors are jubilantly insolent,
every officer feels it his duty to arrest you and toothpicks and chewing
gum abound. What more—what more!

Life, health, strength
Th D

1. Dreiser may mean "authorial."
2. Dreiser here drew a small figure of a "man tapping on wood."

[UPL]

H. L. Mencken
1524 Hollins St.
Baltimore.

March 23rd. [1914]

Dear Dreiser:-

I have just finished "The Titan". Believe me, it is the best thing you
have ever done, with the possible exception of "Jennie Gerhardt", and the
superiority there is only in the greater emotional appeal. "Jennie" is more
poignant—but "The Titan" is better written. In fact, some of the writing
in it is far ahead of any of your past work—for example, the episode of the
honest Mayor snared by the wench. I am delighted that you are striving
hard in this department. You are more succinct, more dramatic, more
graceful. In brief, you are superimposing a charm of style upon the thrill
of narrative.

Let Lane have it, by all means. There is not a word in the book that
will give Comstock his chance. He must go into court with some specific
phrase—something that will seem smutty to an average jury of numskulls.
The fundamental and essential unmorality of the book is beyond his

reach. Believe me, the whole thing has made me kick up my heels. It is the best picture of an immoralist in all modern literature—at least, since Thackeray's "Barry Lyndon". You are not standing still: you are moving ahead. I wish you would print that book of serious philosophy. And the essays you once told me about.

Curious note: "A Traveler at Forty" made such a hit with Chas. H. Grasty, publisher of The Balto. Sun, that he has applied to the Century Co. for permission to reproduce extracts from it.[1]

More anon.

Yours,
Mencken

1. There is no record of such a publication.

[NYP]
March 25—1914.

My Dear Mencken:

Thanks for your letter—forceful & honest as usual. The Lane Company have taken the book—$1000 down, 20%, etc, etc. A three page letter written by Frederic Chapman, the London adviser to John Lane will explain why.[1] I want you to see the enclosed telegram sent to me at Chicago which shows the firms attitude.[2] I think a stand like this deserves recognition. The Chapman letter goes to you under separate cover. I am really too tired to think but your view of it cheers me because I have such implicit faith in your honesty—intellectual & every other way.

The carbuncles are better though another may develop at any time. No prevention is known. The germ (like that of cancer) has never been isolated. They are very, very painful. I learned today that Doran dislikes me personally, having met me, but more than that he thinks Yerkes an abnormal American business type and not worth discussing.[3] I should write on less abnormal themes. Mitchell Kennerley tells Knopf that I have handled Emily Griggsby[4] in a cheap, slanderous & sensational way, rehashing old fables. In justice to her he could not publish it. The truth is the book was never offered to him at all by me. I permitted Knopf (now associated with him) to read it as a favor and he handed out this comment to Chapman of John Lane Sunday at dinner. The latter then told him he had already taken it. Result——? The Century Co insists that the study is abnormal & impossible. Ditto Harper. There you are. Harper—Century—Doran—Kennerley. I haven't done with the trilogy yet. One more volume—but not immediately. I am preparing The Genius[5] of which more later. Masters[6] says he thinks The Titan is somewhat too long in the first half.

Well enough. I am with my sister[7] on Staten Island for a few days—514 Richmond Terrace, New Brighton c/o A. D. Brennan, where address if you answer this. Dont despair. The philistines will never run us out as long as life do last. Given health & strength we can shake the American Jericho to its fourth sub-story.

Spring is here—carpenters, painters, paper hangers, moving vans, plumbers—all the dainty and fragrant signs. "Hey, Jimmie, take this can an' git a quart of Franciskaner—are you William? Move now"   This from the backroom where the philosophers union is in session at $3.50 per day, the side motif being paper hanging. Happy days abroad.

Th D

Return the telegram & Chapman letter.[8]

1. Frederic Chapman, translator of Anatole France and adviser to John Lane in England, wrote a glowing report of *The Titan* for Lane, calling Dreiser "the leading American novelist." [UPL]
2. The John Lane Company sent Dreiser the following message: "Proud to publish Titan. Accept same on terms offered us through your friend and agent William Lengel. Can publish immediately after transfer is arranged and book can be printed and bound. Will arrange with Mr. Lengel tomorrow details and contract." [UPL]
3. On 16 March 1914 Anna Tatum, following a meeting she had had with Doran, wrote Dreiser of the publisher's opinion. Charles Yerkes is Dreiser's original for the character of Cowperwood in *The Financier*, *The Titan*, and *The Stoic*.
4. The prototype of Berenice Fleming in *The Titan*.
5. Dreiser does not yet place quotation marks in the title.
6. Edgar Lee Masters.
7. Dreiser's sister, Mary Frances.
8. Dreiser wrote this at the head of the letter.

[UPL]

H. L. Mencken
1524 Hollins St.
Baltimore.

March 27th. [1914]

Dear Dreiser:-

Within the Lane telegram. The Chapman letter hasn't come in yet. Lane is in the proper attitude of mind: I'm glad you came to terms with him. It is high time that you stopped listening to the vapid criticisms of publishing donkeys. Such vermin overestimate their own sagacity, and what is more, their own importance. Imagine Kennerley objecting to a book of yours! The impertinence of the fellow makes me laugh. He was scared stiff by the "Hagar Revelly" affair.[1]

The more I think of "The Titan", the more I am convinced that some of your best work is in it. In one thing, of course, it seems to fall below "Sister Carrie" and "Jennie", and that is in its lack of poignancy. In other words, Cowperwood does not appeal to the sympathies; he does not grip the more responsive emotions, as Carrie and Jennie do. But I think the book is better planned and better written than either of the others. You are making progress in workmanship, or to use critical cant, in technic. You get your effects with greater ease, and they are subtler effects. I have tried out the book on a typical novel reader, and he is enthusiastic. I see no hook for Comstock to hang upon: he must go before a jury with some definite phrase. The profound unmorality of the book is beyond him. It is a great Nietzschean document.

Willard Wright (who has just gone to Europe) lately made a book out of various travel articles that he, Geo. Nathan and I wrote for the Smart Set, and Lane, I hear is to do it.[2] I have not seen the final ms. and know little about it. My own share in it is slight. The Smart Set is now as pure as the Christian Herald. I am doing nothing but my monthly book article: my contract runs to next Oct.

An eternal curse upon the Harpers. Give them a chapter in your reminiscences, following the Doubleday chapter. Beware of Knopf: he is representing himself as your intimate friend.

I sail on the Laconia April 11th.

Yours,
Mencken

1. See Mencken to Dreiser, 10 December 1913, n.l.
2. Lane did publish the book, *Europe After 8:15* (1914).

[NYP]
March 31—1914

My Dear H. L. M:

Enclosed the letter from Chapman (Frederic) to John Lane in London. Please return it as I have no other copy. If you will believe it Harpers have asked me to permit them to publish ~~The Titan~~ The Genius. This sounds wild but it is true and they backed it by an offer of aid   They feel that they have made a mistake. Neither will they part with the published volumes now in their possession[1]—at least not yet—the same people who think me unfit for publication. Am I mad or is this good red earth we are standing on. Its a long story. If you come through N.Y. breakfast or dine with me and I will tell you the whole story. Scheherazade has got nothing on me.

But I wont go back.

My permanent address is P.O. Box 39—Hamilton Grange Branch N.Y.C. where address me except for special addresses I may give you. Small Maynard & Co offered to take me over but I dont care for them. A pleasant voyage—if I do or dont see you.

Th. D

Let me say one word to you. I have thought of it often. Write an intellectual farce. You will do it brilliantly—exquisitely. Write a two three or four act farce. Why not "The White Slavers"—or "The Vice Crusaders".

---

1. Harper's claimed Dreiser owed them $2,000 in advances.

[UPL]

H. L. Mencken
1524 Hollins St.
Baltimore.

April 5th. [1914]

Dear Dreiser:-

The Chapman letter is a corker, by my troth. The impudence of the Harpers passeth all belief and understanding. Do those swine seriously believe that you would touch them with a ten-foot pole? What a chapter for your memoirs!

I'll get to New York Friday night, and leave for the pier early in the morning, so there is small chance of meeting. I'll put up at the Woodstock in 43rd street.

Curiously enough, the very sort of farce you propose has been in my mind for some time. Maybe I'll try to write it during the autumn, once I get my book done.

Yours,
M

[NYP]

4142 Parkside Ave
Phila, Pa.

April 5—1914

My Dear Mencken:

I am over here for a few days quiet work. Dont give this address to anyone. If you chance to come through Phila & I see you alright. If not— Bon Voyage. Luck to the thriving book.

Th.D[1]

1. Dreiser wrote "Phone Belmont 2813W" at the top of the page.

[NYP]

4142 Parkside Ave.
Phila, Pa

April 11th 1914

My Dear Mencken:

John Lane want to & will publish <u>The Titan</u> May 10th. Harper's have put an almost prohibitive price on my other books to prevent me from moving. The Genius will surely come out next spring. Rand McNally & Small Maynard write to ask privilege of publishing. A soul above naps.

Th. D

Let no scoundrelly European rob you.

[UPL-HPc]

Rome

[27 April 1914]

The more I think it over, the more I believe that "The Titan" is great stuff. Here on your track. Just saw report of Richards divorce.[1]

Mencken

1. Grant Richards.

[UPL-HPc]
Munich, May 5 [1914]

Back to the old town, but only for a few days. Rome tickled me as it did you. But Venice is the queen!

M

[UPL]

H. L. Mencken
1524 Hollins St.
Baltimore.

Sunday. [7 June 1914]

Dear Dreiser:-

My best thanks for the copy of "The Titan", awaiting me on my return.[1] It was my bad luck that the book came out just as I was preparing to clear out. The result is that my S.S. review is much delayed.[2] But I am going to write it immediately, and will also get a good notice into Town Topics.[3] The enclosed, published in the Evening Sun, was done by one Sherwood, a very moral fellow.[4] It has the merit of being absolutely sincere. The book fairly knocked him in the head.

What is the news?

Yours,
Mencken

1. Dreiser's inscription in the book reads: "To Henry L. Mencken from Theodore Dreiser—to add to his collection of Dreiseriana. N.Y. May 13, 1914."
2. The review appeared as "Adventures among the New Novels," *Smart Set* 43 (August 1914), 153–57 (see Appendix 2, pp. 748–53).
3. Under the pseudonym of The Ringmaster, Mencken wrote "The Literary Show: Dreiser and His Titan," *Town Topics* 71(18 June 1914), 17–18.
4. H. S. Sherwood, "Theodore Dreiser's 'Titan,'" Baltimore *Evening Sun*, 23 May 1914, 4; repr. in Salzman, 172–73.

[UPL]

THE SUN
Baltimore, Md.

June 10th. [1914]

Dear Dreiser:-

The news that Kennerley is playing the louse brings no surprise.[1] I had to do with him on one occasion, and came away with the firm conviction that he is a cheap and evasive creature, with no notion of the truth. And I hear the same thing from others who know him. His standing is shown by the fact that when Comstock began his "Hagar Revelly" prosecution only one New York publisher offered any help.

I note that George Howard's[2] card is chiefly devoted to his own virtues. His Broadway stories were well written, but rather pointless. Of his novel I know nothing: I have not seen it, not any part of it. But he seems to be making a sincere effort to put his Popular Magazine stuff behind him, with what success I can't say. Howard has no little talent, but he is constantly quarrelling with one person or another, usually for small reasons. His latest "enemy" is Willard Wright, who did a lot for him. The childish spatting that goes on in New York is amazing.

I have done part of my Smart Set notice of "The Titan". Let me keep the clippings for a few days. I want to read them and refer to them. I'll send them back next week, and if you want them in the meantime you can get them immediately by dropping me a wire.

I have had a couple of letters from Jones.[3] His enthusiasm for "The Titan" seems to be undamaged by Kennerley's efforts.

It is my damnable luck that "The Titan" came out just as I was cleaning up to go to Europe, and that I thus missed the chance to get ahead of the newspaper reviews. Let me see "The Genius" as soon as possible.

Yours,
Mencken

1. The editor and author Alexander Harvey sent Dreiser a letter he had received from Mitchell Kennerley in which Kennerley says, "in my opinion it [*The Titan*] should never have been published in America, and cannot possibly be published in England without incurring legal liability." [UPL] Kennerley's objections had to do with Dreiser's fictional treatment of a number of the originals for the novel, particularly the career of Miss Griggsby.
2. George Bronson Howard (1884–1922), journalist, novelist.
3. J. Jefferson Jones (1880–1941), the American director of the British publishing house of John Lane.

[NYP]

109 St. Marks Place
New Brighton, S.J.

June 15—1914

Dear H. L. M:

I gave the duplicate of the letter I sent you—"The Titan in England"—to Alexander Harvey who is a friend of Kennerleys to give to Kennerley in order to draw him out if possible. Enclosed is Kennerleys letter.[1] I am sending it because I imagine you might care to glance at it. Outside of trying to prevent the suppression of the book over there, I am through.

Th.D

1. See Mencken to Dreiser, 10 June 1914, n.1.

[UPL-H]

THE SUN
Baltimore, Md.

[after 15 June 1914]

Dear Dreiser:-

Kennerley's letter gives him away. Imagine such a fellow chattering about the proprieties! He is really too absurd. All this will make a capital chapter in your reminiscences.

Harvey's offer is friendly enough, but what could you gain by a treaty of peace with Kennerley. The one thing he can do is to apologize unreservedly for his invasion of your affairs.

I'll return the clippings shortly. My Smart Set notice goes in tomorrow. How are you, anyhow?

Mencken

[UPL-H]

H. L. Mencken
1524 Hollins St.
Baltimore.

[before 22 June 1914]

Dear Dreiser:-

By this mail I am returning the reviews. I have copied a sentence or two from each of them, and shall print these extracts together as a sort of exposé of American newspaper reviewing.

My Smart Set notice—about 3,000 words—will be printed in the August number, out about July 12. I am doing Wright's Town Topics stuff for him while he is away, and have a notice of the book in the current number—June 18, page 17.

What progress with "The Genius"?

Yours
H. L. M.

[NYP]
June 22nd 1914

My Dear H. L. M:

Thanks for the reviews which came safely and for word about the T.T.[1] I had some good laughs out of that. You write with a rolling abandon which gets better as you get older. The Genius of which I lost two complete typewriten copies worth $175^{00} all told is nearly recopied. I am to try to edit it next month—and I am such a poor editor. Things are much the same as ever. It's nice where I am—a splendid view of the bay—but I'm going to move back into town or over to Phila. I have many schemes or plans but only one pen hand—and meanwhile my allotted space ticks swiftly by. Greetings—and lets pray we keep good stomachs and avoid religion. The ills that affect man are truly mental and not material. Mostly they are damned theories that blow like diseases on every wind.

Yours as ever

Th.D

Kennerley now says he has no personal objection to the publication of the Titan in England but he lies.[2]

1. *Town Topics*.
2. On 17 June 1914, Kennerley wrote Alexander Harvey that Dreiser could get an English publisher easily if Lane decided not to issue the book in England. "I personally shall have nothing further to say, but to congratulate Mr. Dreiser upon his publisher." [UPL] Harvey sent this letter to Dreiser.

[UPL]

H. L. Mencken
1524 Hollins St.
Baltimore.

June 26th. [1914]

Dear Dreiser:-

If ever you want a strange eye to look at "The Genius" I'll be very glad to read it. Put up your whoops about allotted spans, etc. We are both still youngsters, scarcely past the age of consent. Wait until prohibition is in force all over the country, and every man is a fugitive from justice!

Yours,

M

[NYP]
July 2nd 1914

My Dear Mencken:

All of this 2nd typing of The Genius isn't here yet. When it comes and I have had a chance to run over it myself I will send it on. I am most anxious to know what you think and that long before I publish it.

Th.D

By the way can I get 50 copies of The Sun containing your critical comparison.[1] They will be of use to me.

---

1. Mencken had printed selections from both laudatory and hostile reviews of *The Titan* in the Baltimore *Evening Sun* of 27 June 1914.

[NYP]
July 14—1914

My Dear H. L. M:

My address for the present is 165 W. 10th Street—N.Y.C. How are you? I do not seem to be able to convince J. Jefferson Jones that I had nothing to do with that col. of critical excerpts which he greatly admires. So you see how greatness can be really thrust upon one.

Th D

[NYP]

165 W. 10th St.—N.Y.C

July 20—1914

My Dear Mencken:

I noticed on the page which contained your summary of American criticisms of The Titan your very warm praise of the verses of Louis Untermeyer. I wonder if you know of the work of Arthur Ficke or Nicholas Vachel Lindsay. I have read Lindsays "San Francisco", "Mumbo Jumbo", "The Santa Fe Trail" and several others and consider them lyrical and full of color—rich color. I doubt seriously whether Untermeyer could do near as well in anything—moralic—po-ethical or otherwise. Anyhow I am sick of ethical verse.

Ficke hails from Davenport Ia. This months Forum has something   I have listened to some 30 unpublished sonnets—not recited by Ficke—which I commend to your attention. When an American poet—a writer of short poems arises I instantly think of Herrick, W. E. Henley, Thomas Hardys brooding volumes and A. E. Housmann (The Shropshire Lad) Lindsay and Ficke have the tang of these people and Ficke strongly suggests Keats, Housmann and Iowa combined in a new, tender & delicate way. Also—look over Masters—(Edgar L.) "The Spoon River Anthology" now running in Reedys Mirror—

ThD

You might do something on all three at once.
And what of John G. Neihardt. His verses are pagan & lovely at times.

[UPL-H]

H. L. Mencken
1524 Hollins St.
Baltimore.

[after 20 July 1914]

Dear Dreiser:-

I know little about Lindsay, @ nothing about Ficke, but I have often written about Neihardt. If you are in communication with these fellows, tell them to send me their books. Some of Untermeyer's stuff is very good, indeed. He is inclined to parlor socialism, but it seldom shows in his verse.

God help the rich!

Yours
M

[NYP]

165 W. 10th St. N.Y.C

July 29—1914

My Dear H. L. M:

Under separate cover I am sending you 15 or 16 reviews which have blown in since the major batch you examined. Because of their continued divergence they may interest you. What I am writing to ask however is— can I get you to read a two part philosophic article and three one act plays which I have just completed? The philosophic article—"Saving the Universe"[1] I may publish in one of the magazines if conditions permit. The three one act plays are reading plays only to be a part of group of five or six to be published in book form under the title "Plays of the Natural and the Supernatural"[2] I am not turning esoteric, metaphysical or spiritualistic.

These are merely an effort at drama outside the ordinary limits of dramatic interpretation. If you can find time to read them & will let me know what you think, I will be grateful.

It rains here everyday now. I have a box of morning glories but they dont need watering. I know a place where swell lobsters are sold at 50 cents per, delightfully broiled & with drawn butter. Underneath my table is a bottle of Gordon Gin & a syphon of selzer. Life is difficult & I must keep up.

Th D

The plays are
1. The Blue Sphere
2. In The Dark
3. Laughing Gas

1. "Saving the Universe" has not been identified.
2. The John Lane Company published *Plays of the Natural and the Supernatural* (1916).

[UPL]

H. L. Mencken
1524 Hollins St.
Baltimore.

July 30th. [1914]

Dear Dreiser:-
    Send on the plays and the article, by all means. I have a particular reason for wanting to see them. And when am I going to get the ms. of "The Genius."

Yours,
Mencken

[UPL]

H. L. Mencken
1524 Hollins St.
Baltimore.

August 2nd. [1914]

Dear Dreiser:-
    These reviews merely poll-parrot the earlier ones. It is curious to notice how many of them belabor you for writing, not "The Titan", but some other novel. Such is criticism in These States.

By the way, I was in the Congressional Library the other day, palavering with some of its pundits. They showed me some manuscripts and I asked them how they would like to have yours on your departure for the right hand of God. They were delighted.

Let the plays and the essays come along.

Yours,
Mencken

[NYP]
Aug 3rd 1914

My Dear H. L. M:

Whatever your prejudices against this type of stuff (the playlets) see if on second consideration it hasn't some appeal. If you see any method of editing the philosophic article to advantage do so. I am now engaged in leading the German army on to Paris.

Th.D.

I have all the mss originals. I may be very glad to turn them all over if they will keep them together. The trilogy especially. I will add something to this statement a little later.

[NYP]

165 W. 10th St. N.Y.C

Aug 10—1914

My Dear Mencken:

As I told you I think I am contemplating a small book of these plays—5 or 6—to be brought out this fall unless I serialize them. I have just finished a fourth called "A Spring Recital" and am beginning the last one—"The End." Jones of Lane is willing to publish them. Do you think the adventure in book form worth while? Will be grateful if you will read the other two a little later. I have doped out a fantastic scheme whereby "In the Dark" could be produced at "The Princess" [1] but who would say a good word for me?

—Th.D

I am over half way through Vol 1 of a three volume "History of Myself" Vol 1—ends naturally at 20. Vol II at 40—and volume III will be written and end Chance knows when. On the conclusion of this 1st volume or before—in September I presume, I am going to make a stab at "The Bulwark" If I have any luck, that ought to be a dandy story. I hereby offer you the original pen copy of anyone of my mss—Sister Carrie, Jennie Gerhardt, The Financier, The Titan The Genius (when done with) A Traveller, or this set of one act plays to be disposed of at any time as you see fit. The trilogies ought to kept together.

1. The Princess Theatre was located on Broadway between 28th and 29th streets. *In the Dark* was never produced there.

[UPL]

H. L. Mencken
1524 Hollins St.
Baltimore.

August 11th. [1914]

Dear Dreiser:-

In plain truth, you overcome me with the offer of one of your mss. There is nothing I'd be more delighted to have: it would be the arch of my collection of Dreisereana. But can it be that you really mean it? Trying my damndest to think evil of no man, I am filled with suspicions that you have taken to heroin, Pilsner, formaldehyde. Purge your system of the accursed stuff—and then offer me "Sister Carrie". And see me jump!

By all means, do the plays as a book. And meanwhile, do me this favor: give me an option on them for two weeks. The reason must be kept confidential: I am at work on a plan which may give me editorial control of the Smart Set, and I want to blaze out with some Dreiser stuff.[1] The chances, at the moment, are rather against success, but I am hanging on, and may know the result in a day or two. George Nathan is with me. He, in fact, is doing all the final negotiating. If the thing goes through there will be a future in it for both of us. The S.S. is losing very little money, and the cutting off of certain excessive overhead expenses—high rent, extravagant salary to Thayer, etc.—will quickly make it self-sustaining. And we are associated with a truly excellent man of business—one who is no mere talker, but has actually made a success elsewhere.[2] Thayer is a sorry quitter. He got into a panic at the first fire.

All this for your private eye. If our scheme fails, I want to be in a position to make decent terms with the new boss, whoever he is. Hold up the plays for two weeks. I think we can easily come to terms.*

I offer no formal thanks for the ms. offer. I would esteem it more than the gift of a young virgin. (Thus we old fellows talk! Diablerie senilis!)

Yours,
M

*That is, cash on the block.[3]

1. Later in the month, Mencken and Nathan took over editorial control of *Smart Set*. Colonel Eugene R. Crowe and Eltinge Warner had recently taken over the magazine from John Adams Thayer, and the two men established a triumvirate ownership. Crowe and Warner each held one-third part in the enterprise, and Mencken and Nathan shared a third between them. In effect, Crowe and Warner financed *Smart Set*, and Mencken and Nathan ran it.

2. Eltinge Warner, who made a large success of *Field and Stream* before buying into *Smart Set*.

3. This is in Mencken's hand.

[NYP]

165 W. 10th St. N.Y.C
Phone 7755 Chelsea

Aug 12—1914

My Dear Mencken:

The mss in question is in a box in a storage vault: I'll go up the first chance I get & dig it out. I dont know whether to send it by mail or not. I lost two large mss that way. Perhaps it would be best to leave it at Smart Set office for you. I shall hold the plays in question for the time mentioned and I wish you luck. I am sure if you assume personal charge you will make a go of it.

Th.D.

[UPL]

H. L. Mencken
1524 Hollins St.
Baltimore.

August 13th. [1914]

Dear Dreiser:-

Thanks for your good letter. I am going to New York Saturday afternoon to meet Nathan and Warner, the latter the business man of the combination. Unless something interferes I'll call you up Sunday morning. But if you have any plans for Sunday, don't bother: I'll probably be in New York often during the next couple of months. The scheme is working out very well—so far. We are practically in charge of the magazine. Thayer has packed his goods and left.

If I find you entirely free from poisons when we meet, I'll grab the ms. on the spot. What a gift! Believe me, I'm tickled to death.

Auf wiedersehen!
M.

[UPL]

THE SUN
Baltimore, Md.

August 17th. [1914]

Dear Dreiser:-

With my usual stupidity I went to N.Y. without the memorandum that I had made of your address and telephone number, and so I couldn't get to you Sunday. My news is brief: if all goes well, Nathan and I will be in full editorial control of the Smart Set this week. Nathan, in fact, is already in the office, and I have gone through a lot of ms. The Thayer regime is at an end. We are putting up no money and taking no financial risk except the loss of our time. Warner, who has made a success of Field & Stream, starting on a shoe-string, is in charge of the business office, and gives signs of making it a go. He has backing. I am to stay in Baltimore. My chief job will be to get and read ms. and negotiate with authors. Nathan will look after the office work, which is very slight.

Both of us want at least two of your plays. In fact, we simply <u>must</u> have something from you. It goes without saying that we are not rich, but if you will give us a couple of weeks to turn around, it will be possible to get you your money out of the first cash available. I therefore exercise the option you gave me, and hold the plays that long. What will you take for "The Blue Sphere"? Make it as cheap as possible, if you have a heart. This looks like an excellent fighting chance. The magazine, with our retrenchments, has income enough to keep it going. Give us a lift now, if you can, and I think there will be good times ahead. All our plans, of course, include the theory that we will get copy from you pretty regularly. We want to make this magazine thoroughly first class.

This in a great rush. I'll probably be in N.Y. again next week, and I'll make sure that I don't forget the memorandum.

God's benison upon the Kaiser. He will lick 'em all.

Yours,
H. L. M.

[NYP]

165 W. 10th St: N.Y.C
Phone 7755 Chelsea

Aug. 22nd 1914

My Dear H. L. M:

It's needless to say that I will do anything I can—"within reasal" as someone I knew used to say. Yesterday I mailed you "A Spring Recital" and "The Light in the Window"—one a supernatural skit—the other a disguised melodrama. I would like to know what you think of those. There is one more supernatural which with a little work may prove best of all—and it may not.

I will explain my situation exactly and then you can judge what ought to be done. I need about 1,500 to finish The Bulwark this winter.[1] It is very plain from one or two tentative opinions I have secured that I could get about $1,000 for the first three things from the Century or Metropolitan. After hearing from you I sent them to Doty & DeCamp[2]—not as mss offered for sale but for an opinion. Both have indicated that they think their respective magazine ought to be allowed to consider them—which is neither here nor there in so far as the final disposition is concerned. I would be glad to have the S.S. run anything I have and aside from this situation price is no factor. I sold The Girl in the Coffin for 150⁰⁰ when I paid someone else $50 for work of various kinds on it.

The truth is, as you know, that the last two books haven't sold very well—much talk & low sales. I owed Harper $3000 and before they would transfer The Titan without suit they demanded that the first $3000 in royalties be paid to them, which is being done. I should like to see the first three run as a group, one month after the other, wherever they appear.[3] If you take anything of mine the payment can be made in anyway agreeable to you—so much per week, two weeks or per month in installments. I owe you one good skit for the one you lost through me on The Bohemian[4] and so if you want A Spring Recital or The Light in the Window—you may have it—free & with my best wishes beside. If I do anything else I will be glad to let you see it.

By the way if you don't like the philosophic stuff fire it back without comment. I will understand. Am holding the mss of Carrie subject to your orders.

Hail—

Th. D.

That $50,000,000 tax on the Belgians, if true, is too rich.[5]

1. Though Dreiser began planning *The Bulwark* in 1913, he worked on it only intermittently, completing it just before his death in 1945.
2. Douglas Doty (1874–1935), editor, publisher. At this time, Doty was editor of *Century Magazine*. Charles B. DeCamp, at this time, was editor of *Metropolitan* magazine.
3. *Smart Set* published them in this order: "The Blue Sphere," 44(December 1914), 245–52; "In the Dark," 45(January 1915), 419–25; "Laughing Gas," 45(February 1915), 85–94. They are reprinted in *Plays of the Natural and the Supernatural* (1916).
4. "The Artist," *Bohemian* 17(December 1909), 805–8. See Dreiser to Mencken, 16 December 1909; and Mencken to Dreiser, 17 December 1909.
5. On 20 August 1914, Germany captured Brussels in its march across Belgium. On 21 August, Germany demanded payment of a $40,000,000 tax on the city—the

equivalent of $55 for every man, woman, and child in Brussels. In addition, the German military governor imposed a war levy of $10,000,000 on the province of Liege.

[NYP]
Aug 29—1914

My Dear Mencken:

The attached pleases me much because it is so truly oriental & so unmoral.[1] I found it very roughly sketched (nothing like it is here) among some Greek folk tales at the Public Library and elaborated it—as a stunt largely—for the movies.[2] Since then I offered it and it has practically been accepted by Pathé Freres but as I read it over I see a magazine stunt in it. It reads so well that it can be run as it is. I show it to you largely because I know you are looking for novel effects & if you can secure them the method is not much. Read it anyhow, for if you cannot run it I believe Long[3] of the Red Book might. He is seeking something. Under separate cover I mailed you The Lost Phoebe. I wish I could turn out a play.

Th.D.

1. Dreiser enclosed "The Born Thief," an earlier version of "The Prince Who Was a Thief," later published in *Chains* (1927).
2. "The Prince Who Was a Thief" was produced as a film by Universal-International in 1951.
3. Ray Long.

[UPL]

H. L. Mencken
1524 Hollins St.
Baltimore.

August 29th. [1914]

Dear Dreiser:-

"The Lost Phoebe" is fine stuff—a story in your best style. Is it just finished? And have you entered into any negotiations for its sale? If not, maybe we can come to terms over it. Let me know what you think.

Yours,
M

[NYP]

Sept. 2nd 1914

Dear H. L. M:

The Lost Phoebe was written while I was writing The Titan. I started another thing called The Father at the same time which I expect to finish one of these days.¹ Yes, you can have The Lost Phoebe or for that matter the three 1 act plays as we talked.² The Century Company appears to be in a bad way internally. They don't know whether to sell the magazine or what. Let me know what you think of The Born Thief & return this clipping at your leisure.

ThD.

The selection of criticisms of The Titan which you published in the Eve. Sun is to be republished in The International as I understand it

1. The manuscript of "The Father" is among Dreiser's papers at the University of Pennsylvania.
2. Mencken took the plays for *Smart Set*, and Dreiser eventually published "The Lost Phoebe" in *Century* 91(April 1916), 885–96.

[UPL-H]

H. L. Mencken
1524 Hollins St.
Baltimore.

[after 2 September 1914]

Dear Dreiser:-

I am delighted, @ will go over the whole matter with Nathan on Sunday. A report on "The Born Thief" anon: I am up to my eyes—and have hay-fever!

Why not add more extracts to my digest of reviews? I made it before more than half were in.

Yours

M

[UPL]

H. L. Mencken
1524 Hollins St.
Baltimore.

Monday. [7 September 1914]

Dear Dreiser:-

If it be Goddes will we want to use all three of the plays, beginning with December. As you know, we are damnably shy of money, but a little is coming in, and the transaction will be cash. That is to say, you will get the money for each play <u>before</u> the form is locked, and so you will lose nothing, even if we go up—which now seems improbable. I wish you would fix such a cash figure per each, so that I can go to the office with it. Nathan is as eager as I am to print the plays, and you may trust us to do justice to them.

I have sent him "The Lost Phoebe". My own plan is to run it after the plays. "The Born Thief" is excellent stuff, and as for me, I like the form of it. But here is something to be taken into account: By the schedule outlined above we could'nt reach it until the April number. What if the Pathe Freres should have it on the films before then?

Let me hear from you as soon as possible. The November number is closed and we are at work on December. We got enough new stuff in November to give it some flavor, though some of the matter in type had to be used. October is still wholly Thayer.

Yours,
M

[UPL-H]

H. L. Mencken
1524 Hollins St.
Baltimore.

[before 11 September 1914]

Dear Dreiser:-

Who the devil wrote this?[1] It is a fine piece of writing—the best thing about you ever printed. Let me know his name?

Yours
M

1. Mencken is referring to "From an Old Farm House, XI," *Reedy's Mirror* 33(21 August 1914), 7–8. It was written by the writer and critic Harris Merton Lyon (1883–

1916). When Dreiser was editing *Broadway Magazine* in 1906, he met and hired Lyon. Dreiser believed Lyon's early death was a genuine loss to literature, and for years he sought a publisher for Lyon's manuscripts. He wrote a sketch of Lyon, "DeMaupassant, Jr.," which is in *Twelve Men* (1919).

[NYP]
Friday, Sept. 11th [1914]

My Dear Mencken:

In regard to the mss you said that you did not see how you could pay more than $100 per mss. I accepted that with one mental reservation—that the ten per cent which I shall have to pay my dear, useless agent be added—otherwise I should only clear 90^{00} & I need such cash as I can get.

In regard to The Born Thief—I meant to suggest that its scene numberings (for magazine publication) come out & that in their places stars be placed—* * *   Personally I see no reason why a magazine should not use an mss of that kind even if it had been done in the movies though you may think differently. Editors differ. But I am sure no movie would object to its having been done in a magazine. They rather like that sort of thing.

In regard to the estimate of me in The Mirror—I assumed at first that it was one of three—anyone of whom might have done it—Fritz Krog, Harris Merton Lyon or Raymond Lee Harriman. All have farms—or their parents or relations have & all have worked for me.[1] A letter from Masters says Harris Merton Lyon did it. I wish you would find out if you can. It would please much if Lyon had done it.

Th.D

1. Fritz Krog had worked for Dreiser on the *Delineator* and had been nominal editor of the *Bohemian*. Raymond Lee Harriman had been editor of Butterick's *Designer* when Dreiser was editor-in-chief of that firm's three magazines.

[UPL]

H. L. Mencken
1524 Hollins St.
Baltimore.

September 13th. [1914]

Dear Dreiser:-

I am putting the matter up to Nathan. I don't know at the moment how much money is in sight in the office. I fear it is not much, but there should be more shortly. We had to pay off $3,000 this month.

I'll try to find out about the Mirror article.
More anon.

Yours,
M

Is there any chance of getting a few chapters of "The Genius" for our Dec. no.?

[NYP-T]

165 West 10th St.

Sept. 17th, '14

My Dear Mencken,
Please let me have galley proofs of the particular play you propose to use first. Did you write Jones[1] to hurry up the copying of the remaining chapters of "The Genius"? I doubt whether anything can be done about that for the Smart Set. If I could cut a salable serial out of it I would want to get a reasonable price for it. More as to that later.

Yours,
Dreiser

1. J. Jefferson Jones.

[UPL]

The
SMART SET
John Adams Thayer Corporation
452 Fifth Avenue, New York

Baltimore, Friday. [18 September 1914]
Dear Dreiser:-
There seems to be some misunderstanding. Haven't <u>you</u> got the mss. of the plays? Or have you sent them to Nathan? My own choice is "The Blue Sphere" for No. 1. It's too bad we can't get a hack at the Genius. We don't want a serial, but merely an episode.
I am coming to New York tomorrow and will settle the matter with Nathan.

Yours,
M

[NYP]
Sept 21st 1914

My Dear H. L. M.

My mistake. I had forgotten you had given the mss back to me. Am sending them to the new S.S. address—456—4th Ave. N.Y.C—this a.m.!

Yours

Th.D.

Things like "The Reframe Up" and "From The Cusp of the Moon" by Benjamin De Casseres[1] are worth reprinting in S.S. His address is 11 West 39th St.

1. Benjamin DeCasseres (1873–1945), journalist, drama critic, poet, biographer. DeCasseres was a prolific writer with radical political leanings. In this period, Dreiser tried to advance his career, but it was only in later years that DeCasseres found a market for his work.

[UPL]

H. L. Mencken
1524 Hollins St.
Baltimore.

Monday. [21 September 1914]

Dear Dreiser:-

I saw Nathan in New York yesterday and we went over the situation. Money is still very scarce, but things seem to be slowly and surely improving and I am now very hopeful.

As for the mss., if you can let us start off with "The Blue Sphere" we can take it for $110, payable October 20. The play will not be set up until it is paid for. The other two in regular order, November 20 and December 20, at $110 each. And then probably "The Lost Phoebe", or whatever else is in sight.

If this is all right, please rush "The Blue Sphere" to Nathan at once. The new S.S. address is 456 Fourth avenue.

I have written to Reedy about the anonymous Dreiseriad.

We have the copy of "The Lost Phoebe" and of the oriental fantasy, but you have that of the three plays.

Yours

M

[UPL]

H. L. Mencken
1524 Hollins St.
Baltimore.

October 6th. [1914]

Dear Dreiser:-

Without question, this is good stuff,[1] but I continue to be full of doubts whether it fits into our plans, and so I hesitate to schedule it. Remember this: we have three plays already that present an altogether new Dreiser. What we'd like to get now is something that goes back to the Dreiser of the novels—the Dreiser the public knows. Even "The Lost Phoebe" doesn't strike that note. All this explains my eagerness to get a hack at "The Genius".

I have stirred up Jones, by the way, and he promises to rush the manuscript.

If you get time, take a look at our November number, out in about ten days. It is a very imperfect first attempt, but it shows the way we are trying to head.

Yours
M

1. *The Lost Phoebe.*

[NYP]

165 W. 10th St. N.Y.C

Oct 8—1914

My Dear H. L. M:

Thanks for your note. I shall look over the November number. Are you announcing the one act stunts in any way. I do not know what to say about The Genius. Will think it over & let you know. I need something to carry me through The Bulwark.

Th D.

[UPL]

H. L. Mencken
1524 Hollins St.
Baltimore.

October 13th. [1914]

Dear Dreiser:-

Nathan is so full of the notion that this "Lost Phoebe" lies far off of the Dreiser that we want to play up that I begin to agree with him. Ah, that we could get a chunk of "The Genius" to follow the plays! Those plays are fine stuff, but they involve, as it were, winning a new Dreiser audience. What we ought to have, to follow them, is a return to C major—that is, to the Sister Carrie-Jennie Gerhardt—The Titan style. Is any such stuff in sight? I wish Lane would hurry up "The Genius". I believe I could saw out an isolated episode or two that wouldn't spoil the serial rights in the slightest. What else is in sight? Is there any left-over matter from "The Titan"?

Nathan tells me that the plays are mentioned in all advertising sent to other magazines. There was to have been a page announcement in the Nov. number, but it was killed at the last minute by an unexpected adv.

Yours,
M

[NYP]

165 W. 10th St. N.Y.C

Oct 13—1914

My Dear H. L. M:

Unless I am a poor reader of signs there is a distinct disagreement as to my material between you and Nathan. I know you and anything that I now say bears no personal feeling toward you whatsoever. If you think so, you are going to do me a great injustice. But I do not believe you will really think so. In the first place I recalled The Lost Phoebe from Red Book as Miss Welchs[1] letter files will show after I had been offered $125 by Ray Long and after Miss Welch had urged me to let him have it. She has been peeved over that action because she saw no reason why I should prefer the S.S. to the Red Book although I explained that it was a personal matter. That was before I took the three plays finally out of the hands of The Century and The Metropolitan.

In regard to the three plays I asked both the Century & Metropolitan to drop further consideration of them when there was strong chance that I would get $900 from one or the other and a reasonable amount of publicity. My whole feeling in turning them over to the S.S. was that you (I mean the S.S.) really wanted them and would give them definite publicity of an intelligent, critical character. Evidently for some reason I am not to have that. Now in going as far as I have I think I have done my whole duty. I have lived up to friendship in this matter and in your private conscience you will have to absolve me. Therefore I think that under the circumstances I am justified in calling this deal off and asking that the three plays be returned. I base it on a failure of understanding between us—but there is absolutely no personal animus behind this and in any other deal which may be made at any time I will try and be as fair and self-sacrificing as I know how. However I wanted something definite said, I asked that it should be and all things considered I feel that I am entitled to cancel the deal since it has not been done

Greetings.
Th.D.

1. Galbraith Welch, Dreiser's literary agent.

[UPL]

H. L. Mencken
1524 Hollins St.
Baltimore.

October 14th. [1914]

Dear Dreiser:-

I take all the blame and offer my apologies. But you are quite wrong as to any doubts about the merit of the plays, or, for that matter, of the story. I think the plays are excellent in plan and execution, and Nathan quite agrees with me. They are sure to make a strong appeal to the very sort of people we want to have in our audience. But at the moment we are still confronted by the Thayer audience, and until we get rid of it and build up our own, we will obviously have to handle the situation with some discretion. That is the sole basis for my eagerness to print something in your more familiar manner. We want to get as much wind from "Sister Carrie" and "The Titan" as we can. Once we get going we'll have them ready for anything you want to do, and even now we are willing to take every chance, but when the choice offers we naturally turn to the stuff which comes closest to the public notion of you, and so takes full-steam advantage of your following. Hence my eagerness to get an episode or two out of "The Genius", or even something cut out of "The Titan". I knew you probably had some such stuff on hand, and I also knew that it was otherwise unsaleable, and so I made my suggestion.

But the thought now sticks in my mind that we made a definite arrangement about "The Lost Phoebe". If that is your recollection also, we'll run it directly after the plays, and take our chances on the other stuff later. My confusion must be blamed on the damnable load of negotiations and counter-negotiations I have been carrying on—and writing a load of copy to boot, as the Nov. S.S. will show you.[1]

As for the plays, I sincerely hope you don't push your demand for their return. Believe me, I appreciate your goodness in letting us have them, and if there was the money in the drawer I'd cheerfully pay a lot more for them. "The Blue Sphere" is already in type for December, and it was only an unexpected emergency that kept out a large announcement of it. I think you know how such things can happen, particularly when an office is upside down. We got out the Nov. number by the skin of our teeth. But the Dec. number will have hard and earnest work in it, and I think that you will like it. I needn't tell you that a Smart Set without your stuff in it would lose a good deal of its interest for me.

If I go to Nathan with such a demand as you make, it will kick up the very row that we must now avoid. Let me have "The Lost Phoebe" and forget it. And don't get the notion that I am sniffing at anything you write. If I could get a novel of yours, and had the money to buy it, I wouldn't hesitate to devote a whole number to it, and Nathan would go along.

Yours,

M

1. The November *Smart Set* was the first complete issue edited entirely by Mencken and Nathan. They wrote half the pieces themselves under a variety of humorous pseudonyms. At the same time they sent out the message that *Smart Set* was looking for young and unconventional talent. (For a detailed account of these events, see Carl R. Dolmetsch, *The Smart Set: A History and Anthology* [New York, 1966], 43–66.)

[NYP]

165 W. 10th St. N.Y.C

Oct 15–1914

My Dear Mencken:

As regards "The Lost Phoebe"—we will forget it. Someone will want it and I am sorry I spoke. It was the surprise of its return after I had manipulated matters to get it free that irritated me. In regard to the three plays keep them. My purpose in asking for them back, aside from vindicating my belief in their merit was to give you a chance to step out of the whole thing gracefully, in case, as it looked to me that they were objected to. It seemed to me that Nathan or someone was attempting to shove them in the background and, all things considered, since I had gone out of my way to turn them over it seemed a little unfair. Also I felt that someone up there might be thinking that you were making a mistake in your interest in the matter. But if you really want them it is done.

Be that as it may there is no feeling toward you and even now I feel sorry that I did not pocket my pride and let the matter drop for we always get a second chance at things if we wait. However, it is all over now. As regards The Genius—would you prefer to set aside the plays to run an episode or two, or would you run the plays first.

Th D

[UPL]

H. L. Mencken
1524 Hollins St.
Baltimore.

Saturday. Oct 17th [1914]

Dear Dreiser:-

Thanks for your letter. We are in your hands, and damned glad to be. I have a letter from Nathan this morning assuring me anew that he is with me absolutely. He agrees with me that the plays are full of fine stuff, and looks for them to make a success.

Our plan, of course, is to run them seriatim. The first is in the December number. This will put the third into the February number, out January 15. If "The Genius" is a Spring book, this will give us room for two episodes—in March and April, out February 15 and March 15 respectively. Or we can run "The Lost Phoebe" in March, and the episodes in April and May—assuming that the book is not published before April 15. On this matter I'll call you up next time I get to N.Y., maybe in two weeks.

It would not do to break into the continuity of the play series. There is a connection between them that ought to be preserved.

Finally, why not "The Lost Phoebe" after the episodes? We hope and expect to be in business a long while.

Yours,

M

You say nothing about any left-over stuff from "The Titan". It stuck in my mind that there was some.

[UPL]

The
SMART SET
A Magazine of Cleverness
452 Fifth Avenue, New York

November 8th. [1914]

Dear Dreiser:-

Don't forget that I am to get a reading of "The Genius". You have the place of honor on the front cover of this month's (December's) S. S., and on the third advertising page, in the southwest corner, you will find the stuff, slightly changed, that Nathan intended for a full page in Nov. As you will see, advertising is still damnably scarce, and so there is not much space. But beginning with the Jan. no. there will be a substantial jump. A number of new contracts are already signed.

How do you stand on this war? As for me, I am for the hellish Deutsche until hell freezes over.

Yours,
M

[NYP]

165 W. 10th St. N.Y.C

Nov. 10th 1914

My Dear Mencken:

I have on hand chapter 1 to 61 inc of "The Genius"—rather badly pencil marked because (for serial purposes), certain things were marked to be left out. I am promised 62 to 104 this Saturday—marked in the same way. Now I could wait until I get all of this stuff in hand and having turned it over to Lane for safe keeping send you the unmarked copy they have, but Jones rather objects to that. If you think you could wade through the marked copy I can send you what I have now and the balance when I get it. Nothing is cut out—only portions marked out.

In a way I shall be sorry to have you get your first impression of this book from this unedited mass. I have been going over one copy but I am not near done and when I am it will be somewhat better pulled together than it is now and better written. If you judge anything but the general thread of the story from this you will be doing me a technical injustice— but I suppose you understand just about what will happen between now and publication. "The Titan" was in much worse shape than this when I began editing it.

By the way have you noticed "The Spoon River Anthology" running in The Mirror (St. Louis)   It is by Masters, of Chicago. You ought to take a look at that. Masters, Nicholas Vachel Lindsay, Arthur Davison Ficke & De Casseres might contribute some worth while poetry to the Smart Set. They may not represent ultimate perfection but they are good.

I am leaving tomorrow for Poultney Bigelows farm up on the Hudson for a few days. He is an old friend of the German Emperors having staid at Potsdam for months but he is against militarism. Personally I think it would be an excellent thing for Europe and the world—tonic—if the despicable British artistocracy—the snobbery of English intellectuality were smashed and a German Vice-Roy sat in London   I fear so much it cant be but such is life   Unfortunately, for all their amazing qualities the Germans lack appeal to the imagination—that appeal that the French had under Napolean. I am for William R.I. even in defeat

Th.D

Please see that I get proofs of "In the Dark" & "Laughing Gas." I like the first number of S.S. rather well. It needs I think, a wider range of stuff

[UPL]

H. L. Mencken
1524 Hollins St.
Baltimore.

November 12th. [1914]

Dear Dreiser:-

Let me have the pencilled copy, by all means. I am sure I can read it, and I'll bear in mind its roughness. I am very eager to find out what you have put into "The Genius".

I am telling Nathan to send you proofs of the next two plays. I haven't seen Masters' Mirror stuff. Later on I'll approach all of the men you name. The reason I don't do it at once is that we inherited a lot of poetry from Thayer—enough to keep us supplied for four months or more—and so we are buying nothing.

The Germans will fight their way out. My one hope is to see them in London. English pecksniffery must be crushed.

Yours,
Mencken

[NYP]

165 W. 10th St. N.Y.C

Nov. 30th 1914

My Dear Mencken:

By Adams express, today, prepaid I sent you chapters 1 to 66 (I believe) of the typewritten mss—of "The Genius", 2nd carbon, unrevised. Please note that the title, "The Genius" is quoted. In some reference to it in Town Topics it was mentioned as The Genius—unquoted. This reference has been going the rounds as my clippings show. There is another book, still on sale in old book stores called The Genius—a Russian locale.[1] To avoid being bothered by the author and to convey the exact question which I mean to imply I am quoting my title. I have so notified John Lane and if at any time you refer to it please see that the quotes are not left out.[2]

I received your Philadelphia programme clipping. I am told that one John Cooper Powis,[3] an Englishman is to lecture on me there next week— also here and in Chicago. So you see how it is. One can seem more than he really is. "Deutchland über alles."[4]

Th.D.

1. Dreiser is referring to Margaret Potter's *The Genius* (1906), a book that makes his novel of the same name look like a splendid masterpiece.
2. The book would be published as *The "Genius."*
3. Dreiser means John Cowper Powys.
4. Germany above all.

[UPL]

H. L. Mencken
1524 Hollins St.
Baltimore.

December 2nd. [1914]

Dear Dreiser:-

The manuscript is here and I'll fall to it at once. I note what you say about the title. In the Smart Set all book titles are quoted, but to make sure I'll put single quotes within the double ones.

Observe the fruits of that bogus Russian victory last week. The Germans announce that they have taken 80,000 Russian prisoners.[1] Dreimal hoch![2]

Yours,
H. L. M.

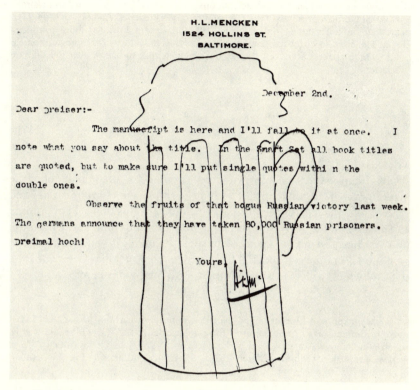

H.L.MENCKEN
1524 HOLLINS ST.
BALTIMORE.

December 2nd.

Dear Dreiser:-

The manuscript is here and I'll fall to it at once.   I
note what you say about the title.   In the Smart Set all book titles
are quoted, but to make sure I'll put single quotes withi n the
double ones.

Observe the fruits of that bogus Russian victory last week.
The germans announce that they have taken 80,000 Russian prisoners.
Dreimal hoch!

Yours,

Mencken letter: 2 December 1914 (University of Pennsylvania Library)

1. On 24 November 1914, the Russian army culminated a ten-day battle in Poland by stopping the Austro-German forces in their push toward Warsaw. The Russian campaign was seen, particularly by Germany, as mainly a defensive victory. In addition, on 27 November Germany reported the capture of 40,000 Russian prisoners in Poland; Russia, on the other hand, remained cautious about announcing a victory and claimed only 4,000 German prisoners. On 2 December reports reached America that the Germans had broken through the Russian lines and captured 12,000 more prisoners. Hence Mencken's gleeful reference to a bogus Russian victory of the previous week.

2. Three cheers. Mencken drew a beer stein with a full head over the body of this letter.

[NYP]
Dec. 8th 1914

My Dear H. L. M:

By Adams express tomorrow I expect to send you the remainder of the marked mss of "The Genius"   I hope you manage to retain an unfixed state of mind as regards the ultimate technique of this thing. I am pruning and editing all the way through taking out a number things which, in the mss you have, stand as severe blemishes. I wonder if you would care to give me an opinion on the 100,000 word serial which has been cut from this and which will shortly be offered to two magazines here?[1]

Th.D.

1. Mencken and Dreiser talked over the manuscript early in January 1915. Because of the censorship problem after the publication of *The "Genius,"* there was no serialization of an abridged version of the novel until 1923, when it appeared in *Metropolitan Magazine* 56(February-March 1923), 57(April-September 1923), 58(October-November 1923).

[UPL]

H. L. Mencken
1524 Hollins St.
Baltimore.

Wednesday. [9 December 1914]

Dear Dreiser:-

The remainder of the ms. will come just in time for me. I have been taking the first part slowly, reading five or six chapters each evening. Surely I'll be glad to go through the proposed serial. The crude cuts, of course, leave the thing as it stands rather disjointed, but I think I grasp its general drift. Two criticisms by the way:

1. I think Witla's artistic progress is under-described in the first part,

that is, down to his New York days. The successive steps are not very clear. Suggestion: Start him in Chicago, cutting out the Alexandria part, and then go back to it briefly later on, a la Joseph Conrad.

2. There is no such word as "alright". I notice that you correct it to "all right" in one place, but elsewhere it stands.

More anon.

Yours,
M

[NYP]
Dec. 10th 1914

My Dear Mencken:

You seem to be under the impression that the cuts which appear in the mss you are examining have something to do with its preparation for book form   They have nothing to do with it whatsoever. I merely sent you that because the clean mss which is being edited for book purposes is in use. Those cuts, in so far as the book is concerned <u>do</u> <u>not</u> <u>go</u>. They relate to a 100,000 word serial which was cut out of the mss. In reading that mss read through cuts and all. Disregard all changes except where they are made in my own hand. Then if you have any cuts of your own to suggest do so. If it is too difficult to read through these pencil cuts wait a little bit and I will try and let you have a clean mss of the whole thing as it will go into type. I think your suggestions are good.[1]

Th. D

1. Dreiser, however, did not incorporate Mencken's changes into the text of the novel.

[UPL]

H. L. Mencken
1524 Hollins St.
Baltimore.

Friday. [11 December 1914]

Dear Dreiser:-

Yea; I understand. As a matter of fact, I have been reading all the cut-out parts. The balance of the ms. has not yet reached me.

On to London!

Yours,
M

[NYP]

Dec 12th 1914

My Dear Mencken:

I forgot to ask you to read the various pencil cuts made in the effort to extract a 100,000 word serial with a view to seeing whether a number of them might not advisedly be retained. Where you think the story is obviously better for the cutting, large or small—give me chapter and page number—all providing you have the time and only so.

Second half went as I said—Adams Express.

Greetings

Th. D.

[UPL]

H. L. Mencken
1524 Hollins St.
Baltimore.

December 15th. [1914]

Dear Dreiser:-

The ms. is all here, and I'll go through the second part as you say, marking possible cuts. At the moment my eyes are overworked and tired, and so it may be four or five days before I can resume.

May all Englishmen roast forever in hell!

Yours,

M

[UPL]

The
SMART SET
A Magazine of Cleverness
456 Fourth Avenue, New York

December 23rd. [1914]

Dear Dreiser:-

So far as I know Powys is not to lecture in Baltimore.[1] If you hear of him heading this way, let me know of it, and I'll stir up the animals a bit. I enclose a report of his lecture from the Philadelphia Record.

Who the deuce is Mordell? I get letters from him occasionally and once he sent me a pamphlet that he had written. He seems to be a pushful sort of person. His writings on Nietzsche are worthless.

Let us join in three cheers for Jesus Christ. Great days for him—and for Karl Marx!

Of "The Genius", something anon.

Yours,
Mencken.

1. Dreiser had forwarded Mencken a letter he had received (dated 21 December 1914) from the critic Albert Mordell, in which Mordell speaks of hearing John Cowper Powys lecture in Philadelphia, praising Dreiser and Henry James as the best contemporary American writers. Mordell wrote, "He mentioned your name in the same breath with Lincoln and Michaelangelo. . . . He compared your personal appearance with the ponderous Samuel Johnson." Dreiser wrote in the upper left-hand corner of the letter, "Do you know of this lecture? Does he come to Baltimore?" [UPL]

[NYP]
Dec. 24—1914

My Dear H. L. M.

Your question in regard to Mordell is the same as the one I asked you over a year ago   Your answer then is the information you supply now. Sometime early last fall he wrote me a long letter & sent me his book which seemed rather heavy & commonplace.[1] Then he called from some Phila. paper to get an interview which I gave him. Once again last summer he called to learn what I was doing. He is short, dusty, Hebraic, from many points of view impossible but wildly enamored apparently of letters & literary repute—a plodder. That is all I know. This letter of his comes after six months of silence.[2]

Curiously today I learn that Powys lives in this neighborhood or rather his sister[3]—along with a hundred other theatrical and art personages. She is a friend of the Wilson-Perkins group right around the corner here, of whom of course you are ignorant. I work like a slave, alas, and have damned few enjoyments. May all Germans thrive.

Th. D.

Leave tomorrow A.M. for Malden-on-Hudson—Poultney Bigelows[4] country place. There until Jan. 2nd next. If you write me, address me there, but hang onto mss until you can send it here. And send it C.O.D. Express—putting a $300 value on it.

1. Albert Mordell (1885–1965), lawyer, critic, author, first wrote Dreiser on 19 September 1913 to praise *Jennie Gerhardt*. Mordell sent Dreiser his "book," an eighty-four-page pamphlet entitled "The Shifting of Literary Values." [UPL]

2. See Mencken to Dreiser, 23 December 1914, n.1.
3. Marion Powys.
4. Dreiser knew Poultney Bigelow, who had contributed to the *Delineator* since 1907. He often visited Bigelow's house at Malden-on-the-Hudson, New York.

[UPL]

The
SMART SET
A Magazine of Cleverness
452 Fifth Avenue, New York

December 27th. [1914]

Dear Dreiser:-

I am coming to New York next week (January 4th) to stay all week, and shall bring the ms. with me. I have a few kicks and suggestions. If you have the evening of January 1st open, why not a meeting?

Don't let Bigelow make an anti-German of you. The Kaiser must and shall win.

Yours,
M

[NYP]

BIGELOW HOMESTEAD
MALDEN ON HUDSON, NEW YORK

Tuesday, Dec 29th 14

My Dear H. L. M.

You say "I am coming to N.Y. next week (Jan 4th)" which would be Monday and then you say "if you have the evening of Jan. 1st open how about a meeting?"

Jan 1—is Friday next & I cant be in N.Y. Do you mean—what? Please let me know. If it is after this coming Friday I'll try & be there. Bigelow fulminates like a blunder buss but he can't convert me. Russo-German assaults take place every morning at the breakfast table.

Th D

H. L. Mencken
1524 Hollins St.
Baltimore.

December 29th. [1914]

Dear Dreiser:-

My apologies: can it be that Christmas cheer corrupted my faculties? I meant, of course, next Tuesday, January 5th. But if that will be inconvenient, don't bother. I'll be in town all week. When you get back to N.Y. drop me a line to the S.S. office, 456 Fourth avenue. I shall name my next child Hindenburg, whether it's a boy or a girl. A pox upon the English!

Yours,
M

3

The Country Is in a State of
Moral Mania
(1915–1918)

"The country is in a state of moral mania and the only thing for a prudent man to do is to stall off the moralists however he can and trust to the future for his release."
—HLM to TD, 28 July 1916

"I owe you too much to turn on this or any other occasion and say the few ugly things we can say when hurt."
—TD to HLM, 9 October 1916

By 1915 Dreiser and Mencken had identified themselves as principals in an ongoing cultural rebellion. They matched each other's commitment to revolt against the national order of things as the abiding metaphor of their careers. Over the years, this identification stimulated a friendship that was as stormy as it was full of sentiment. The storms were predictable. Any deviation from the precepts of their public stance—as in Mencken's concessions to public opinion in the editing of *Smart Set* or Dreiser's experiments in nonrealistic forms—was taken as a personal betrayal. It was a tension that both men contended with, in complex ways, for the next thirty years. For better and worse, it dominated the friendship and gave it a singular style and tone, a mixture of principled rebellion and rancorous mischief, that became the trademark of their joint endeavors.

The first big storm is not recorded in the letters. After reading the manuscript of *The "Genius,"* Mencken broke his routine of sending one of his letters of criticism and instead asked for a private meeting to discuss the book. This took place in early January 1915, and, years later, Mencken recalled that they had had such a "friendly row" that "Kirah Markham apparently horrified by the thought of two Christians murdering each other, rushed out of the house" (5 September 1925). The infrequency of the exchange during the first half of 1915 suggests how much the argument over *The "Genius"* meant to them. It dramatically confronted them with the extent of their fundamental differences and was a sore spot in the relationship for years after. It also led to other confrontations. Dreiser's testy response (20 April 1915) to Mencken's request for a few kind words in support of *Smart Set* makes more sense when seen against this background. And, in his published comments on the novel, Mencken was willing—another first—to use his reviewer's hammer to bludgeon his friend. Dreiser's most unwieldy and sexually explicit novel was, Mencken thought, his poorest book; and the *Smart Set* review, "A Literary Behemoth," remains a classic—and comic—analysis of Dreiser at his worst (see Appendix 2, pp. 754–59). While conceding that "this Dreiser is undoubtedly a literary artist of very respectable rank," Mencken dwells on his "barbarous" manner, his "oafish clumsiness and crudeness," and fills the pages with terms of ridicule. Understandably, the humor was lost on Dreiser.

The temptation, clearly, was to retreat into separate corners. The war in Europe came upon them with such force, however, that they put aside personal battles for the time. In important ways, the international conflict intensified the bond between them, even as they began the protracted squabbles of the next three decades. American reaction to the war reinforced the friendship at a crucial moment, and the exchange became a bonding ritual in the face of what they saw as a common enemy. From 1914 to 1919 they encountered a challenge from the critical old guard, which in those years aligned itself with latter-day know-nothings who worked openly and proudly in the name of patriotic nativism and literary censorship. This placed Dreiser's and Mencken's private life under considerable strain, and it gave a political dimension to their work. The challenge drew its strength from the intense and widespread anti-Germanism of the period, which saw, among other things, thousands of Germans arrested on presidential warrants and thrown into internment camps, pronouncements to equal Theodore Roosevelt's advice that disloyal Germans be hung or shot, the banning of German language and music, and even mob lynching.

Two years before the country went to war, Mencken and Dreiser began comparing notes about the personal toll they, as noncombatants, would pay if the country fought against Germany. Their jokes reflected the fears they lived with: "I believe that both of us will be killed by patriots within six months," wrote Mencken in 1916, as bravado mixed with wartime hysteria. And he added, "you will be lucky, with your German name, if you are not jailed the day the U.S. enters the war." Dreiser followed Mencken's lead and started closing his letters with "Deutschland über alles." When the United States declared war on Germany in 1917, Mencken shared with Dreiser his fears of mob violence against his family in Baltimore, and Dreiser escaped stress by retreating to Maryland's farm country, where Mencken would join him to discuss their fates over gin highballs.

They were, the record shows, easy marks for wartime mania. Especially Mencken who, with his attachment to Baltimore and its old-world ethos, had flaunted his taste for German music, food, and beer in his earliest essays, while his books on Nietzsche and the frequent use of the philosopher in reviews earned him the title of the "American Nietzschean." Moreover, Mencken was not particularly cautious. Shortly after the war began, he took his stand in the "Free Lance" column: "I am for Germany . . . and not only for Germany, but also for the Kaiser, and not only for the Kaiser, but also for the *Junkertum*. And to that I pledge my parts of speech."[1] In February 1917, when America severed diplomatic relations with Germany, he was on the eastern front with General Eichhorn's troops, writing reports as war correspondent that left little doubt about which side he supported. Dreiser had less chance (and little desire) to publicize his views, but he did not hesitate to inform readers of *A Hoosier Holiday* (1916) of "my German ancestry . . . my German name and my German sympathies." (173)

For years Mencken had underscored Dreiser's Teutonic qualities, particularly before 1914 when it was still legitimate to trace the origins of liberty to the dark woods of Germany. Moreover, Dreiser's first readers were sensitive to the ethnic implications of *Jennie Gerhardt* and the Nietzschean chapter titles of *The Titan*. They were aware, if only in a vague way before the war, that Dreiser was, in F. O. Matthiessen's words, "virtually the first major American writer whose family name was not English or Scotch-Irish."[2] And Mencken himself often pointed out—by way of explaining how dead his friend's ear was to standard prose rhythms— that he was the first American novelist of importance to grow up speaking a language other than English.

After 1915 their public profile put them—and other German-American intellectuals like George Sylvester Viereck and Ludwig Lewisohn—on the defensive. Dreiser and Mencken did not suffer the public indignity of, say, Karl Muck who, as conductor of the Boston Symphony Orchestra, needed a police guard to direct concerts, until he was interned in 1918 for the duration of the war. Yet Mencken's refusal to follow the official line lost him his job on the *Sunpapers*. He went over to the New York *Evening Mail* on the condition that he not write about the war; but he was fired in 1918, when the paper's publisher was arrested as a German agent, and the new management tried to implicate Mencken. At this time, he and Nathan felt compelled to keep any hint of the war out of *Smart Set*, though Mencken reduced his frustration somewhat by taking on Woodrow Wilson and his administration at every chance. Dreiser too felt the pinch of wartime editorial practice. To this day, long pieces like "American Idealism and German Frightfulness" remain in manuscript. He argued there that the war, conducted by "pro-moralistic Puritans" and Anglophiles, would "force two or three or four or five million American boys to face an almost impregnable autocratic firing line," and that "we are sending them to die in an unjust cause." [UPL]

By 1917 one did not have to be German to suffer for such views. Randolph Bourne's antiwar articles in *Seven Arts* brought charges of pro-German sympathies and spelled the end of an important journal; *Masses* folded after the trial of its staff, including Max Eastman, Floyd Dell, and Art Young, for violating the Sedition Act of 1917. In this climate, the stigma of his German heritage followed Dreiser into the critical arena, where critics like Paul Elmer More and Stuart Sherman lambasted him for his mixed loyalties. Sherman's famous attack on his "barbaric naturalism" stressed its roots in Dreiser's German-American background, and he held up Dreiser's books as the signal of "a new note in American literature, coming from the 'ethnic' element in our mixed population."[3] Later, when Mencken published his first book of criticism, *A Book of Prefaces* (1917), Sherman took the chance to club him as well: "Mr. Mencken," he wrote with mocking irony, "is not a German. He was born in Baltimore, September 12, 1880. That fact should silence the silly people who have suggested that he and Dreiser are secret agents of the Wilhelmstrasse."[4] As descendants of German immigrants, Dreiser and Mencken in effect shared in the nativist backlash that, before the war, had been reserved for more recent southern and eastern European groups.

Never known for their tolerance, the two men found no reason to practice it then. Mencken sent Dreiser hostile reviews with glosses designed to keep the novelist on edge: "The Atlantic Monthly review [of *The "Genius"*] is typically and beautifully Anglo-Saxon. . . . I notice the accusation of Teutonic deviltry. Ah, the brave loyalists!" Mencken had a point. *The "Genius,"* which was quickly linked to the "Hun Menace," gave both sides the chance to blur the distinctions between literature and social fact. "We hope," one reviewer said in 1915, "that *The 'Genius'* will immediately appear in a German translation. That's how kindly we feel toward the Germans!"[5] Mencken had been one of those who had found the novel unpalatable. But when, in the summer of 1916, the Western Society for the Prevention of Vice united with John Sumner's New York branch to suppress the book and everyone ran for cover, including Dreiser's publisher John Lane, Mencken went on the offensive. He realized that the novel "has exactly the right defects to invite such an attack, but none the less the attack itself is dishonest." He solicited the aid of the Authors' League of America, and the case became an international *cause célèbre*.

Mencken generously spent time, and his own money, organizing an offensive and collecting signatures for the *"Genius"* protest. Since he was on record as no admirer of the novel, he could argue for Dreiser on the merits of literary freedom; and he was thereby able to get support from conservative as well as progressive artists and critics. The enterprise had mixed results for the friendship. As usual, they disagreed on methods. · The disagreements offered an excuse for airing two issues that would become constant motifs in the letters for the next three decades: the argument over Dreiser's connections to literary Bohemia and to the political left; and the more allusive but persistent tension over Dreiser's expression of sexuality, both in his work and in his personal life.

These private quarrels had little effect on the outcome of the case. In the end, the trial of The *"Genius"* proved a dramatic but futile exercise. Since the publisher had withdrawn the novel without contest, no indictment had been issued, and the case failed to establish a precedent for judgments on literary censorship. Despite this, the whole affair added a measure to Dreiser and Mencken's public image, as it crystallized the view of them as shapers of a major literary revolution. The terms, so heightened, encouraged them in a dialogue that reflected the charged nature of their cause. Their professional battles became inseparable from larger social issues. By the summer of 1916, Mencken could write Dreiser, "The thing I am most afraid of, as I wrote you, is the introduction into the case of the German spy fear." To counter this, they gave their activities the trappings of a spy novel, speaking of "smuggling" the plates of The *"Genius"* across state lines, publishing "subversive" articles, and checking mail for signs of official tampering. They exchanged congratulations as German troops drove into France, and, after some of the most tragically bloody battles in military history, they toasted to British military ineptitude.

In this period, the rhetoric of war conditioned the style and tenor of literary debate. Metaphors of the battlefield came easy to them. When Mencken wanted to caution Dreiser against having radicals join the *"Genius"* protest, he simply asked, "Why start a fight in the trench while bombardment is going on?" The private exchange, which set the tone for their public posture, illustrates how the conflict encouraged their tendency to conflate military and cultural issues. How such a tendency can turn a relatively harmless bias—before the war they traced the ills of American culture to its imitation of priggish English models—into something else is seen in a typical comment in one of Mencken's letters: "The British loss at Neuve Chappelle: 11,850. Gott strafe the dirty lice." Or this from Dreiser's "American Idealism and German Frightfulness": he hoped the country would put aside its infatuation with England, recognize its real enemies, and then "arm, *arm*, *arm*, and when ready, and unfairly treated, strike." [UPL]

The two men supported each other in a paranoiac style that is perhaps endemic in all wartime societies. Mencken had aired pro-German sentiments in his "Free Lance" column, but after that outlet was denied him in October 1915, he turned to Dreiser, who shared his belief that German-Americans were being forced into "a separateness which, before the war, had never marked them."[6] Their letters became a secret weapon, a form of defense against an escalating sense of social marginality. The old formulas took on new meanings. Before 1914 the familiar straw man, the American as puritan, functioned largely as a rhetorical device; by 1915 Mencken was writing Dreiser about "The Puritan mind . . . and its maniacal fear of the German." They met slander with slander, and the former nemesis, the native American, took on new racial coloration: Mencken urged no "compromise in future between men of German blood and the common run of 'good,' 'right-thinking' Americans," while Dreiser began signing off letters with "Success to all Hyphenates." And, as comic relief for their tensions, they turned to swapping pro-German oaths in pidgin German and composing German macaronic verse.

Dreiser and Mencken seldom wrote this way to others. There are many reasons for this (some having to do with the mysteries of friendship), but the fact remains that no other American writer—certainly not one of Dreiser's stature—gave Mencken the occasion for a fight with such personal meaning for him. More than before, and despite the noisy quarrels, the two men provided each other with mirror images. The novelist's predicament energized Mencken's strenuous effort to find a critical language that would capture both the temper of his time and his own angst. The correspondence suggests the extent to which this was a joint effort. Mencken reinforced Dreiser's tendency to discover puritanism everywhere, urging battle against conservative publishers, the censors, and hostile reviewers. And Dreiser, sensing that Mencken was his best advocate, not his best critic, sent letters to Baltimore filled with the stuff of literary fable.

With these letters—and old reviews—at his side, Mencken wrote the impressive *Prefaces* essay of 1917, in which he gave classic expression to the image of Dreiser as a primitive, isolated, and beleaguered writer made to survive on nothing but genius. In his hands, the novelist became the model of the artist for whom creative expression was inseparable from the politics of cultural confrontation. He defined Dreiser's practice as he did his own, with stunning images drawn from the language of the battlefield. "He blasts his way through his interminable stories by something not unlike main strength; his writing, one feels, often takes on the character of an actual siege operation, with tunnellings, drum fire, assaults in close order and hand-to-hand fighting. . . . The field of action bears the aspect, at the end [of *The "Genius"*], of a hostile province meticulously brought under the yoke, with every road and lane explored to its beginning, and every crossroads village laboriously taken, inventoried and policed." Such lines, in the context of the time, identified Dreiser's work as a form of cultural aggression. And the essay itself achieves its credibility and power from Mencken's ability to find a language for the personal threat he felt, believing that "the effort to depict Dreiser as a secret agent of the Wilhelm-strasse, told off to inject subtle doses of *Kultur* into a naive and pious people, has taken on the proportions of an organized movement."

One of the sources for the *Prefaces* essay was "The Dreiser Bugaboo," which appeared in *Seven Arts* (August 1917) (see Appendix 2, pp. 768–75). In it Mencken gave much space to *The "Genius"* and its trials. Putting aside the mocking tone of "A Literary Behemoth," he argued for Dreiser's work as a whole and against the academic and thin-skinned criticism that denied his achievement. He praised the early books, from *Sister Carrie* to *The Titan*, which he noted "were done in the stage of wonder, before self-consciousness began to creep in and corrupt it." It was Mencken's way of articulating an idea that appears often in the private dialogue he had been having with the novelist since 1915. "Greenwich Village pulls as Chautau-qua pushes," Mencken laments, and "the passionate skepticism that was his original philosophy begins to show signs of being contaminated by vari-ous so-called 'radical' purposes." Mencken here is arguing that most central of all American doctrines: the necessity of radical and unfettered individu-alism as a psychic precondition for the artist. In the letters this appears—as it did to Dreiser, and as it often in fact was—as mere cranky complaint about the novelist's lifestyle and association with "jitney liberals."

Mencken's complaints increased as Dreiser, partly out of fear that his novels would not sell in wartime, devoted his energies to short stories for the magazines, a travel book, and to genres that are not major forms for him: plays like *The Hand of the Potter* and philosophical essays—for which Mencken expressed his distaste privately and in print. Dreiser began slowly to reverse his usual pattern, asking the critic to hold back his re-views or at least not to "lead the procession." Despite ritual gatherings at Lüchow's, the spirit of the old beerhall camaraderie began to fade. As Mencken wrote Ernest Boyd, "Dreiser, it appears, is subtly outraged by certain passages in my prefaces," and he added in another letter, "he is full of some obscure complaint against me, which I can't understand, and so I don't see him. In brief, I suddenly find myself very lonely in New York." [7]

At the time, Dreiser felt more dejection than outrage. Mencken's re-views left him depressed and unsure of himself as a writer. Thoroughly devoted to the novelist's vision from *Sister Carrie* to the Cowperwood books, Mencken read almost as a personal affront Dreiser's thematic concerns in more controversial work like *The "Genius"* and *The Hand of the Potter*. Though Dreiser would not admit his true feelings in letters to Hollins Street, his diary during this period shows the degree to which he took to heart his friend's changing opinion of him.

[Merton S.] Yewdale calls up, wants me to get proofs of Mencken's *Book of Prefaces* and persuade him to modify his estimate of me. Asserts it is all unfavorable and untrue, that he dismisses *The "Genius"* as a mass of piffle and that he states that my first work was the best and that I have steadily deteriorated since. Urges me to point out [Randolph] Bourne's estimate, which is better, but tell him I can't influence Mencken. Get the blues from this. Bert [Estelle Bloom Kubitz] adds to them by saying that such a criticism will fix public belief, that it is always anxious to believe the worst. . . . Have fierce case of blues all day. At 4 P.M. am sick at stomach. . . . I am horribly blue and sad, feeling eventual failure staring me in face. (13 August 1917)[8]

Both men played true to form, opting for periods of silence instead of an airing of grievances. From December 1916 to March 1917 Mencken was in Europe covering the war, but the usual rash of travel postcards and joking notes is now conspicuously absent. Following the fall 1917 publication of *A Book of Prefaces*, there is no extant correspondence until 10 May 1918. So connected were novelist and critic in the public mind that such rows became news. Offers by concerned parties to help mend the friendship did not produce complete candor on either side. Dreiser, for instance, wrote to the publisher Benjamin W. Huebsch, thanking him for trying "to straighten out any seeming difference," and adding:

I want to disabuse your mind of the idea of a personal quarrel. . . . Where we diverge, and only there (and there is no personal feeling in this), is in regard to my work. . . . I fancy for years to come I shall be severely and conscientiously attacked by him for methods different to, and in my humble judgment, somewhat above his present intellectual mood and taste.

Despite Dreiser's insistence that "I am overly fond of Mencken, literally," his complaint to Huebsch reveals the hurt he felt over Mencken's "drifting into a position where he feels it incumbent upon him as a critic to place me in a somewhat ridiculous light."[9]

The shift in Mencken's public stance stemmed from a combination of broad intellectual differences with Dreiser and a number of deeply personal motives. Dreiser's attraction to the avant-garde in New York and Chicago, particularly to its enthusiasm for the new sexual and literary freedoms, annoyed Mencken, who demanded independence from fashionable coteries of all kinds. One of the critic's arguments with *The "Genius"* was that "it somehow suggests the advanced thinking of Greenwich Village." [10] Mencken thrived in Baltimore's hearty middle-class confines and, combining propriety and a suggestive, racy humor, separated his manly indiscretions from his public life. As he later insisted, "In all matters of manners I am, and have always been, a strict conformist. My dissents are from ideas, not from decorums." [11] Nothing could be further from Dreiser's style. As an uprooted midwesterner living in West Tenth Street, the novelist's sympathies were with the artists and intellectuals who openly challenged the nation to a radical shift in social mores. Like many of his contemporaries, Dreiser looked to libidinous drives to inspire his art. In essays like "Life, Art and America," he quoted Freud and Krafft-Ebing and contended that sexual repression destroyed creative expression in America. In "Neurotic America and the Sex Impulse," he announced—to Mencken's dismay—that from "sex gratification—or perhaps better, its ardent and often defeated pursuit—comes most of all that is most distinguished in art, letters and our social economy and progress generally." [12]

Mencken had little patience for such ideas. He was more comfortable with a pragmatic, skeptical, and essentially comic view of the battle between the sexes, as he expressed it in, for example, *In Defense of Women* (1918). Yet there was more to their conflict than intellectual differences. Dreiser sensed, in Mencken's criticism of the sexual element in his work (and of the related issue of his Greenwich Village friends), "something that does not appear on the surface." The evidence suggests he was correct. First of all, Mencken associated Dreiser's more experimental writing with his increasing reliance on women friends both for subject matter and for critical confirmation. Especially after the blowup over *The "Genius,"* Dreiser stopped sending manuscripts to Baltimore for a first reading. None too subtly, the critic urged: "Take the advice of men with hair on their chests—not of women." To Huebsch, he complained of Dreiser's susceptibility "to the flattery of self-seeking frauds, particularly those with cavities between their legs." [13]

Mencken was irked by the loss of Dreiser's confidence and by the equally embarrassing perception of himself as, in Nathan's formulation, "Dreiser's most faithful critical mount, private shimmy dancer and rajpoot at large." [14] Moreover, Dreiser's large sexual appetites, and reputation to match, irritated and perhaps even challenged his friend who, with all his muscular bluster, was more inhibited in this regard. More than ever before, Mencken focused on Dreiser's sexual behavior and became strident in his denunciations. To friends, like Ernest Boyd, he wrote that Dreiser "is doing little writing, but devotes himself largely to the stud." [15] Even mere business contacts, like the San Francisco bohemian poet George Sterling, might gather from Baltimore the latest news about Dreiser: "he still keeps his manly powers and is first cock in Greenwich Village." [16] To complicate matters, the critic's prejudices began to color his perception of Dreiser's writing: *The Hand of the Potter*, he wrote Huebsch, is "a cheap piece of pornography." [17] And to Boyd he announced that the novelist "is at work on a 'philosophical book.' You may guess that fornication will be defended in it." [18]

Whatever their disagreements in principle, they might have avoided such extremes but for the peculiar relation between them and the sisters Marion Bloom and Estelle Bloom Kubitz. Between 1914 and 1923, Mencken and Marion Bloom were on intimate terms, at times contemplating marriage in an erratic relation that lasted longer than any other before Mencken's marriage to Sara Haardt. Dreiser met Estelle Kubitz through Mencken, and they lived together intermittently from 1916 to 1919. Mencken was very fond of Marion Bloom's sister, who was called "Gloom," ostensibly because of her taste for heavy Russian novels, but also for her somewhat somber disposition. Their correspondence shows the degree to which he maintained the rather paternalistic role she encouraged, becoming her chief counselor in the matter of handling Dreiser.

The critic's letters to Estelle Kubitz suggest how much Dreiser's often callous treatment of her infuriated Mencken. This correspondence is somewhat surprising, since the two men themselves always went out of their way to maintain a cautious reserve about their intimate affairs. By early 1917, Mencken was offering her money to leave Manhattan (that is, Dreiser) and pleading with her to resettle in Washington, D.C. Since he and Dreiser often took the sisters out together in New York, the novelist's cavalier treatment of women lost its romantic glow for Mencken: "I was staggered," he wrote Kubitz, "when I heard that you had gone back, following the episode of which I was witness" (20 July 1917 [NYP]). Until 1919, when Dreiser left for California with Helen Richardson, the letters between Mencken and Estelle Kubitz centered on Dreiser's amorous vagaries. Especially in the years when he was contemplating marriage to her sister, Mencken responded with angry indignation to every detail: "I class you among the damned fools. You put that ancient guinea pig above your own fair little sister, your best friend" (19 October 1917 [NYP]); "You have allowed the old boy to make a doormat of you, and yet you have gone back every time" (23 January 1918 [NYP]). At times Mencken reveals how deeply this peculiar triangle had cut into his friendship with the novelist: "Down in his heart he probably believes that you and I have betrayed him" (6 November 1918 [NYP]).

There was a betrayal of sorts, and Mencken, with his constitutional distaste for intimate confessions, certainly felt uncomfortable with this backdoor access to his friend's private life. On one occasion Kubitz sent to Baltimore a minidrama in the form of a dialogue between "Damn Phool" and "SOB," which recreates a scene in which Dreiser is shown plotting to sneak off to one of his many trysts. When she secretly copied and typed Dreiser's personal diary for 1917–18 and sent it to Mencken, he obviously understood more about his involvement than he admits in the note he pinned to the diary years later: "Whether she gave it to me because she was then on bad terms with Dreiser and eager to make him look foolish or because she thought that the diary would aid me in my writings about him I don't know." [NYP] What seems clear is that Dreiser had good reason to suspect something unspoken behind the peculiar turn that Mencken's personal and professional criticism took in these years. Although the air cleared considerably when Dreiser left for California and after Mencken's relation with Marion became less intense, the two men would never regain the feelings of mutual trust that marked their early friendship.

Notes

1. Mencken, "The Free Lance," Baltimore *Evening Sun*, 15 September 1914, editorial page.
2. F. O. Matthiessen, *Theodore Dreiser* (New York: William Sloane, 1951), 4.
3. Stuart Sherman, "The Barbaric Naturalism of Mr. Dreiser," *The Nation*, 2 December 1915; repr. in *The Stature of Theodore Dreiser*, ed. Alfred Kazin and Charles Shapiro (Bloomington: Indiana Univ. Press, 1955), 72.
4. Stuart Sherman, "Beautifying American Literature," *The Nation*, 29 November 1917, 594.
5. N. P. Dawson, "Books of the Week," New York *Evening Globe*, 30 October 1915; repr. in Salzman, 226.
6. Mencken, "The Free Lance," Baltimore *Evening Sun*, 16 February 1915, editorial page.
7. Both letters to Boyd are undated; Guy J. Forgue places them in the fall of 1917 and winter of 1918: *Letters*, 111; 113.
8. Dreiser, *The American Diaries*, ed. Thomas P. Riggio, James L. W. West III, Neda Westlake (Philadelphia: University of Pennsylvania Press, 1982), 181.
9. Dreiser to B. W. Huebsch, in Elias, *Letters*, 1 : 250–51.
10. Mencken, "Theodore Dreiser," *A Book of Prefaces* (New York: Alfred A. Knopf, 1917), 124.
11. Quoted in Sara Mayfield, *The Constant Circle: H. L. Mencken and His Friends* (New York: Delacorte Press, 1968), 167.
12. Dreiser, *Hey Rub-a-Dub-Dub* (New York: Boni and Liveright, 1920), 134.
13. Mencken to Huebsch, 16 March 1918, in Bode, *Letters*, 84.
14. George Jean Nathan, "Dreiser's Play—and Some Others," *Smart Set* (October 1919), 131; repr. in Salzman, 351–52.
15. Mencken to Boyd, 20 April 1918, in Forgue, *Letters*, 120.
16. Mencken to Sterling, 18 March 1918, in Bode, *Letters*, 85.
17. Mencken to Huebsch, 16 March 1918, in Bode, *Letters*, 83.
18. Mencken to Boyd, 27 May 1918, in Bode, *Letters*, 89.

The Correspondence
(1915–1918)

[UPL]

SMART SET
A Magazine of Cleverness
456 Fourth Avenue, New York

Wednesday. [after 14 January 1915]

Dear Dreiser:-

I'll look into the matter of literary clubs in Baltimore and let you know by Monday. There is an organization called The Saturday Night Class which used to invite me to eloquence, and I think there are several women's clubs which run to beautiful letters. If the worst comes to the worst I'll get an invitation for Powys[1] from the Brew-Workers' Union, No. 22.

The Rogers case is a mere beginning.[2] The uplifters have sworn to put down the villainous practice of copulation in this fair republic, and I begin to suspect that they will do it, just as they will put through prohibition and prevent any increase of the army. Their ideal is a nation devoted to masturbation and the praise of God. The American of the future will do his love-making in the bath-room, and he will be found in the same place when his country is invaded. If I ever get out of my present morass I shall begin the serious study of German, to the end that I may spend my declining years in a civilized country.

A letter from Harry Leon Wilson[3] yesterday lavishing high praise on your plays. Not the first, by any means. They have made an unmistakable hit, and it is worth noticing that the persons best pleased by them have been writers. I think the banzais that should please a man most are those of his own profession.

Long live Pilsner! Did you notice what old Kluck did to 'em at Soissons?[4]

Yours,
M

1. John Cowper Powys (1872–1963), English author and lecturer who had been promoting Dreiser in his lectures.
2. The Rogers case had to do with adultery and murder.
3. Harry Leon Wilson (1867–1939), best-selling humorist, novelist, playwright.
4. On 14 and 15 January 1915 the Germans won the battle of Soissons, and the French sustained losses of over 4,000 men killed and 5,000 captured. General Alexander von Kluck (1846–1934) was commander of the German First Army.

[UPL]

H. L. Mencken
1524 Hollins St.
Baltimore.

February 20th. [1915]

Dear Dreiser:-

I congratulate Ibsen upon getting into your class. What play is Reicher using?[1] And how are you coming on with that novelette you told me about? It sticks in my mind.

Germany will declare war upon the United States within two weeks, and there will be a hot old time here if Bryan & Co. try to embark any troops for France.[2] I expect to go to jail with the first batch of Baltimore suspects. Maybe we can contrive to be incarcerated in the same dungeon. Deutschland ueber alles![3] Damn neutrality!

Yours,
Mencken

1. Emmanuel Reicher, who founded and ran the Modern Stage Theater at 55 West 86th Street. At this time Reicher was planning to produce Dreiser's play *The Girl in the Coffin*, but nothing came of this project.
2. William Jennings Bryan (1860–1925) was secretary of state.
3. Germany above all.

Mencken in his Hollins Street study (Enoch Pratt Free Library)

[UPL]

SMART SET
A Magazine of Cleverness
456 Fourth Avenue, New York

Sunday. [after 10 March 1915]

Dear Dreiser:-

A thought: you are constantly coming into contact with aspiring authors. Why not spread the following whisper: that I'll be glad to see the manuscript of any ambitious new one, buck or wench, and to give them my prompt and personal attention? This may develop something and so help both the magazine and the authors. In particular, I'll be glad to read any novelette or play. Even on the red-ink question I am still willing to be convinced. All I say is that the stuff actually sent in by the tabble doty revolutionists was uniformly feeble and empty.

Incidently, what has become of your own novelette—the one about the man condemned to the chair?[1]

The English loss at Nueve Chapelle: 11,850.[2] Gott strafe the dirty lice![3]

In nomine Domini!

M

1. In 1915, Dreiser began a novel called "The Rake," based on the Roland Molineux murder trial in 1899. He completed six chapters and abandoned the project.
2. On 10 March 1915, the British took the French village of Neuve Chapelle from the Germans; however, the French and English losses were heavy.
3. God punish the dirty lice.

[NYP]

165 West 10th St.
New York

Mch 22nd 1915

My Dear Mencken:

Barring Howells, James, Norris, Phillips, Mrs. Wharton, Garland, Herrick and London are there any fugitive realistic works of import. I want a list. I should exclude Whitlock, H. B. Fuller & Stephen Crane.

Oblige Yours
Theodore Dreiser

Make it as comprehensive a list as you can.

[UPL]

SMART SET
A Magazine of Cleverness
456 Fourth Avenue, New York

March 25th. [1915]

Dear Dreiser:-

Counting out the authors you mention, and yourself, there have been very few realists in this fair land. Kennerley is just bringing out a very remarkable book, "One Man", by Robert Steele (pseudonym), but it is too full of autobiography to qualify as a novel, though it is called "a novel" on the title-page. Don't miss it. Others:

"Love's Pilgrimage" and "The Jungle", by Upton Sinclair.

"A Song of Sixpence", by Frederick Arnold Kummer.

"The Inside of the Cup," by Winston Churchill.

"The Golden Age",[1] by Mark Twain and Chas. Dudley Warner.

What else? Damme if I know. Realism doesn't seem to appeal to most American writers.

What are you doing? Are you making any progress with that story of the condemned man? It sticks in my mind.

Yours,
M

1. Mencken means *The Gilded Age*.

[NYP]
Mch 29—1915

My Dear Mencken:

Harry Leon Wilson wrote a novel "The Spenders." Is that without sound realistic value. Is no one of Will Lenington Comforts works sound, realistically speaking? Did Alice Brown ever write a realistic work?—or Mary E. Wilkins—one that was good all through? And how about Margaret Deland? The Iron Woman?

I enclose reviews just received of The Titan in England. Thought they might interest you for the moment. Am working, as usual.

Th. D.

[UPL]

SMART SET
A Magazine of Cleverness
George Jean Nathan
and   }Editors
H. L. Mencken
456 Fourth Avenue, New York

April 1st. [1915]

Dear Dreiser:-

If I left out Harry Leon Wilson's "The Spenders" it was an oversight. Comfort's stuff is gorgeously romantic, and even fantastic. He deals with Mystic Motherhood, the Fourth Lustrous Dimension and other such bosh, and is a crazy gynophile. Alice Brown, Mary Wilkins and Margaret Deland I don't know.

The London reviews, on the whole, are very decent. Locke's is excellent.[1] It is amusing, by the way, to see how the English fear and hatred of Germany bob up, even in book reviews. The English Review is full of it every month. The English are beginning to realize what it means to fight Germans. They are finding that this is no Boer war, and the discovery is paralyzing them. I have a tip from the highest sources that a Zeppelin raid on a grand scale will be undertaken shortly, and that it will be a lulu.

"Working as usual". But on what? What of that story of the condemned man?

The Smart Set, by the way, seems to be making progress. The returns are declining steadily and the advertising department is bringing in new contracts for 6, 9 and 12 months. I begin to believe that we'll put it over. But what a sweat!

Yours,
M

1. W. J. Locke, "A Colossus of Finance," London *Pall Mall Gazette*, 6 March 1915, 5.

[UPL]

SMART SET
456 Fourth Avenue, New York

April 6th. [1915]

Dear Dreiser:-

If you have ever given the resurrected Smart Set a glance, and can do it without injury to your conscience, and have no scruples otherwise, I wish you would dash off a few lines saying that it has shown progress during the past six months and is now a magazine that the civilized reader may peruse without damage to his stomach. This for chaste publication in refined announcements, along with the statement that you are a high-class novelist, a faithful Elk and a swell dresser on and off the stage. We are turning the corner and a help will actually help. But if the lie is too vast for you, say Nix in a loud tone, and no one will every hear it save myself. Meanwhile I continue to pray for your conversion to orthodox Swedenborgianism and Lake Mohonkery.

Yours,
M

By the way, the New Republic approached me lately with a proposition to do an article on you. The sheet is so damnably slimy and pecksniffian that I bucked, thinking it would injure both of us, but I may go back to it during the summer.[1] There is no more oleaginous and forward-looking gazette in These States.

---

1. Mencken never wrote this piece for the *New Republic*.

[UPL]

SMART SET
456 Fourth Avenue, New York

April 7th. [1915]

Dear Dreiser:-

I forgot to add one of the best realistic novels done in this country in late years: "Rebellion", by Joseph Medill Patterson. Patterson afterward dramatized it. Don't miss "One Man". The last few chapters, in their crude artlessness, will delight you.

Yours,
M

[NYP-T]

165 West 10th Street
N.Y.City.

April 20th,'15

My Dear Mencken:

I wish that I could say whole-heartedly that I liked the Smart Set, or that it has shown the kind of progress that I like in the last six months.

Under Mann[1] in its profitable social days it had a glittering insincerity and blasé pretence which I rather liked, shallow as it was.

Under Wright, when the society act had become a chestnut, it reflected a kind of shameless blood-lust, too fulgurous and unrelieved to suit me entirely, but still forceful and convincing.[2]

Under you and Nathan the thing seems to have tamed down to a light, non-disturbing period of persiflage and badinage, which now and then is amusing but which not even the preachers of Keokuk will resent seriously. It is as innocent as the Ladies Home Journal. Really, the thing is too debonair, too Broadwayesque, too full of "josh" and "kid", like a Broadway and Forty-Second Street curb actor. Everything, apparently, is to be done with a light, aloof touch, which to me is good but like a diet of souffle. I like to feel the stern, cool winds of an Odessey now and then. Why publish so many things in one number? Wouldn't it be better to have one or two occasional very fine things than so many trivial ones? Why couldn't you have published "Crainquebille" by Anatole France, or Flax's study of Octave Mirbeau? (See Greenwich Village) or De Casseres' "From the Cusp Of The Moon" or Masters' "To a Greek Altar"?[3] I called your attention to Masters months ago and you pass him over completely for third-raters like Witter Bynner and Untermeier. When you started six or seven months ago I was hoping that along with the touch that you now have—just a touch, however,—you would take a tip from Reedy and "The Masses" and The "International", and do the serious critical thing in an enlightening way. There are splendid indictments to be drawn of a score of things before the world right now—things which could be sandwiched in between the things you do use and real literary achievements, such as a play by Tchekof or a satire by Andreyeff. Once I was on the point of writing you. I felt that you were helplessly in tow of the Broadway-bebraided George Jean, for whom I have some respect as a lighter touch. But I decided not. Now, since you ask it I offer this as a purely personal opinion and one which, if followed, might cause your circulation to drop. Personally I think you are sound as a critic of books and that the magazine as you are doing it has some interest, but not enough to call forth from me the praise you want. The things haven't enough real interest for me.

Take the April number. Your leading story is entitled "When Fancy Leaves the Narrow Path." To me it is thin stuff, poorly done—traditional to the point of weariness and mediocre in style. The next thing that arrested my attention was "The Windy Shot". It was only fair—lacking in poetic poignancy—but fair. Then I went back and read "The Uplifters". It seemed trivial and along a line which is now becoming a little thin. Then, for interlude, I read the three things by Lord Dunsany who is good as a philosopher-humorist, but not fascinating enough to warrant three contributions in one volume. Also I read "Cameron's Conclusion", (fairly clever) "Jealousy"—William Anderson, (not worth doing) "Grandmother" Woljeska (fair) "Flirt", Thomas Ransford—(trivial but good for the society game and as a filler.) Then I stopped and turned to the poetry. "Annunciation"—Witter Bynner, (truck—uninspired) "Evening"—Martin Grief (a useless filler) "Transposition"—Thompson Rich (rather good—traditional) "The Victory"—Whitford (a dull mechanical idea—made to sell) "April Song" (charming but the eightieth millionth of its kind) "Love's Pilgrimage" Middleton (mediocre) "The Last Poet"—Johns (not bad at all—rather good) "The Ancient One" (truck) "In Donegal" (truck—lost space) "Certainly, It Can Be Done", (Should have been done in prose and then torn up) "Lines for Music" (only fair—sweet old style) "Disembodied"—H. K. (not worth space) "Love's Need"—Scollard (a dull rhyme) "The Reason"—A. W. Peach (suitable for Godey's Lady Book.)

To finish I read "A Careful Surgeon"—clever but in the same joshing vein as eight or nine others in the book and not to be included with so many of its kind. "The Moral Defeat"—Harvey—(clever but in the same vein—good another month) "The Flight"—(without serious charm) and finally "With The Minstrels Of The Moment" (I don't think George Jean is mentally in a position to pass on Granville Barker) and "The Grand Stand Flirts With The Bleachers" by Henry L. Mencken—whose diatribes I always enjoy and whose strictures in the main I accept as sound.

Does this sound severe? I don't mean it to. Frankly I think you are infinitely better than the paper you produce. Why is this?

Dreiser

And how I long to write another kind of letter—one which would express my good will. By the way if you have done with those two clippings let me have them.[4] The English journals are foaming at the mouth. The St. Louis Post-Dispatch could do no worse than the Saturday Review.[5]

1. Colonel William D'Alton Mann founded the *Smart Set* in 1900. The magazine's loyal but limited audience did not make it a financial success, and Mann sold it in 1910.
2. Willard Huntington Wright edited the magazine successfully in 1913, but the cautious owner, John Adams Thayer, replaced him with Mencken and George Jean Nathan when Wright's avant-garde policy disturbed conservative advertisers.
3. Dreiser is referring to work he admires that had been published recently in other journals: the pieces by Anatole France and Benjamin De Casseres in *International* and that by J. Flax in *Greenwich Village*; Edgar Lee Masters's poem has not been identified.
4. The English reviews of *The Titan*.
5. The postscript is handwritten.

[UPL]

SMART SET
A Magazine of Cleverness
456 Fourth Avenue, New York

April 22nd. [1915]

Dear Dreiser:-

These notices are marvellous revelations of English pecksniffery. They are obsessed by moral phantasms—and the other fellow, of course, is always wrong. The Germans are putting holes through that philosophy, and they will put a lot more before this war ends.

I am sorry that The Smart Set doesn't please you. As it stands, of course, it represents a compromise between what we'd like to do and what the difficulties that we face allow us to do. We had to buck a falling circulation and a bad reputation. The former has swung back; the latter we are trying to live down. We haven't money enough to take long chances. We have to give them, to some extent at least, what they seem to like, and more particularly, what we are able to get. I agree with you that "When Fancy Leaves the Narrow Path" was an execrable novelette. But, believe me, it was the very best that we could get. We got promises of stuff on all sides, but not a line of actual copy. The May novelette is very much better, and so is that we have scheduled for June. Where July's is to come from I haven't the slightest idea. Nothing whatever is in sight. Read the novelettes in the other magazines: you will find that they are even worse than ours. I know it because I have read most of them in ms. and declined them.

But the light touch that you protest against is what we want. The Smart Set—consider its title!—is no place to print the revolutionary fustian of De Casseris and company. One of the first things I did last August was to invite De Casseris, Dell, Herts and all the rest of the red-ink boys to send in stuff.[1] I read it diligently and hopefully, but found it inexpressibly empty. These fellows are all sophomores; they have nothing to say, and they say that nothing very badly. My study of their stuff cured me of all belief in neglected geniuses. The whole red-ink bunch, and particularly the International bunch, is hollow-headed and childish. I couldn't find a single intelligible idea in 50 mss. Harry Kemp is the only tabble doty genius who has given us anything fit to print.[2]

As for Masters, I bought a long ballad from him three months ago, and only recurring make-up difficulties have kept it out so long. It is scheduled for the July number. Harris Merton Lyon has sent us two good stories.[3] We printed one, "The Pact", in December; the other dealt with an abortion, and, though well done, was quite impossible. A novelette that he submitted was full of faults; he is still tinkering with it. Nothing else from the Reedy crowd.⁴ You missed the best two stories in April, "Little Girl" and "Felix and Carlotta". It was, however, a bad number.

But let it go! We are not trying to shock 'em, but to entertain 'em. The June number will be better.

Yours,

M

1. Benjamin De Casseres; Floyd Dell; and Benjamin Russell Herts, Socialist author and journalist.

2. Harry Kemp (1883–1960), poet, novelist, biographer. Kemp was a romantic bohemian who was known as the "Byron of the Village."

3. Harry Merton Lyon (1883–1916) was a protégé of Dreiser and the original for "De Maupassant, Jr." in *Twelve Men*.

4. William Marion Reedy (1862–1920), journalist, editor, critic. His St. Louis newspaper, *Reedy's Mirror*, introduced many new writers, including Dreiser, in the first decades of the century.

[NYP-T]

165 West 10th Street
N.Y.City.

April 26th, '15

My Dear Mencken:

You make a mistake in regard to my supposed interest in "the red ink fraternity", as you call them. I hold no brief for the parlor radical. Viereck, Rethy, Herts¹ and a score of others whose names have come and gone are of a thin cloth, but when you mix in Dell and De Casseres with them, and then pause to praise Lyon and George Bronson Howard you are sound asleep, also having taken over into your camp the empty Kemp. Produce me a poetic philosophic dissertation (recent) the equal of "From The Cusp Of The Moon," by De Casseres, or better poems than some of Dells, and I will eat these words without salt.

The trouble with you is that in the fury of your riding you plunge over all merit on foot. "The International", "The Masses", "Rogue", "Greenwich Village", "The Mirror", and the like are, let us say thin things. Admitted. Yet if they can pick things like "Crainquebille" "From The Cusp Of The Moon", "The Spoon River Anthology" and things of that sort, and you can't or don't, where do you get off? A man like Max Eastman,² radical though he is, lays his finger on notable pecksnifferies, sores and shames. You don't. Yet they are everywhere at hand. It may be important for circulation to print gay trifles—I know it is in part—but why attempt to ride down the other fellow until you are sure that he is not doing some of the things you ought to be doing. I am genial—not angry.

I sometimes think that because I have moved into 10th Street and am living a life not suitable to the home streets of Baltimore that you think I have gone over to the red ink family and "the brothers of the hollow skull." Give yourself one more guess. I have never had a better line on myself than at present, and the advice I am giving you is straight from the shoulder. You may increase your circulation and make some money by the unrelieved "light touch" you mention—(the "unrelieved" part being the only thing I complain of)—and the desire not to shock is comendable where the cash drawer is concerned, but it is not necessarily at war with the desire to entertain. Personally I would say that if you would mingle a severe jolt now and then, or a loud shrill scream, you really would entertain and keep up your good character in the bargain. But for a man with your critical point of view the stuff you are publishing is not literature and there are those who are getting it under your nose. But—But here's to all storm and sudden death! I see that the Catholics are quoting you.

Dreiser

If I can think of anything to suggest I will do so with pleasure. It is helpful criticism you want, not grape juice.[3]

1. The poet and journalist George Sylvester Viereck (1884–1962) edited the pro-German *International*; the Socialist writers Joseph Bernard Rethy and Benjamin Russell Herts were his associates.
2. Max Eastman (1883–1969), poet, critic, teacher who edited the radical journals *Masses* and *The Liberator* during these years.
3. The postscript is handwritten.

[UPL]

SMART SET
A Magazine of Cleverness
456 Fourth Avenue, New York

Thursday. [29 April 1915]

Dear Dreiser:-

Pish! What slush is this about "living a life not suitable to the home streets of Baltimore?" Do you take me for a Methodist deacon—or a male virgin? For far less insults I have had gentlemen killed by my private murderer, a blackamoor but a deft hand at the garrote.

Moreover, your allegations are chiefly damphoolishness. I tackle Masters the moment I heard of him (through you), and bought a long ballad from him out of the first and only batch he offered. He tells me he has been sick all winter. His Spoon River stuff was all printed when I got to him. I read all the stuff that De Casseras sent in, and bought the only good thing in the lot. I read all of Dell's stuff and found nothing. I have bought three or four things from Kemp, not one of them "a gay trifle". I did not mention George Bronson Howard in my last letter, and have bought nothing from him. I have read The International for three years and have seen nothing in it worth a dam save a philippic against Maeterlinck by André Tridon.[1] I have read Rogue, and found nothing in it save the sort of "wit" that school-boys chalk on pissoir walls. I have read all the books published by the Nortons, etc., and told the truth about them in the Smart Set.

I grant you that there has been a decided lightness in the magazine— but we had a condition, not a theory, before us. The experiment with whores and horrors had failed; the experiment with cheap melodrama had failed; we had to try a new tack or go down. On August 15 The Smart Set owed $24,000 and was losing more than $2,000 a month. The circulation was cut to pieces; there was no advertising at all; we actually had to borrow money to pay interest on the debt. We guessed that satire would save it, and we guessed right. But we have steadily endeavored to lift the thing as much as possible. April was our worst number, and you picked out the worst things in it. For example, you missed the two stories by James Joyce[2] (his first published in America), the excellent "Little Girl", by Lee Pape; "The Man Who Waited", by Lina Bernstein; "Felix and Carlotta", by Edna Marion Hill (sentimental stuff); and "The Desert is Not Fifth Avenue".

But away with debates! We'll prove it to you yet, old top! If you see anything likely, for Goddes sake sound the alarrum! I have no prejudices, save against the Methodists.

In nomine Domini
M

1. André Tridon (1877–1922), journalist, psychoanalyst.
2. "A Little Cloud" and "The Boarding House," two of the *Dubliners* stories.

[UPL]

H. L. Mencken
1524 Hollins St.
Baltimore.

May 18th [1915]

Dear Dreiser:-

This notice is supreme![1] Not for one minute are the English able to forget the immorality of the Germans. Say what you will against the gospel of frightfulness, it has at least turned the bowels of J. Bull to water.

I look for war within ten days.

Yours,
M

1. This has not been identified.

[UPL]

H. L. Mencken
1524 Hollins St.
Baltimore.

September 29th. [1915]

Dear Dreiser:-

My best thanks for "The Genius". Even with the cuts it is a whale of a book, but I shall go through it with eagle eye—and eager to be converted. My Smart Set review will be in the December number, out November 15th.[1] My November copy went in a week ago.

How art thou, anyhow, and what dost thou? I think the war is nearly over. The Germans have given them all a belly-full. To invade Germany now appears as practicable as to put out the fires of hell.

Yours,
M

1. "A Literary Behemoth," *Smart Set* 47(December 1915), 150–54 (see Appendix 2, pp. 754–59).

[NYP]

165 West 10th Street
New York City

Oct. 9—1915

My Dear H. L. M—

At present I am working on two things—"The Bulwark" and "A Hoosier Holiday"—the latter an account of a 2000 mile auto trip I made to Indiana in August—looking over me native heath. Franklin Booth has made some remarkable charcoal sketches—about fifty.[1]

Reviews of "The Genius" are beginning to pour in—most of them favorable. The ass in the St. Louis Globe is sure that it ought not to be put in the public libraries.[2] Favorable reviews in this case no doubt indicate the inherent weakness of the book to you—and no doubt you are right. The applause of hacks is the proof of a failure. I most of all am aware of that.

I look to the Germans to win & bring better days.

Th D

Will you please return quickly such reviews as I may send.

The book of plays may come out this winter.[3]

I haven't a thing on hand to offer outside of The Light in the Window & A Spring Recital.

1. Franklin Booth (1874–1948), artist. Like Dreiser, Booth was born in Indiana and came to New York to work. In 1915 the two friends took an automobile trip to Indiana, and they published *A Hoosier Holiday* (1916), with text by Dreiser and illustrations by Booth.

2. Anon., "Theodore Dreiser Writes Story of Genius Whose Life Was a Failure," St. Louis *Globe Democrat*, 2 October 1915, 6.

3. *Plays of the Natural and Supernatural* was published on 18 February 1916.

[NYP]

165 West 10th Street
New York City

Oct. 10—1915

Fairest Mencken:

I am thinking of accepting a directorship in a new and somewhat imposing film corporation.[1] Can you recall a story which would make a suitable film offering for my first. I cant begin by ramming naturalism down their throats—not at least until I get my hand in but I can make such incidents as will go over appealing.

Greetings. In a separate envelope I am sending you a one act nothing, dashed off in an hour.[2] If it disappoints you greatly, let me know. I was not attempting anything more than something faintly amusing.

Th.D

Would that the rumor about [word illegible] were true.

1. William Lengel approached Dreiser for the Hoggson firm, which wanted to form a moving picture company called Mirror Films. The idea was to make Dreiser scenario director. Dreiser was enthusiastic about the project, but it was never developed.
2. *The Spring Recital.*

[UPL]

H. L. Mencken
1524 Hollins St.
Baltimore.

Thursday. [14 October 1915]

Dear Dreiser:-

I think you will find the very thing you are seeking in "The Song of the Lark", by Willa S. Cather, just published by Houghton-Mifflin. It is, in brief, the old Cinderella story, which never fails to wring tears from the osseocaputs. The scene shifts from the Colorado hills to the Metropolitan Opera House, and includes a glimpse of the Cliff Dwellers of Arizona. Go to it. There is also an excellent sentimental film in a story called "Bill and George", published in the September Smart Set. Also, observe the possibilities of "Thirty Days Hath September" and "At the Club" in the same number. I am having the office send you a copy.

The ms. you mention has not yet reached me, but my eye is alert for it. Why not have dinner with me next Tuesday or Wednesday—you and Miss Markham?[1] I'll be in New York until Wednesday. Don't reply to Baltimore, but to The Smart Set office, 331 Fourth avenue, for I may reach New York Sunday, or even Saturday.

Yours,
M.

1. Kirah Markham, art student and actress who took part in the little theater movement of the nineteen-teens in Chicago and New York. At this time, she and Dreiser were living together in New York and providing a weekly open house for artists and intellectuals.

SMART SET
A Magazine of Cleverness
452 Fifth Avenue, New York

Friday. [15 October 1915]

Dear Dreiser:-

Frankly, I am against using this, and for a simple reason.[1] It would strike a note of anti-climax after the other three and spoil their affect, both for you and for us. The difference between it and them is plain enough. In each of the three there was a definite transaction, and a resultant dramatic suspense. In "The Blue Sphere" there was curiosity as to what would become of the imbecile child; the atmosphere grew steadily more sinister. In "In the Dark" there was the conflict between murderer and police, with the issue in doubt until the end. And in "Laughing Gas", of course, there was that poignant suspense which always hangs around a surgical operation. But in "The Spring Recital" there is no suspense at all. It is atmospheric, not dramatic. And so I think, as I say, that it would be very injudicious to print it after the other three. The effect would inevitably be disappointment.

I am not arguing, mind you, that the play is bad. Not at all. On the contrary, I think there is a good deal of color in it. In the book, sandwiched between two of the other plays, it will go down. But standing alone in a magazine I am convinced that it will seem weak, and I believe you will agree with me when you think it over.

By the way, you have forgotten to put in the name of the composition the organist "drifts" into at the bottom of page 4.

What of the novelette you mentioned—the electrocution story? Is it coming on? I begin to hope that we will have a few bucks in bank by the time it is ready.

Thine,
H. L. M.

1. Dreiser's play *The Spring Recital.*

N.Y. Oct 13—1915

Have I grounds for a libel suit in connection with this particular statement in your judgement.[1]

Th.D

1. Dreiser sent Mencken the *Globe-Democrat* review (see Dreiser to Mencken, 9 October 1915, n.2).

[UPL]

H. L. Mencken
1524 Hollins St.
Baltimore.

October 17th. [1915]

Dear Dreiser:-

I doubt that you have any ground for a libel suit in this Globe review.
At all events, the business is not worth pursuing: nobody reads the Globe.
I hope you made note of the English losses at the Dardanelles.[1]

Yours,
M

Will you be in N.Y. the week of Oct 25?[2]

1. The English losses in the Dardanelles were so heavy that by the end of October
Sir Charles Munro, who was in charge of the campaign, recommended total evacua-
tion of the British forces from the area—a recommendation that was acted upon in
early 1916.
2. The postscript is handwritten.

[NYP]
Oct. 20—1915

My Dear H. L—

Yes, I will be here all this week—possibly not Friday P.M. unless you
notify me at once. Phone—7755 Chelsea. The enclosed two flights may
amuse you.[1]

Th. D

1. Dreiser is referring to reviews of *The "Genius."*

[UPL]

H. L. Mencken
1524 Hollins St.
Baltimore.

Wednesday. [20 October 1915]

Dear Dreiser:-

This World notice is the usual cheap and empty stuff.[1] The Tribune
boy, on the contrary, offers a coherent and intelligible review—an unusual
thing, I believe, in the Tribune.[2]

So far, I haven't had a chance to go through the book properly; I'll get to it within the week. When is the play book to be published? And have you anything resembling a novelette?

Hochactungsvoll![3]
HL Mencken

The war is in its last stage, and the Germans have knocked the ahss off'n 'em.

---

1. The anonymous New York *World* review mentions that *The "Genius"* is 736 pages long, weighs a pound and three-quarters, and contains some 350,000 words—and then proceeds to say that it could be cut by all these measurements (see New York *World*, "Mr. Dreiser's 'Genius,'" 2 October 1915; repr. in Salzman, 212–13).

2. Anon., "Views and Reviews of Current Fiction: The 'Genius,'" New York *Tribune*, 2 October 1915, 8; repr. in Salzman, 212–13.

3. With great respect.

[UPL]

H. L. Mencken
1524 Hollins St.
Baltimore.

November 2nd. [1915]

Dear Dreiser:-

The secret of the Globe braying lies in the last paragraph: the grand crime, in these days, is to bear a German name. Unluckily, "The 'Genius'" has exactly the right defects to invite such an attack, but none the less the attack itself is dishonest. Who is this N. P. D.?[1] I have a little list. There can never be any compromise in future between men of German blood and the common run of "good," "right-thinking" Americans. We must stand against them forever, and do what damage we can to them, and to their tin-pot democracy.

I needn't say that the fair Bloom,[2] having venerated you from afar and as if you were some gaseous E flat amateur Jesus, emerged from your presence in a state bordering upon maryolatry. Hence I do not apologize for the invasion, particularly since you were sober and Miss Markham was so charming to us. Scratch upon the wall this fact: you and she have a dinner engagement with H. L. M. along about Nov. 15th, the exact date to be at your convenience. Meanwhile, God's benison.

Yours,
M

The more I think of the anti-German snorting now going on, the more I larf and larf.

M.

1. Mencken is referring to a review of *The "Genius"* signed by one "N. P. D.," "Books of the Week: Theodore Dreiser," New York *Globe and Commercial Advertiser*, 30 October 1915, 8. N. P. Dawson wrote it and used the occasion to remind his audience, by association, of Dreiser's German heritage: "We hope that 'The Genius' will immediately appear in a German translation. That's how kindly we feel toward the Germans!"
2. Mencken met Marion Bloom in 1914 and they later developed a close relationship, at times contemplating marriage. Mencken encouraged her in her writing career and published her work in *Smart Set*.

[UPL]

H. L. Mencken
1524 Hollins St.
Baltimore.

November 11th. [1915]

Dear Dreiser:-

Can you and Miss Markham dine with me Monday evening, instead of Tuesday or Wednesday, as I suggested? If so, rush me an answer as above, and it will reach me before I leave Baltimore. I propose the change because I want to bring a fellow who should be able to do a lot for you in England.[1] He is a close friend of George Moore's and a contributor to The New Age; also a very decent citizen, once you get used to his sepulchral voice.

If Monday is inconvenient, make it any night that suits you.

Gott hat England gestraft![2]

M

1. Ernest Boyd (1887–1946), Irish-born critic, diplomat.
2. God has punished England. This is probably a reference to the English military misfortunes in the Dardanelles in the fall of 1915.

[UPL-H]

H. L. Mencken
1524 Hollins St.
Baltimore

[after 12 November 1915]

Dear Dreiser:-

Make it Tuesday. I'll call you up Monday morning to arrange the time and place.

In His Name

Yours,
M

[NYP]

165 West 10th Street
New York City

Nov. 17—1915

My Dear H. L. M:

After mailing "The Scavenger" today it occurred to me that perhaps children would never use a cry like "Scavenger" but rather something like "Rag picker" which would be more within the range of their intelligence.[1] Also that the thing might be made more poignant by having him actually struck by a can, thrown by a boy. For these reasons and several minor ones, I have decided to revise the mss. So if you haven't read it don't bother, but ship it back, and I'll ask you to look at it a little later. Greetings & thanks for the kindness.

Th D.

Miss M. includes her good wishes.[2]

1. This is a reference to Dreiser's play, which he eventually called *Old Ragpicker*.
2. This is placed above the salutation, and refers to Kirah Markham.

[UPL]

SMART SET
A Magazine of Cleverness
George Jean Nathan
and   } Editors
H. L. Mencken

Friday. [19 November 1915]

Dear Dreiser:-

I agree with you on both points. It would be more effective to have some sort of overt action, and "Ragpicker", or, better still, "Ragman", would seem more child-like than "Scavenger". The two cops are done to the life; it is actually a defect in the sketch that they are more interesting than the old man. But I think the thing might very well go into the book. It is not open to the objections that lie against the other one.

By the way, there is no such word as "alright". It should be "all right", two words. I filed a caveat on this subject some time ago; I see that I must proceed to a formal suit.

Wright is coming down to Baltimore tomorrow.[1] I wish you were coming too. My new jitney bus makes at least 12 miles an hour on level roads, and I have laid in some synthetic red wine. Give us your prayers.

Yours,
M

1. Willard Huntington Wright, at this time the literary critic of the New York *Evening Mail*.

[UPL-H]

SMART SET
A Magazine of Cleverness
452 Fifth Avenue, New York

[after 20 November 1915]

Dear Dreiser:-

Who in hell is N. P. D?[1] Some lousy old maid?

The Bourne notice shows careful thought @ has more than one good touch. The paragraph next to the last is exactly right.[2] Curiously enough, Wright[3] said the same thing some time ago.

Yours,
M

1. See Mencken to Dreiser, 2 November 1915, n.1.

2. Mencken is referring to the review of *The "Genius"* by Randolph Bourne, "Dreiser as Hero," *New Republic* 5(20 November 1915), 5–6. The passage he is pointing to reads, in part, "And for all its dull and rather cheap texture, the book is set in a light of youthful idealism. Nobody but Mr. Dreiser could manage this fusion, but it is there."

3. Willard Huntington Wright.

[NYP]

Nov. 28—1915

H. L. M.

The two stories you pointed out to me in the Smart Set are clever after their kind but not very important.[1] I may seek the rights for them a little later, assuming that I take over the art and literary direction of this institution which seems probable. But have you any larger theme in mind—something with poetry and poignance in it—to last 5 reels.

By the way "Old Ragpicker" will be produced here February next by a new theatre movement.[2] Incidently I have a two years vaudeville contract for it offered me but I am not certain that I want it butchered by a clown.

Hoch Hindenburg! Von Besseler! Von Mackensen! Von Tirpitz! Hock![3]

Th.D.

1. See Mencken to Dreiser, 14 October 1915.

2. *Old Ragpicker* was not produced in New York.

3. Dreiser is toasting German military leaders: Generals Paul von Hindenburg, Haus von Besseler, August von Mackensen, and Admiral Alfred von Tirpitz.

[UPL]

H. L. Mencken
1524 Hollins St.
Baltimore.

November 29th. [1915]

Dear Dreiser:-

At the moment I can think of nothing that would last 5 reels. But I rather believe the fantastic tales of Lord Dunsany,[1] poetically done, would make a colossal success in the movies. Do you know them? I am acquainted with Dunsany, and, if he is not already killed in the war, I rather think I could get you his permission to use his stuff. So far as I know, no one else has ever touched it. And even if you don't use it, it should suggest other fantastic stuff. Get his book, "Tales of Wonder."

Go slow in the vaudeville matter. Vaudeville is a fearful mess.

Exit Serbia! Ta-rah!

Yours,

M

1. Edward John Morton Drax Plunkett, eighteenth Baron Dunsany (1878–1956), author, playwright, sportsman, soldier. He was closely associated with Dublin's Abbey Theatre and, with the support of Mencken and Nathan, achieved a great popularity in America.

[UPL]

H. L. Mencken
1524 Hollins St.
Baltimore.

December 6th. [1915]

Dear Dreiser:-

Please don't forget to exhume that poetry.[1] I am very eager to see it.

By the way, the man I spoke to you about lately, Ernest A. Boyd, will probably be in New York December 19th, and if you say so I'll bring him to your house. Wright knows him. This Boyd writes for the New Age and for various French reviews, and is about to do an article on you for one of the latter. More, his wife,[2] a clever Frenchwoman, is eager to translate "Sister Carrie". Altogether, I believe that it would help the cause along to be polite to him. Fortunately, he is an excellent fellow, and I am sure you will like him. But if you'd rather put him off, say so. I can always handle him.

I am getting too old to sit up all night. Sunday I slept until 11 A.M., and all day today I have heard my arteries hardening and clicking.

Highly confidential detail: Boyd is the British Vice-Consul at Baltimore, but is of safe and sane views. He has lived in Germany and speaks the language almost as well as he speaks French. He got into the consular service on account of his linguistic talents.

Hochactungsvoll!

M

1. Dreiser had promised Mencken a number of his poems for *Smart Set*.
2. Madeleine Boyd, who later became literary agent for, among others, Thomas Wolfe.

[NYP]

Tues Dec 7—1915

Dear H. L. M.

Bring Boyd along. If he fails to fit in we'll chase you to the nearest dock where the water is deep.

Th.D.

The enclosed letter came this AM.[1]

1. The letter has not been identified.

[UPL]

SMART SET

A Magazine of Cleverness

George Jean Nathan

and   } Editors

H. L. Mencken

December 8th. [1915]

Dear Dreiser:-

The Nation article is a masterly exposure of what is going on within the Puritan mind, and particularly of its maniacal fear of the German. Let the degraded swine squeal! We can stand the noise—if they can stand what is coming to them. Compare Wilson's amazing exhibition of alarm and hatred in his harangue to Congress. Such things fill me with the utmost delight. I am sending the Nation article to Wright, and asking him to return it to you promptly. Let us discuss it December 18th.

As for Lengel's suggestion, let us go over that, too.[1] I have a plan for a sort of review of reviews.[2] But not, assuredly, for the Atlantic Monthly! But of this, more anon.

Yours in Xt.,

M

What of your poetics?[3]

1. William C. Lengel, at this time editor of *Hoggson Magazine* in New York (see Dreiser to Mencken, 10 October 1915, n.1).
2. Mencken's idea was to do a humorous overview of the reviews of *The "Genius."*
3. The postscript is handwritten.

[UPL]

H. L. Mencken
1524 Hollins St.
Baltimore.

December 20th. [1915]

Dear Dreiser:-

This Peattie stuff is a scream.[1] The fair wench is a novelist herself, and her last one was sweetly praised by Hildegarde Hawthorne.[2] By all means, let me have this masterpiece of the ovarian school when the time comes to write the review of the reviews. What a noble world we live in! The loveliest part of all I have marked with a pencil, in the second column. Note the maddening dilemma of poor Ella! The horrible thought that God, after all, <u>may</u> be a comedian darn nigh drives her crazy.

I enjoyed Saturday night's session immensely. But I should have gouged that poetry out of you while the chance offered. Where is it? By this mail I am sending a copy of Nathan's book.[3] It is light-headed, but full of good stuff. Don't try to read it at a sitting. It is for odd moments.

May the birthday of our late Lord and redeemer find you boozy and happy.

Yours in Xt.,
M

1. Mencken is referring to Elia W. Peattie's moralistic review of *The "Genius,"* "Mr. Dreiser Chooses a Tom-Cat for a Hero," Chicago *Daily Tribune*, 4 December 1915, 5; repr. in Salzman, 242–44.
2. Hildegarde Hawthorne (1871–1952), novelist and biographer who was the granddaughter of Nathaniel Hawthorne.
3. Nathan's *Another Book on the Theatre*.

[NYP]
Dec. 24—1915

Fairest Mencken:

Here are seven poems. They are submitted subject to these conditions. (1) That all seven be published at the same time, as a group   (2) That they be published in the order numbered. If you feel that any of them will do me harm let me know. I rather like them, as a group.

Th.D.
Phauna Kuchen, Miss Twitez
Lengelhengel,
Hands Knocken, Affel Strudel.[1]

1. Life
2. There Was a Girl
3. The Waterside
4. Woodnote
5. Ye Ages, Ye Tribes
6. For A Moment The Wind Died
7. They Shall Fall as Stripped Garments

1. Dreiser here is imitating Mencken's habit of listing gag names.

[UPL]

H. L. Mencken
1524 Hollins St.
Baltimore.

December 25th. [1915]

Dear Dreiser:-

This is the impression the group of poems makes on me: the first three are hopelessly commonplace, and two of them open with intolerable banalities, but the last four are truly excellent. "Wood Note" is genuinely superb; I am enthusiastic over it. "For a Moment the Wind Died" is almost as good. "Ye Ages, Ye Tribes" is a fine statement of your philosophy. Even "They Shall Fall as Striped Garments", despite the obviousness of the thought, is a sound poem. But why hook these with such obvious and hollow stuff as "Life is so Beautiful" and "How pleasant is the waterside"? I am wholly unable to understand the idea beneath the grouping. My recommendation is that the first three be dropped entirely and the last four be made into a group. The former will hurt you; the latter will be sure to do you good. I am so strongly of this opinion that I urge it with the utmost vigor, and if you dissent from it call for arbitration by some disinterested party, say Masters or Wright. Believe me, "Wood Note" is first-rate stuff. If you have more things of its kind you should print a volume of them, by all means. Nobody in this country is doing better. But please don't tie up your best with things so empty as "Life".

I hold the copy for your decision, which I hope will be favorable to my contention. If not, I'll come to New York week after next and tackle you head-on.

Yours in Xt.,
M

[NYP]
Jan 1—1916

Dear H. L. M.

    Let the four poems go as a group.

    Return the others.

    All my best wishes for 1916—Every one.

Th. D.

[UPL]

SMART SET

A Magazine of Cleverness

George Jean Nathan

and   } Editors

H. L. Mencken

January 4, 1916.

Mr. Theodore Dreiser,
165 West 10th Street,
New York City.

Dear Dreiser:

    Thanks very much for your letter. I am returning the first three poems and shall run the last four in a group.[1] I believe that this arrangement will be greatly to the advantage of the sequence. The highest price we can pay is 50c a line. Is this satisfactory?

    I enclose a letter head found upon a manuscript sent in by one of your contemporaries in Michigan.[2] The manner in which the gentleman designates his profession seems to me very sweet and delicate.

    Here's hoping that you passed through New Year's day with no more than the usual debauchery!

Sincerely yours,
H. L. Mencken

    1. The poems were published in *Smart Set* 49(May 1916), 277–78. They were republished in *Moods, Cadenced and Declaimed* (1926).

    2. This has disappeared.

[NYP]
Jan. 19—1916

My Dear Mencken:

    Thirty dollars is little enough for that group. Don't let your German war-time thrift get the best of you.

Look who's here. Theodore Dreiser, whose power and force have placed him in the forefront of American novelists, and who has demonstrated that he can write a realistic novel with something real in it.

Dreiser caricature with message to Mencken, 1916
(Astor, Lenox and Tilden Foundations)

Mr. Sherwood Anderson of Chicago tells me he is sending via you an mss which he wants me to get the Lane Co to publish.[1] Have you it?

I expect to go to Savannah, Ga. shortly for a time.

Th. D.

N.B. I wonder if you could get for me from the one or two leading book stores in Baltimore the exact number of copies of The "Genius" sold to date. A very important reason impels me to you to get the information as exact as possible.

1. Sherwood Anderson's first novel, *Windy McPherson's Son* (1916), which Dreiser helped to get published. Mencken reviewed the novel in the October issue of *Smart Set*.

[UPL]

H. L. Mencken
1524 Hollins St.
Baltimore.

January 21st. [1916]

Dear Dreiser:-

The market price for first-class verse, dear heart, is 50 cents a line. At this rate we are offered endless consignments of sound goods by the best firms in the business. But the finances are up to Nathan and if he finds it in his heart to throw away money I'll go with him. I am writing to him by this mail. I was in New York yesterday.

I'll send you the Anderson stuff shortly. But why Savannah? It is beautiful, but the Methodists are very strict down there, and every newcomer is carefully investigated. A cocktail breath is enough to damn a man.

I'll try to get the sales of "The 'Genius'" in Baltimore, but the thing presents difficulties. The bookstores are very tight with such information, and will lie nine times out of ten.

Yours in Xt.,
M

[UPL]

SMART SET
A Magazine of Cleverness
George Jean Nathan ⎫
and ⎬ Editors
H. L. Mencken ⎭

February 2, 1916

Dear Dreiser:

I find that it will be quite impossible for us to go beyond 50c a line for poetry at this time. If this seems too little, I can only return your four poems. Please let me know what your decision is. In any event, I shall surely not abandon my daily supplications for your salvation.

Yours in Xt,
HLM

Oh, the Appam! [1]

1. On 15 January 1916, a German cruiser captured the *Appam*, a British merchantman, and took the ship into Hampton Roads, Virginia. The American government released the English crew, and the courts decided that the ship and cargo should be returned. The German government appealed the decision to the Supreme Court, but it was turned down on the grounds that the action was a breach of American neutrality.

[NYP]

P.O. Box 282
Savannah, Ga.

Feb. 4—1916

My Dear H. L. M:

Friendship alone prevents me from cursing you out. I don't really give a damn about having the poems published. I rather not than otherwise. But because you were interested and not because of the $19 or $30 we will let it go as it stands. Or better yet, I'll make you a present of the horrible things with my compliments and paternal blessing. But why talk of 50 cents a line as a standard American price. There is no standard.

Th.D.

The Appam is the best yet: a howling German joke.

[UPL]

SMART SET
A Magazine of Cleverness
George Jean Nathan
and ⎱ Editors
H. L. Mencken ⎰

February 5, 1916.

Dear Dreiser,

I was already privy to this negotiation between Anderson and Jones, and have sent the manuscript to Jones.[1] Unfortunately my eyes were in such bad condition while I had it that I could not read it but I am asking Jones to send me an early proof.

I wrote to you from New York the other day about the poems. Frankly I believe that they are worth more than we offer and I rather suspect that you may be able to get more but we are fearfully short of money at the moment and Nathan insists that 50 cents a line is the best we can pay. Let us not quarrel about such a small matter. The manuscript is safe and its disposition is for you to determine.

What are you doing in Savannah? Acting in the movies? If so, I shall cheerfully risk a nickel to see you in your young beauty.

I need not add of course that my domestic chaplain has instructions to sing at least five masses for you every week, including two high masses of requiem.

Sincerly yours,
M

1. J. Jefferson Jones, the American representative of the John Lane Company.

[NYP]

P.O. Box 282

[after 5 February 1916]

My Dear Mencken:

Am just here writing & waiting for the moving picture situation to clear up. Only now I have finished a book ("A Hoosier Holiday"[1] I have named it tentatively) which I have been wanting to do for years—a sort of native heath, back home—here I once spent my boyhoods happy days stunt, only in this case I have used it as a means of sizing up the middle west and interpreting American character as well as tossing in a little personal history. It's not unsatisfactory to me—and cut some—it's not so very long will make an intermediate or change volume.

Incidentally I am working on "The Bulwark,"[2] and with this other thing out of the way will be able to give it my full attention. I have schemes for several plays but somehow don't get to them. Miss M is in New York playing with The Weavers.[3] I don't think she's coming down this way—not soon anyhow.

Much luck & please don't bother over the poems. They are yours as a gift. Let sleeping poems lie. The book of plays should be out by now. Will unload a <u>marked</u> copy if I may.

von Dreiser

1. *A Hoosier Holiday* was published on 17 November 1916 by John Lane.
2. According to Donald Pizer, who has made the most complete study of the evolution of *The Bulwark*, Dreiser started the novel in the fall of 1914. He expected "to complete the novel during the winter of 1915–16, and in response to this expectation John Lane prepared a salesman's dummy of the book which specified a 1916 publication" (*The Novels of Theodore Dreiser* [Minneapolis: University of Minnesota Press, 1976], 302). Dreiser worked sporadically on the novel until 1920 when he put it aside to undertake *An American Tragedy*. He did not return to the project in any sustained way until 1942 and finally finished it in 1945.
3. Kirah Markham was studying for a New York production of Gerhart Hauptmann's *The Weavers*.

[NYP]

Box 282
Savannah, Ga.

Feb. 8—1916

My Dear Mencken:

Let us have no more correspondence over the poems. They are yours as a Christmas present—Publish them at once.

While I read reports of men dying in blizzards in Cleveland Ohio, I sit on my balcony, watch ambling negroes with buckets on their heads selling apples and look at palm trees and flowers.

And all for a 20 hour run due south. Sometime in bitter weather try it: It's like throwing off a big, material load.

Th. D.

I am wrestling with <u>The Bulwark</u>.

[UPL]

SMART SET
A Magazine of Cleverness
George Jean Nathan
and   } Editors
H. L. Mencken

February 9, 1916.

Dear Dreiser,

Let the poetry matter go over for a couple of weeks, I want to consult my spiritual adviser.

What are you doing in Savannah? Be careful. The presence of barbarian Germans in any American seaport provokes grave suspicion and you may find yourself in jail on the charge of trying to mine the forts in the harbor.

Down at Tybee Island, 6 or 8 miles below Savannah, I came very near being drowned in the year 1902. Perhaps you will care to go to the spot and throw a beer keg overboard in memory of that historical event. The water, I dare say, is still dirty.

The Appan overfilled me with such mirth that I was quite unable to work for two days. Two or three more such jocosities and even Lansing[1] will be forced to snicker.

Sincerely yours,
H. L. M.

1. Robert Lansing, secretary of state.

[UPL]

SMART SET
A Magazine of Cleverness
George Jean Nathan
and   } Editors
H. L. Mencken

February 12, 1916.

Dear Dreiser,

What are your relations with the John Lane Co.? That is to say, are they satisfactory? I ask because I am thinking of offering Jones a small book. I don't want to do it if he has turned out badly. Wright tells me that his relations with Jones are satisfactory so far but that Jones is an American patriot of the worst type. Don't bother to answer this if you are busy; all I want is four or five words. The manuscript is not yet ready and there is plenty of time.

The Garrison episode shows how things are drifting in Washington.[1] Garrison was the only intelligent member of the cabinet and the fact that the army drew him was a source of much discontent in the navy. It would be a capital joke if Woodrow now promoted Daniels from the navy to the army.[2] I know at least 20 naval officers who would get drunk at once and stay drunk for at least a month. Daniels is the most thoroughly hated secretary the navy has ever had, and for sound reasons. He represents the filthiest type of ignorant American.

Sincerely yours,

HL. M.

1. On 10 February 1916, Lindley M. Garrison (1884–1932) resigned as secretary of war as a result of a disagreement with President Wilson over national defense legislation. Garrison favored a strong military establishment (a continental army of 400,000), while Wilson leaned toward what he called a "half-federalized militia" centered around state governments.
2. Secretary of the Navy Josephus Daniels. Newton D. Baker succeeded Garrison as secretary of war.

[NYP]

P.O. Box 282
Savannah, Ga.

Feb. 14—1916

Dear H. L—

My only complaint against the John Lane Co is this—that while the books with Harpers and the Century Co continue to sell—The Titan and The Genius—both more talked about than any of my books so far have fallen off. This in the face of a growing volume of private support which I hear from directly. After I had connected with The John Lane Co.—Poultney Bigelow told me that Gertrude Atherton has sued Lane in London and compelled him to disgorge.[1] Several years ago when a woman cashier walked off with $15,000 they let her go compromising as I understand it for a portion of the money. The question arises, did she know anything which caused them to be lenient? Again Jones—apparently not a bad fellow in his way—is only literary manager on a salary. The financial department is in the hands of an Englishman or two, personal representatives of Lane. Whether Jones personally had access to the books or not I don't know. I have a great aversion to changing publishers again. It looks so bad. And yet it seems to be my fate to be pursued by most irritating conditions.

Mind you I am not reflecting on Jones in person. He may be a victim of circumstances. Again I may be mistaken but my private advices from dealers indicate more sales than I have been paid for. That was why I asked you for information from Baltimore. I do not propose to change or to say anything to anyone outside yourself unless I obtain indisputable proof that I have been done. You will not, of course, hint of this to anyone. Aside from these facts my relations have been entirely agreeable.

Th. D.

I liked your two column article. This American situation is one of the most disagreeable I have lived through, politically. All letters addressed to me from Holland, where I have friends, are regularly taken off lines sailing directly from here and Holland and read and resealed by the <u>English</u> Censor. In other words we are a political appendage of John Bull. I have protested to the Postmaster General at Wash. but as yet have heard no reply

---

1. Poultney Bigelow had been Dreiser's friend since he began contributing to the *Delineator* in 1907. Gertrude Atherton (1857–1948), best-selling novelist, biographer, historian. In the late 1880s, she was part of what conservative critics termed "The Erotic School," that is, a group of writers who rebelled against the suppression of erotic love in fiction.

[UPL]

SMART SET

A Magazine of Cleverness

George Jean Nathan

and } Editors

H. L. Mencken

February 18, 1916

Dear Dreiser:

I am here in New York and have gone over the financial situation with Nathan. I seize and embrace your offer to give us your poems free of charge, cost or expense and accept it with respect to three of them. With respect to the fourth entitled "Wood Note", we find ourselves unable to see our way clear to take advantage of your kind hospitality. We therefore insist upon paying $25 cash for this poem, which works out to $3.62-1/2 a line. With the cheque, which will reach you next week, go the blessings and prayers of the firm.

Your book of plays has reached me this very minute from Jones, and I shall bury my snout in it on my way home tomorrow.

Let us pay strict attention to our religious duties during the next month or two. I believe that both of us will be killed by patriots within six months.

Yours,

HLM.

P.S. I notice that opposite to the title page of the book Jones gives a list of your works included in the "Trilogy" and that the third volume of the "Trilogy" is represented by a row of stars.[1] The thought seizes me that it would be a capital idea to use this row of stars as the title of the third volume. The novelty would be sure to interest and inflame the boobs. Jones, by the way, has made a very beautiful book.

I saw Wright last night and he, too, is preparing for death.

HLM

1. The third volume of the Cowperwood trilogy, *The Stoic*, was published posthumously in 1947.

[UPL]

SMART SET

A Magazine of Cleverness

George Jean Nathan

and } Editors

H. L. Mencken

February 21, 1916.

Dear Dreiser,

Thanks for your letter regarding Lane. It has made me give thought to some scheme for checking up his returns from Baltimore, but the more I think of it, the more difficult the thing seems. There are at least a dozen book stores here and even if one or two of them tell the truth about their sales, the rest would probably lie. All who would do so, it goes without saying, would lie on the side of exaggeration and the result might be embarrassing. It is conceivable, of course, that Lane may be making honest returns and that the difficulty may lie in the inefficiency of his selling force. In the absence of specific evidence against him, it would be difficult to do anything of value. It is simply the repetition of the old story: the author is at the mercy of the publisher.

I agree with what you say about Jones and it also coincides with Wright's opinion. Wright tells me that Jones is an American patriot of the purest ray serene, and hence somewhat foolish in certain directions, but that he is an honest man and sincerely eager to print good books. When I see him in a couple of weeks, I shall ask him about the sales of "The Genius" and shall try to pump something out of him.

Your complaints regarding interference with your mail from Holland will not get you much satisfaction; on the contrary you will find your name inscribed on the roll of traitors. It is now a dangerous thing for any American to complain against England in Washington. Lansing[1] has come out frankly on the side of virtue, honesty, justice and righteousness, and I hear that he never lets a day go past without giving out some story or other unfavorable to the Germans. Most people who complain about interference with the mails do not even get answers. It is Woodrow's settled determination to do nothing to embarrass and inconvenience England, and he does not care a hoot who objects. You will be lucky, with your German name, if your are not jailed the day the United States enters war.

Sincerely yours,
M

My best thanks for the autographed play-book, just in.[2] Jones made a very good looking book.[3]

1. Robert Lansing, the secretary of state.
2. Dreiser had written in a copy of *Plays of the Natural and Supernatural*, "For Henry L. Mencken, from Theodore Dreiser. With all my good wishes."
3. The postscript is handwritten.

[UPL]

SMART SET
A Magazine of Cleverness
George Jean Nathan
and   } Editors
H. L. Mencken

February 22, 1916.

Dear Dreiser,

My sincere congratulation to Miss Markham on the good job she made of the book. It is a really distinguished piece of work, particularly in the binding. I lent my first copy to a fair friend to read, but shall try to get it back this evening and send it to you.

Your specimen of Chicago German reminds me of a celebrated Baltimore example, to wit, "es gebt gar kein use das man talka tut".[1]

I understand, by the way, that you and I are to be penned up in the same detention camp. I only hope that it will be in St. Louis, or, failing that, in Union Hill, N.J.

Yours,

HL. M.

Remington, the leading Baltimore bookseller, told me today that he has sold 150 "Titans" and 75 "Geniuses" so far. He says that this is a fine sale for serious novels, and that Baltimore is a Dreiser town. He says "Gerhart" is his best regular seller, but that everyone of your books, including "A Traveler at 40," has sold well here. He is very eager for the book of plays @ for "The Bulwark", of which he seems to have heard. This Remington is an American patriot and down in his heart, I suspect, an uplifter, but he regards you with veneration. He is not to be confused with the Remington typewriter, which is a mechanical device.[2]

1. A macaronic phase: "there is no use, the man talks nonsense."
2. The postscript is handwritten.

[UPL]

H. L. Mencken
1524 Hollins St.
Baltimore.

March 11th. [1916]

Dear Dreiser:-

The only answer to the Anglo-Saxon is artillery. Let us await Der Tag[1] in patience. The Dillman letter[2] makes me weep, particularly the affecting tribute to Mrs. Cowperwood No. 1. What a country!

I heard Billy Sunday[3] the other night. You should have seen the converts—adolescent, chlorotic girls; silly-looking middle-aged women; men with blank eyes and no chins. In brief, a convention of masturbators. Of such is the Kingdom of Heaven!

Yours,

M

1. The day.
2. Willard Dillman, a businessman from Minneapolis, began writing to Dreiser about his books in 1916.
3. The evangelical preacher William A. Sunday (1862–1935).

[NYP-Pc]

Savannah

Wed. Mch 29—1916

Mail no more screeds to this charming place. Am leaving here Friday or Saturday for Washington and Philadelphia. May see you, for a moment, in passing. Should any mail, perchance, arrive detain it—I dont expect any.

Greetings
Th. D.

My old address in Washington for a day or two will be Gen. Delivery.

[UPL]

H. L. Mencken
1524 Hollins St.
Baltimore.

April 3rd. [1916]

Dear Dreiser:-
I'm very sorry I missed you yesterday.[1] I was in New York. Nathan is ill with neuralgia, and I brought him down to Baltimore this afternoon, and put him in the Johns Hopkins Hospital, where he will stay for four or five days for observation. Senility is what ails him, I dessay. I met Miss M. at Wright's Sunday night, and she said you would be in Washington for the rest of the week.

Yours in Xt.,
M

1. On his way back from Savannah, Dreiser had stopped in Baltimore to see Mencken.

[NYP]

165 W. 10th St.
N.Y.C

April 10—1916

Heinrich Leon:
I forgot to thank you for those two books on the war:—until I got to reading in one last night. Thanks very much. I propose to read further.

And—one more favor—could you find a copy of the review of the plays you wrote and let me have it.[1] I'll be grateful.

Th. D.

This I saw, in Washington—
Edgar A. Poe—
    Practical Horseshoer
And this in Philadelphia
    "The G.B.S. Brewery."

1. Mencken's review appeared later in the year: "A Soul's Adventures," *Smart Set* 49(June 1916), 154 (see Appendix 2, pp. 759–60).

H. L. Mencken
1524 Hollins St.
Baltimore.

April 11, 1916.

Dear Dreiser:

Within you will find a copy of "The Play Book Review". If you ever want any more, let me know.

The G. B. S. Brewery is a Baltimore corporation, and its former President, Frederick Gottlieb, is an old friend of mine. He retired from the company about two years ago and since then its brew has greatly deteriorated. I tell you this so you may not drink it incautiously and so destroy your kidneys.

Edgar A. Poe is another Baltimorian. He appears in many editions. One of them was, lately, Attorney-General of Maryland.

Yours in Xt.,
HLM

H. L. Mencken
1524 Hollins St.
Baltimore.

April 22, 1916.

Dear Dreiser:

From some unknown hand I receive notice that you have taken to the stump and will read one of your plays before an intellectual gathering next

Sunday. In vicarious expiation of this crime, I am going into a monastery to serve ten days. Moreover, I shall have my ruffians at the meeting and in the midst of your eloquent burbling, a dead cat will approach you at terrific speed. This is too, too much; henceforth, I consign you to hell along with Alfred Noyes and Henry Van Dyke.[1]

Yours in Xt.,

M

1. Alfred Noyes (1880–1958), English poet and educator who gained a wide popularity in America. Henry Van Dyke (1852–1933), author, educator, preacher. Both were literary conservatives who attacked naturalism.

[NYP]

165 W. 10th St.

April 23—1916

H. L. M.

Why does the heathen rage and imagine a vain thing. I am not going to read my plays to any gathering of any kind nor have I given anyone any authority so to say. When I was in Savannah Madge C. Jenison[1] an old friend of mine—(why do friends take such an intense delight in trimming you on occasion) wrote me that she was opening a book shop to sustain her in her old age and wanted me to read. I groaned in pain. Then she wanted me to be present with a "select group" when my plays were read. I fled in horror. Then she intrigued K. M.[2]—in my absence—to read them. Result this circular which I saw for the first time last Saturday.

I have threatened and stormed. The lady has been on her knees. I am telling all and sundry there is nothing to it but what can a poor scribe do. She has put one over on me. I shall not be present nor give aid or comfort but I fancy the plays will be read, willy-nilly some of them. In the meantime the thought of your vicarious atonement for old sins or new cheers me. Grant me a 900 days indulgence. Pickle the dead cat and save it for friends who betray friends. You will need it. And betimes I will provide you with a much better reason for attacking me you may be sure.

Alexander VIth

1. Dreiser first came to know Madge C. Jenison when she wrote for the Butterick magazines.
2. Kirah Markham.

[UPL]

H. L. Mencken
1524 Hollins St.
Baltimore.

May 12, 1916.

Dear Dreiser:

I have been working on a chapter about you for a book that I have under weigh and find myself stumped for one or two facts.[1] In the first place, I have been unable to make out to what extent, if any, you were influenced in your early days by Frank Norris. "McTeague" was published in 1899 and "Sister Carrie" in 1900, but it sticks in my mind that you once told me that you had not read "McTeague" when you wrote "Sister Carrie." Is this true? The two books, in many ways, show a similar attitude of mind though the differences between them are numerous and important. What is your remembrance of the influences you stood under at the time you began to write? You have told me that you had not read Zola or any of the Russians. Did Hardy influence you? I know that this is difficult ground, for a man can scarcely determine such things himself, but it occurs to me that you may remember some enthusiasm of that period and that it may account, to some extent, for your utter divergence from what was then the main stream of American fiction. Saving H. B. Fuller, I can think of no American novelist of the 80's or 90's who steered in anything even remotely approaching your own direction.

Incidently, what was the name of that novel by Arthur Henry which you spoke of in your house the other night?[2] I don't know that I will mention it at all but if I should happen to do so, I will want to get its title accurately.

Another thing: how long after the suppression of "Sister Carrie", by Doubleday, Page and Company, did William Heinemann bring out his London edition?[3]

Yours in Xt.,
M

Again, let me have that long Sheridan review in the Nation,[4] and that Chicago wench's review—the one in which parents are warned to defend their children against German kultur.[5]

M[6]

1. Mencken's *A Book of Prefaces* (1917). See Appendix 2, pp. 775–90.
2. Mencken is probably referring to *A Princess of Arcady* (1900), the novel Arthur Henry was working on while Dreiser was writing *Sister Carrie*.
3. The Heinemann edition appeared in 1901.

4. The reference is probably to the anonymous review in the London *Nation*, "A Methodical Novel," 18(8 January 1916), 550, 552.

5. Elia W. Peattie, "Dreiser's Plays, Natural and Supernatural," Chicago *Daily Tribune*, 18 March 1916, 7.

6. The postscript is handwritten.

[UPL]

H. L. Mencken
1524 Hollins St.
Baltimore.

May 13, 1916.

Dear Dreiser:

1. My advice is that you have nothing to do with Harré's committee.[1] Such manifestos only achieve the end of making Woodrow[2] more violent, and Harré himself is a fourth-rater and surely not worth following. I am told in Washington that Woodrow is walking around in a sort of Puritanical ecstasy and that his delusions of moral grandeur grow worse every day. What good can be accomplished by tackling such a monomaniac with argument?

2. Your treatise on the effects of laughing gas is interesting but by no means surprising.[3] Precisely the same effects are produced by drinking cocktails served at the Florestan club here in Baltimore.

3. The Boston moralist[4] takes a hack at me about every two weeks. I shall let him run on a while and then open on him with shrapnel. His discovery that there is nothing "sound and sweet" in the philosophy of Nietzsche is a scream. When Boyd read the phrase he almost died of joy.

4. Please rush me the information I asked for in my letter yesterday. My book is over half done and I want to finish it during the summer.

Sincerely yours,

M

1. T. Everett Harré was secretary of the Manifesto for Neutrality Committee, which advocated the maintenance of a strict neutrality in the war. In a letter of 8 May 1916, he asked for (but did not receive) Dreiser's signature. [UPL]

2. Woodrow Wilson.

3. The play *Laughing Gas*.

4. J. Frank Chase (1872–1926), the head of the Boston censorship group, The Watch and Ward Society. In 1926 Mencken would confront Chase directly in the famous "Hatrack" case (see Arthur Garfield Hays, *Let Freedom Ring* [New York, 1937], 164–85).

[NYP]

1̲6̲5̲ W̲. 1̲0̲

May 13—1916

Dear H. L. M:

I feel that you need a serious talking to or with about this whole business but since you are not here I will make a few remarks   Sister Carrie was written in the fall, winter and spring of 1899–1900. I never saw or heard of McTeague or Norris until after the novel had been written and turned in to Harper and Brothers who promptly rejected it with a sharp slap. Then I took it to Doubleday, Page & Co. and left it, curiously, in the hands of Frank Doubleday, who was sitting in the office usually occupied by Walter H. Page.[1] I was as green as grass about such matters, totally unsophisticated and I remember his looking at me with a kind condescending, examining smirk. At that I like Doubleday. He is such a big husky incoherent clown.

Be that as it may.

The week after I took "Sister Carrie" to Harpers, Rose White, a sister of Mrs. Dreiser came to visit us. We were then living at 102nd St. & Central Park West. She was reading a book called "McTeague" and liked it. Rose, who was peach in her way intellectually and otherwise, persuaded me to read it. It made a great hit with me and I talked of nothing else for months. It was the first real American book I had ever read—and I had read quite a number by W. D. Howells and others.

As a matter of fact my reading up to this time had been the standard American school reading of the time—Dickens, Scott, Thackeray, Hawthorne, Poe, Oliver Wendell Doughnut, Bret Harte, E. P. Roe (yes, E. P. Roe) George Ebers, Lew Wallace, Washington Irving, Kingsley, etc, etc, etc etc. At fourteen years of age I was dippy over Washington Irving, Twice Told Tales and Water Babies and used to lie under our trees by the hour and read them. I thought the Alhambra was a perfect creation and I still have a lingering affection for it.

I went into newspaper work (Chicago Globe, June 1—1891)[2] and from that time dates my real contact with life—murders, arson, rape, sodomy, bribery, corruption trickery and false witness in every conceivable form. The cards were put down so fast before me for awhile that I was a little stunned. Finally I got used to the game and rather liked it.

Incidently in Pittsburgh—1894—I discovered Herbert Spencer and Huxley and Tyndall.[3] They shifted my point of view tremendously, confirmed my worst suspicions and destroyed the last remaining traces of Catholicism which I now detest as a political organization or otherwise. At the same time I discovered Honore de Balzac—quite by accident—found one book on him and then got down "The Great Man from the Provinces" and began to read it. Need I tell you that it was a knockout. It was. I was quite beside myself and read three others without stopping. Then somehow I ceased and began reading George Eliot and Lord Lytton and seemed to get along very well. Incidently I made a study of Henry Fielding, who seemed and still does amazing. "Joseph Andrews" and "Tom Jones" have been favorites of mine for years.

Yet as late as 1897 and 1898 I never had the slightest idea that I would ever be a novelist. My bent, if you will believe it, was plays and had I been let alone I would have worked out in that form. As it was I then re-encountered in New York a young fellow whom I had met in Toledo, Ohio, four years before. Arthur Henry   At that time, 1894, he city editor of the Toledo Blade, newly married and very anxious to write. Somehow he had taken a fancy to me and now he hung about me all the time. He was tremendously well read, a genial critic and an able man. I think I told you something about him here. He was then advance agent for "Hermann, the Great"[4] but tremendously interested in the novel as a form and in short stories. He went on the road then but a year later when I had married, came back and camped in my apartment. It was he who persuaded me to write my first short story. This is literally true. He nagged until I did, saying he saw short stories in me. I wrote one finally, sitting in the same room with him in a house on the Maumee River, at Maumee, Ohio, outside Toledo. This was in the summer of 1898[5] and after every paragraph I blushed for my folly—it seemed so asinine. He insisted on my going on—that it was good—and I thought he was kidding me, that it was rotten, but that he wanted to let me down easy. Finally, <u>he</u> took it, had it typewritten and sent it to Ainslees. They sent me a check for $75.[6] Thus I began.

The above is exact and sacredly true.

Later he began to ding-dong about a novel. I must write a novel, I must write a novel. By then I had written four short stories or five, and sold them all.

1. Of the Shining Slave Makers
2. The Door of the Butcher Rogaum
3. The World and the Bubble[7]
4. Nigger Jeff
5. When the Old Century Was New.

He had a novel in mind—"A Princess of Arcady (Doubleday Page—1900—same year as Carrie)   He wanted to write it but he needed me, he confessed, to help him. Finally—September 1899 I took a peice of yellow paper and to please him wrote down a title at random—Sister Carrie—and began. From September to Oct 15th or thereabouts I wrote steadily to where Carrie met Hurstwood. Then I quit, disgusted. I thought it was rotten. I neglected it for two months, when under pressure from him again I began because curiously he had quit and couldn't go on. (Isn't that strange) Then I started and laughed at myself for being a fool. Jan. 25th or thereabouts I quit again, just before Hurstwood steals the money, because I couldn't think how to have him do it. Two months more of idleness. I was through with the book, apparently   Actually I never expected to finish it

About March 1 he got after me again and under pressure I returned to it. This time I nearly stopped because of various irritating circumstances—money principally—but since he was there to watch I pressed on and finally got it done. I took an intense interest in the last few much more so than in anything which had gone before. After it was done considerable cutting was suggested by Henry and this was done. I think all of 40,000 words came out. Anyhow there is the history   At that time, Henry's interest in "Sister Carrie" having been so great his own book was neglected and he could not finish the last chapter. Since he had told it to me so often and I knew exactly what he desired to say, I wrote it. But don't accuse him or me of it in public. It wouldnt be kind, I'm afraid.

In regard to The "Genius", I still feel that you are far astray in that book—and for your own sake, not mine, you ought to get in line. I do not propose to try to make you see what you cannot but I suggest you re-examine it sometime slowly and dispassionately. It will get over, even with you, for the stuff is there and happily co-ordinated, as long as it is. You change your mind as to books occasionally and you might as well consider changing your mind on this one before you record a final judgement.

Sister Carrie I notice gets over with those who love the shine and tingle of Broadway and the metropolitan atmosphere generally.

Jennie Gerhardt with emotionalists—especially women.

The Financier and The Titan uniformly appeal to men and women who have some real knowledge of business and finance and who are beyond good and evil in their views or would like to be.

The "Genius" is appealing to those who know love and sex and life generally—but not life in all its particulars, by any means.

Among the plays, "Laughing Gas" is supremely the best—personally I think the best thing I ever did.

Greeting.

I have just seen my adjectived self in the S.S.

Th D.

1. Walter H. Page (1855–1918), journalist, diplomat, publisher. With Frank Doubleday (1862–1934), Page began the Doubleday, Page firm in 1899.
2. Dreiser means 1892.

3. Dreiser shared with Mencken an early enthusiasm for the British naturalists Herbert Spencer, Thomas Huxley, and John Tyndall.

4. The magician Alexander Herrmann.

5. Dreiser means 1899.

6. *Ainslee's Magazine* published Dreiser's "The Shining Slave Makers," 7(June 1901), 445–50, and "Nigger Jeff," 8(November 1901), 366–75.

7. This title does not appear among Dreiser's published works or in manuscript.

[NYP]

Sunday. [14 May 1916]

H. L. M

I find in glancing over your letter that I haven't answered all your questions. After Balzac, (1894) came first Hardy (1896) and then Sienkiewicz— particularly Quo Vadis (1897) which made a deep impression on me. About this time I did a lot of general reading, Tolstoy, Stevenson, Barrie, Dumas—I cant think of a tenth of the stuff. But Hardy, Tolstoy and Balzac stood forth in my mind all the time. I have never read a line of Zola. Since 1906 or thereabouts I have become acquainted with Turgenev, Dostoyevsky, de Maupassant, Flaubert, Strindberg, Hauptmann etc. etc. but I couldn't possibly call them influences. They came too late. Actually I should put Hardy and Balzac first in that respect, though I seriously doubt whether I was influenced for in St. Louis (1892) I was already building plays of a semitragic character. My mind just naturally worked that way.

Th D

The Heinemann edition of Sister Carrie was published in the spring of 1901—I made a separate contract with him as Doubleday would not handle.

[UPL]

H. L. Mencken
1524 Hollins St.
Baltimore.

May 15th. [1916]

Dear Dreiser:-

My best thanks for your letter. It clears up a lot of dark places and heads me in the right direction. Curiously enough, though I never heard you mention Hardy, I had written a long paragraph arguing that he probably influenced you. The exact facts are excellent. Let me keep the clippings for a while; I won't get back to the essay for a couple of weeks. This afternoon I am going to New York, but whether I'll see you God knows; the office is in a mess. But I'll surely go over the whole thing with you before I send my book to Lane. Four of the eight chapters are blocked out and four-fifths written—those on you, Conrad and Huneker, and one on American best-sellers.

"The 'Genius'" is still my blind spot; more and more I put "The Titan" first, not for its contents, but as a work of art. Your best writing, and by long odds, is in it. Nor do I think that "Laughing Gas" is your best play. "The Blue Sphere" and "In the Dark" seem to me to be much better. If there is time, I want to get the Old Home Week book[1] and "The Bulwark" in.

The San Quentin letter[2] is immense. All the best Americans will be in prison in a few years.

Yours in Xt.,

M

1. *A Hoosier Holiday.*
2. Dreiser received a letter from an inmate at San Quentin prison who called himself Milton Goldberg and wrote Dreiser about the popularity of his books, especially *The Financier* and *The Titan*, among the prisoners. (6 May 1916 [UPL])

[UPL]

H. L. Mencken
1524 Hollins St.
Baltimore.

June 6, 1916

Dear Dreiser:

The Atlantic Monthly Review is typically and beautifully Anglo-Saxon.[1] In particular, I notice its atmosphere of moral deprecation. Please let me keep it a few weeks, as I want to mention it in my book. I notice the accusation of Teutonic deviltry. Ah, the brave loyalists!

Last week's grand victory of the English high seas fleet fills me with indescribable mirth.[2] For the first time in six months I have been reading the newspapers diligently and enjoying them immeasurably. The English explanations belong to high comedy and I shall not forget them when I get to work on my book on the Anglo-Saxon Under the Terror.

Sincerely yours,

M

And now Kitchener![3] Har, har![4]

1. An anonymous review, "Recent Reflections of a Novel-Reader," *Atlantic Monthly* 117(May 1916), 632–42. The piece argues for "literary romances" as an antidote to naturalism in fiction, and it discusses *The "Genius,"* among other books. The article says Dreiser's philosophy reduces life to "filth and froth" and, with pointed irony, praises his industry as "quite Teutonic in fact" (637).
2. The important battle of Jutland ended on 1 June 1916 with English and German announcements of victory; Mencken's laughter is at the expense of the English, who sustained the greater losses.
3. Field Marshall Horatio H. Kitchener was killed on 5 June when his ship ran into a German mine.
4. The postscript is handwritten.

[NYP]
165 W. 10th St.

May 11, 1916[1]

Dear H. L. M:

At the end of this week—June 16 or 17—I will be sending you by express—or if you are over here I will give it you—a complete, typewritten copy of "A Hoosier Holiday"   Do me the favor to read it carefully and advise me as to policy in connection with certain things in it which I am sure will halt your eye without any comment from me. I write this so that in case you are in N.Y. I may turn over the mss here.

Greetings. I am beginning to feel better about life now that the accursed English domination is beginning to turn to a wraith. No peace to its ghost. I want the Germans to come out once more.

Th. D

N.B. Booth's[2] illustrations for this thing—32 full pages—are something to be considered critically. They are very beautiful. Will send you proofs of them later.

1. Dreiser means 11 June 1916.
2. Franklin Booth.

[NYP]
165 West 10th Street
New York, N.Y.

[before 19 June 1916]

Dear Henry L—

This will introduce Anna Tatum,[1] one of the best and sanest brains I know anything about. She can write—and well, if she would, but she wants to editor or advise in a publishing house or magazine office. Entirely aside from this I think you ought to know her. Five minutes conversation will make plain why. And after you've talked with her I am satisfied that you will be pleased to do anything you can. I respect her taste, judgement and general brain force immensely—I really do. No uplift or reaction here.

> Yours
> Dreiser

This is on the level and no private audiences are necessary.

1. Anna P. Tatum (1882–1950) was a bright graduate of Wellesley living in Fall-sington, Pennsylvania, when she wrote to Dreiser on 7 November 1911, telling him of the impact on her of *Jennie Gerhardt* and "The Mighty Burke." In the fall of 1912, after many letters had passed between them, Tatum and Dreiser met in New York for the first time. She told him about her Quaker ancestors—particularly about her devout father's personal career, which moved Dreiser to begin planning a novel based on the story. Thirty-odd years later that novel appeared as *The Bulwark* (1946). Dreiser and Tatum lived together in 1912, and she worked with him on *The Titan*. Later correspondence at the University of Pennsylvania shows that in the 1930s she began again to edit and type his work. Dreiser turned his relation with her into a fictional account in "This Madness: The Story of Elizabeth," *Hearst's International-Cosmopolitan* 86(April 1929), 81–85, 117–20; and 86(May 1929), 80–83, 146–54.

[UPL]

> H. L. Mencken
> 1524 Hollins St.
> Baltimore.

> June 19, 1916.

Dear Dreiser:

The manuscript has not yet reached me. Have you delayed sending it or is the express company at its old trick of holding packages to find out if their contents are spoil?

> Yours in Xt.,
> M

Miss Tatum came in Friday, @ we had a pleasant talk. There is no job for her in the S.S. office, but I think we can come to terms about some stuff.[1]

1. The postscript is handwritten.

[NYP]

<u>165 W. 10th St.</u>

Friday, June 23rd 1916

Sire:

Under separate cover (Adams Express) I am sending you now the 1st carbon of A Hoosier Holiday—complete—62 chapters.

Judgement!

Th. D.

[UPL-H]

H. L. Mencken
1524 Hollins St.
Baltimore.

[24 June 1916]

Dear Dreiser:

The ms. is here, and I shall read it before I get to N.Y. Why not victual with me Friday evening, June 30th; we can then talk it over? I nominate the Lafayette[1] at 6:30.

M

1. The Lafayette Hotel, on 9th Street at University Place.

[NYP]

<u>165 W. 10th St.</u>

June 24—1916

Fairest Ludwig:

Somewhere in the book you will come to a place where the exact title of Kitchener is missing. Here it is

Field Marshall Lord Kitchener, K.G. Will you fill it in.

I read the Vivisectionist of Women.[1] It is a fine piece of work. Plainly you wrote it. If it is intended as a warning to me—cheer up. I will never end that way. I may organize a new order of mystics—non-religious and non-theoretic to which, once you reach seventy, you may be invited by my heirs and assigns or I may turn the order over to you at my death. Unless this is done, I very much fear that after the fashion of most intellectuals (can I claim admission?) I am destined to die alone.

Sometime recently I put into the John Lane safe for present keeping Vol 1 of The History of Myself.[2] I am instructing Jones to this effect: that in case anything happens to me this manuscript is to be turned over to you and your judgement as to its disposition followed. In case anything should happen to you kindly arrange further for its care. You can guess why of course. If it ever fell into the hands of Mrs. Dreiser or some of my relations I am satisfied that they would destroy it at once.

Th. D.

N.B. Jones wants 150 or 200 words or something like that concerning "A Hoosier Holiday" as well as "The Bulwark" to put in a trade circular as well as on the jacket of the book. Could you possibly dope these out for me? I find it almost impossible to do these things intelligently for myself.

Accept my affectionate regard.

1. In *Smart Set* 49(June 1916), 3–33.
2. This appeared as *Dawn* (1931).

[UPL]

H. L. Mencken
1524 Hollins St.
Baltimore.

June 26, 1916.

Dear Dreiser:

1. I have had three copies made of the insert and am inclosing two of them herewith.

2. I shall insert the name of Kitchener in the proper place. I notice several errors and omissions. For one thing, you speak of Gustavus Myers' book on the great American fortunes as in four volumes. My copy is in three volumes.[1] Was a fourth ever published? Curiously enough, I have had it in mind for some time to write an article on this work, which has been so much neglected that it is practically unknown. Despite a lot of Socialist fustian, it is one of the best books ever done in America. Naturally enough, it was not done by an American.

3. I note what you say about your autobiography and shall leave a memorandum among my papers providing for its disposition in case of my death. It is conceivable that we may enjoy the felicity of dying together— for example, in battle for the Republic. Let us discuss the question of a substitute editor when we meet.

4. I will be delighted to do the catalog notes for "A Hoosier Holiday"

and "The Bulwark", but it had better be put off until I see you. I suggest that we meet at the Lafayette at 6:30 on Friday evening and put in the rest of the evening discussing the problems of theology and statecraft. If I don't hear from you, I shall assume that you will be there. Meet me in the entrance hall.

5. No; I didn't write "The Vivisectionist of Women." The thing was actually done by Vere Tyler. But I wrote the whole of the first chapter and re-wrote parts of all the rest. The idea, however, was Mrs. Tyler's and so was the plan of the story in every detail. I didn't insert a single incident. Even in the first chapter, I followed her general idea faithfully. The difficulty with the novelette as it reached us was that it was badly written. But the scheme of it was well devised and the characters well thought out.

I have read about 75,000 words of "A Hoosier Holiday" and I am proceeding forward steadily at twenty-five miles an hour. The book is full of excellent stuff—some of the very best you have ever done. I am constantly outraged, however, by banalities, and it seems to me that they should come out. My hands itch to get at the job. I hope that I will be able to convert you to it when we meet. The pastoral scenes are beautifully written. How long is it? I feel it must run to 200,000 words or even more. This is too much for such a book.

Yours in Xt.,
HLM

1. Gustavus Myers (1872–1942), Socialist historian who wrote a three-volume study of the great American fortunes.

[NYP]

165 W. 10th St.

June 27—1916

Dear H. L. M.

If you can serve me in so definite a way (in regard to the banalities) and will, for heaven's sake do it. Make a list of all objectionable spots and I'll go over it with you swiftly. I doubt there are over 125,000 words. The chapters average less than ten pages of 250 words each. Some have as low as 6 or seven pages. Booth has done a stunning cover for the thing—in fact he has made a fine book in plan anyhow. It depends on Jones[1] now as to execution

Th. D.

1. J. Jefferson Jones.

[UPL]

H. L. Mencken
1524 Hollins St.
Baltimore.

June 28, 1916.

Dear Dreiser:

If the book is 125,000 words long, as you say, the cuts I propose would reduce it to just the right length; that is, between 80,000 and 100,000 words. Most of them are in the early part, though there are a few important ones toward the close. For example, some of your discussion of women in the college chapter seems to me to be very unwise. Also the Day Allen Willy episode had better be changed, at least, to the extent of disguising Willy's name.[1] He is now a highly respectable Baltimorean and a God-fearing man. The slightest suspicion that he had ever engaged in so carnal an enterprise as that you describe would cause his expulsion from the Unitarian church, and probably lose him his home.

I'll bring the manuscript with me and go over it with you Friday night. Many of the changes I propose are verbal and to make them properly would require a thorough re-reading of the manuscript, and at least a week of time. The book contains so much charming and excellent matter that I hate to see it go into type with the slightest blemish.

Yours in Xt.,
M

1. Dreiser changed Willy's name to W—— in chapter 60 of *A Hoosier Holiday*.

[UPL]

SMART SET
A Magazine of Cleverness
George Jean Nathan
and   } Editors
H. L. Mencken

July 5th. [1916]

Dear Dreiser:-

Unexpectedly, I have been able to put in two days on the ms., and so I have got through it, and am returning the last half by express today. The changes I propose are relatively few, and making them will leave no appreciable mark on the book. Most of them involve the excision of repetitions: your discussion of the nature and meaning of life, for example, is repeated a dozen times, and often in very similar words. Again, there are many smaller repetitions. Yet again, certain words are overworked—for example, secure—and I have substituted synonyms. Yet again, I have performed some discreet surgery upon the Day Allen Willy episode, and upon others of its sort. In the main, I have let the discussion of the Catholic church stand. They are against you anyhow. Why not strike back? You do it very effectively. So with the Puritans.

The book, on a second reading, seems very good to me. It contains, in fact, the best writing you have ever done. A genuine feeling for style is in it.

I'll be in New York in about a week.

Gott mit uns!¹
M

1. God be with us.

[NYP]

<u>165 W. 10th</u>

July 6th 1916.

Henry L—
You said you were sending the 1st half on July 4—It hasn't come though I expect it today. Better insure last half for $50 or thereabouts so the dear company will have a slight care.

Hock!
Th. D

[NYP]

<u>165 W. 10th</u>

Friday, July 7—1916

Henry L—
Both Express packages arrived this A.M. and I have just finished examining your cuts and elisions. With all but one or two I agree heartily and I may come to see the others. For all this, thanks—a damned poor reward, isn't it? Well, I'll do you a turn sometime. Meanwhile I can't help slyly chuckling over the spectacle of H. L. M cutting out all lewd, obscene and lascivious references. You must love me a lot, really.

Greeting and much beer

Th D

[UPL]

H. L. Mencken
1524 Hollins St.
Baltimore.

July 11, 1916.

Dear Dreiser:

The Floyd Dell article in The Masses convinces me more than ever that Dell is a hollow fellow.[1] His notion that Cooperwood is not a man worth drawing is a truly amazing piece of criticism. Obviously, he has completely missed any adequate understanding of the stature and significance of "The Titan". I can imagine no more silly criticism. "The Bulwark" should be a sufficient answer to his suggestion in the latter part of his article. But what he wants you to do, plainly, is to compose a prose hymn to some tinpot Socialist.[2]

I am going to New York tomorrow and shall call you up Thursday morning and send for the manuscript.

Yours in Xt.,
Mencken von Deutschland

1. Floyd Dell, "Talks with Live Authors: Theodore Dreiser," *The Masses* (August 1916), 36.
2. Dell concluded the article with a question to Dreiser: "Why do you not write the American novel of rebellion?"

[UPL-HPc]

Baltimore, Md.

July 21 1916

Here are the boys who brought over the submarine.[1] A fine bunch of barbarians!

M

1. The postcard shows a picture of a crew of German sailors.

[UPL]

H. L. Mencken
1524 Hollins St.
Baltimore.

July 26, 1916.

Dear Dreiser:

This fragment is from the rough notes of my book.[1] If you see anything in it that is too absurd, please let me know and I'll make the proper correction. There will be other installments later on.

Perhaps it would be well not to show the inclosed to Jones. There are several references in it that may excite his patriotic ire and he may want to cut them out of the book. It will be easy enough to slip them in the actual book manuscript. I believe that Jones never reads a book manuscript.

Yours in Xt.,
M

1. Mencken here sends Dreiser his article, "Theodore Dreiser," published this day in the Baltimore *Evening Sun*. The article was based on the notes for his chapter on Dreiser that would appear in *A Book of Prefaces*.

[NYP]

165 W. 10th St.

July 27—1916

H. L. M.

Thanks for the clipping. I'll look it over and mark any errors and send it back.

In passing—the censor has descended on The "Genius" and ordered Jones to withdraw it from the market. He claims complaints have been filed in New York and Cincinnati.[1] Dont write Jones concerning this or say anything until I get further details. Jones is apparently anxious to compromise and I do not intend that he should unless I have to but I have promised silence until the specific objections are laid down. So far they are "blasphemy" and "immorality". You may be called upon as an expert, later

By the way send me thirty copies of the article—the full page on which it appears. I can use them now to advantage.

Th. D.

This book was selling the best of any and now this cuts me off right in mid stream.[2] Dont it beat hell.

1. The censorship of *The "Genius"* began in Cincinnati when a Baptist minister, the Rev. John Herget, complained of the book's "immorality and blasphemy" to F. L. Rowe, secretary of the Western Society for the Prevention of Vice. Rowe had the book removed from Cincinnati bookstores and alerted John Sumner, of the New York Society for the Suppression of Vice. On 25 July 1916, Sumner went to the John Lane office and threatened J. Jefferson Jones with criminal proceedings unless he withdrew the book. Fearing charges of shipping obscene matter, after postal inspectors inquired about the book, Jones ordered further shipments through the mail stopped and instituted a nationwide recall from bookstores.

2. By this point, the book had been selling for ten months, and its sale of 6,202 copies in the last quarter of 1915 had dropped to 1,685 in 1916. Still, Dreiser did lose money on royalties when the book was recalled.

[UPL]

H. L. Mencken
1524 Hollins St.
Baltimore.

July 28, 1916.

Dear Dreiser:

Can you get a bill of complaint from the moralists—that is, an exact statement of the passages they object to? In the absence of such details it is impossible to make any plans of defense. As you know, I have been in combat with these gentlemen on various occasions and know something of their methods of work. I needn't tell you that it is an extremely difficult thing to combat them in court, for all judges are eager to appear as moral gladiators, and though they hate the Comstocks, nevertheless, they want to cut a pious figure in the newspapers. The charge of blasphemy need not bother you. No such crime is known to American law. But the charge of immorality is more serious. It seems to me that Jones is approaching the matter in a wise way. The thing to do with the moralists in the case of such valuable a property as "The Genius" is to offer some sort of compromise and so force them into the position of negotiating with you. In the end, if the thing is properly managed, it will be unnecessary to take out more than a few sentences. My feeling is that it is always better to do this than to risk the complete suppression of the book. After all, we are living in a country governed by Puritans and it is useless to attempt to beat them by a frontal attack—at least, at present. The war against them is so badly organized and the average American is such a poltroon that it is next to impossible to get help. I'll tell you when we meet the story of the Parisienne case,[1] and in particular, that part of it dealing with the desertion of the gentlemen we had trusted. The country is in a state of moral mania and the only thing for a prudent man to do is to stall off the moralists however he can and trust to the future for his release. If this attitude may seem to be pessimistic, please don't forget that it is born of extraordinarily wide experience. My whole life, once I get free from my present engagements, will be devoted to combatting Puritanism. But in the meantime, I see very clearly that the Puritans have nearly all of the cards. They drew up the laws now on the statute books and they cunningly contrived them to serve their own purposes. The only attack that will ever get anywhere will be directed—not at the Puritan heroes but at the laws they hide behind. In this attack I am full of hope that shrapnel will play a part.

I shall be in New York on Monday and shall try to get into communication with you. Not a word has come from Jones. Please keep the whole matter quiet.

Sincerely yours,
M

1. To make money, Mencken and Nathan published on the side a number of mildly risqué magazines like the *Parisienne, Saucy Stories*, and *Black Mask*. The censors brought *Parisienne* to court in 1915, but the case was quickly dismissed.

[NYP]

Great Neck, L.I.

July 29—1916

H. L. M.

In re The "Genius".—The Cincinnati Anti-Vice Soicety is at the bottom of it apparently. Has filed charges with the P.O. authorities at Washington and with Sumner of the Comstock Society here. The latter has ordered Jones to withdraw all copies or they will sue. Pending legal advice he has agreed so to do. The Federal Agents have called. One has read the book & thinks its bad. The other, his assistant, as I understand it is for it. He wants to call his chief off.

Jones' first scare has passed & I am doing my best to pump him up to a fighting point   I have a plan. Am perfectly willing to break the postal laws and go to jail myself. It will save me my living expenses this winter   He seems willing to hire counsel and fight now if his directors will agree to it. There is to be a meeting sometime next week at which I am to be present. If you can think of anything that will hearten him act on it. The Lane Co is rich enough to do something for the cause of liberty in this respect

The exact specifications are these.
Lewd:

Pages 20-21-43-44-46-51-52-55-56-70-71-72-78-79- 124-125-126-127-128-129-130   131-150-151-152-154-155-156-158-159-160-161-163- 164-167-168-171-179-180   183-245-246-340 341-342-343-344-345-348-350-351-445-446-531-533-539-540-541-542-551-552-553-554. 555-556-557-558-567-569-585-588-595-596-597-599-

Profane:-

192-335-356-379-389-408 409-410-421-431-469-566-618-678-713-718-722

> Greeting.
> Visit me in my cell.
> Th.D.

[NYP]

165 W. 10th St.

July 31—1916

Dear H. L. M.

I am not for compromise and Messieurs the Anti-Vicers do not want compromise either. So the thing is going to the Courts if I can persuade Jones or I may go to jail for mailing a copy. Only the hot weather deters me.[1] Enclosed is the report. Imagine editing all the pages! Allons, mon enfant. To the pen with me. There is no escape

> ThD

The "Genius"
    Lewd—
    Pages

> 20-21-43-44-46-51 52-55-56-70-71-72- 78-79-124-125-126-128
> 129-130-131-150-151-152-154-155-156-158-159-160-161-163-
> 164-167-168-171-179-180-183-245-246-340 341-342-343-344-
> 345 348-350-351-445-446 531-533-539-540-541 542-551-552-
> 553-554 555-556-557-558-567 568-585-588-595-596-597-599

Profane

> Pages: 192-335-356-379 389-408-409-410-421 431-469-566-
> 618-678-713-718-722

---

1. Dreiser did not mail a copy, even after the weather had cooled.

[UPL]

SMART SET
A Magazine of Cleverness
George Jean Nathan
and   } Editors
H. L. Mencken

August 3, 1916

Dear Dreiser:

I have been trying in vain to get you by telephone. At first the company reported that there was no phone in your house, and now with your actual number they report that they can get no answer. Unluckily, I have to go back to Baltimore today. Please let me know exactly what the status of "The Genius" case is. Have the moralists actually begun proceedings? I hear that Jones is out of town for three weeks. I have no copy of the book here and so I can't check up the complaints until I get home. I am convinced that it will be possible to stall them off without doing the book any essential damage. For many reasons it seems to me unwise to put through the plan you propose. You would not have one chance in a million against them. Immediately you put critics on the stand in your defense, they would get before the judges all the anti-German snorting that has been printed. And the result would be a mad glad time of it for the patriots.

I will return in ten days.

Yours in Xt.,
M

P.S. Don't think I am indisposed to fight the moralists. As a matter of fact I have been fighting them for many years, and in The Parisienne case I helped to beat them. But you would go into battle with very serious handicaps.

[NYP]

165 W. 10

Aug 4—1916

Henry L:

I need 20 more of that remarkable study which you are doing.[1] I wish the whole thing were in my hands now. It will do us both a great deal of good. It is so sound.

In regard to the Vice attack, nothing new. Jones is due back, next Wed. I think. If it were a question of a few changes I would say fine. But consider. And each one is enough according to Sumner to suppress on. A fight

Dreiser in his study (University of Pennsylvania Library)

is the only thing & I want Lane to fight. I hope & pray they send me
to jail

Th. D

That G. J. Nathan study of his own book is antagonizingly bumptious.[2]
You ought to tone him down.

1. The 26 July and 1 August articles ("Theodore Dreiser" and "More Dreiseriana")
in the Baltimore *Evening Sun*, which became part of the Dreiser chapter in *A Book of Prefaces*. On this day, Mencken published a third piece called "Two Dreiser Novels."
2. Nathan's review of his *Another Book on the Theatre*, "And in the Name of Criticism," *Smart Set* 49(July 1916), 283–91.

[UPL]

H. L. Mencken
1524 Hollins St.
Baltimore.

August 4, 1916.

Dear Dreiser:

Going through the pages marked by the moralists, I find they have
fallen into their characteristic extravagances. Page after page marked as
indecent is utterly harmless, and I can't see more than half a dozen pages
that they could reasonably take before a jury. This examination of their
own evidence very considerably augments the chances that they may be
beaten. If, as you say, Jones has gotten over his alarm and is ready to fight,
I begin to believe that your plan may be the best one after all. The chief
danger, aside from those I mentioned in my last letter, lies in the faint-
heartedness of your associate in the defense; that is to say, if Jones is convinced that the moralists have a good case, you yourself can scarcely hope
to beat them, but if Jones is convinced that he can win, then I believe that
the chances of actually doing so are very greatly improved. As for the
charges of profanity, they are childish and need not concern you. The
Postal Act says nothing whatever about profanity. Its exact words are: "any
obscene, lewd, lascivious, filthy, or disgusting book." It would be strain-
ing a point to call such phrases as "God damn it" disgusting. The New
York Act of March 4th, 1909, uses the words "obscene, lewd, lascivious,
filthy and indecent." Here again you will find no mention of blasphemy.
As a matter of fact, I believe that blasphemy is a crime unknown to American law. Surely, the occasional use of "Jesus Christ" in "The Genius" is
not a violation of any existing act. If they base any process on it at all, it
will have to be under the common law and I doubt that the common law
still runs in such matters.

Let me know the result of Jones' conference with his directors. Wright told me on Wednesday that Jones had left town for three weeks and so I made no effort to see him, though I had business with him regarding my own books. After trying in vain to get hold of you, I was told by M[1] that you were out all day investigating records at the World office. I return to New York on August 14th, ten days hence. Let us have a meeting. My experience in the Parisienne case may offer some suggestions. The thing I am most afraid of, as I wrote to you, is the introduction into the case of the German spy fear. A man accused of being a German has no chance whatever in a New York court at this time. He would be better off, if anything, before an English court.

My best thanks for your corrections in my Sun article. I'll make all of them. More installments will reach you from time to time.

Please don't get the notion that I am disinclined to tackle the moralists. The one thing I am against is tackling them with both hands tied.

> Yours,
> M

1. Marion Bloom.

[UPL]

H. L. Mencken
1524 Hollins St.
Baltimore.

Aug. 5, 1916.

Dear Dreiser:

I have been unable to obtain twenty copies of my first article but I am sending fourteen or fifteen today. Worse, it will be difficult to obtain even fifteen copies of the other articles, but I shall go to the Sun office today and send you as many as I can get. I have made the corrections in my book manuscript and shall bear them in mind when I re-write it. When that will be, God alone knows. I am finding work very difficult.

Sumner's contention that everyone of the passages he has marked is sufficient to bar "The Genius" from the mails is no more than his usual bluff. He will compromise readily enough once you show fight. Your yearning to go to jail at this time awakens no responsive echo in my chest. There is very heavy work to be done once the war approaches an end and you are one of the many who are in duty bound to help do it. If Sumner had confined his allegations to a few passages, the case would have been different, but the reckless extravagance of his charges has greatly weakened his own case, and once you come to grips with him, you will find that he realizes it. Sumner is not a man of much courage. It is comparatively easy to bluff him off, and if Jones handles the business properly, he will readily consent to compromise on a few important changes. In so large a book, a few thousand words might be easily cut out without damaging the whole in the slightest.

However, please don't get the idea that I counsel a surrender. If he demands the exclusion of essential things, fight him; but if he can be jockeyed into compromise and discussion, it will be very easy to outwit him. His intelligence is limited. I'll be in New York in ten days. Let us have a meeting then.

Wright is complaining that Jones has done him a dirty trick.[1] I have not heard Jones' side of it but Wright seems to make out a rather good case.

Sincerely yours,

M

1. Wright complained that Jones did not pay him $500 for a manuscript he had delivered.

[NYP]

165 W. 10th St.

Aug 8—1916

Henry L—

There is an effort here to organize a committee of 100 to conduct the defense of The "Genius"   If you are appealed to as you will be of course, lend your critical countenance to the same   Money will be provided from upper aides. I am for a scrap and your letter pleases me much. You must get me at least 17 more copies of the article entitled "Dreiseriana" and 22 of the one called "Two Dreiser Novels." This is very important. Can you get them. I'll pay an extra price if necessary.

Don Marquis[1] had a col. in last nights Eve Sun against this suppression business and pro "Genius"   A pretty storm can be brewed. Personally I'm feeling all right about it but I believe Jones would like to slip out. If you conscientiously give me the details of the Wright case I would like to have them. I may break with Lane yet—and soon.

Dreiser

Your not sick, are you?

1. Don Marquis (1878–1937), journalist, author. At this time Marquis was writing for the New York *Sun,* and he argued for Dreiser's case in his column.

[UPL]

H. L. Mencken
1524 Hollins St.
Baltimore.

August 9, 1916.

Dear Dreiser:

1. I'll do my best to get the extra copies you want, but the Sun keeps such a short stock of back number that they may not exist. Please keep the inclosed corrected copy and make notes of the corrections on any clippings you send out to important men. The errors make me look very absurd.

2. It goes without saying that I shall be delighted to join the Committee of One Hundred. My connection with the Parisienne case may weaken my usefulness in one direction, but the experience I there gained may increase it in another. Please be careful to keep down, as much as possible, the number of professional radicals. They are necessary, of course, and some of them are first class men, but a few mountebanks may do great damage. Let me know exactly what is being done and I shall try to get some recruits.

3. I am writing to Wright today asking him to send you a full account of his affair with Jones. His statement of it to me showed Jones in a very unfavorable light, but I have not, of course, heard the other side.

4. I'll be in New York next Tuesday morning. Let me know when you will be free on Tuesday, Wednesday or Thursday.

Sincerely yours,
M

[NYP]

165 W. 10th St.

Aug 10—1916

Henry L.

I will correct the copies as suggested before sending them out. Wright just called up and we are going over that matter in the morning. In regard to Jones he has come around to my side completely and has now decided to fight. The lawyers, today or tomorrow, are going to notify Sumner of this decision and give him a chance to back out if he will. If not a statement is going into the papers as an advertisement and the fight is on. I wish you would write Jones a good stiff letter of encouragement such as you wrote me after your examination of the charges. He will appreciate it and it will do us all good. The Committee of One Hundred is in process of trying to form itself as it were. I'm afraid I wont have as much to say as I would like if it goes through but I'll pull a long face over too many dynamiters.

Do get me those extra copies. You have done a masterly peice of work here and those who know and care for that sort of thing ought to see it— and I propose that they shall.

Pick any day you want and have dinner with me. And bring your girl.

Th.D.

I wish you would spread the news of this scrap as far and wide as you can. I'm going to win it in the open, if I can.

N.B. Do you know where and in what condition are Harris Merton Lyons stories?[1] I want to get hold of them.

N.B.2   Without connecting me with it in any way please send a set of your articles to Anna Tatum, Fallsington, Pa. Shes down on me at the present writing so I cant.

Jones is after me heavily about that jacket stuff for The Bulwark and "A Hoosier". Will you send it?

An thou lovest me, respond

Dreiser

I know the undersea freighter arrived but pull yourself together.

1. Dreiser believed that Harris Merton Lyon's early death from a kidney ailment was a genuine if minor loss to literature, and for years he sought to collect and publish Lyon's manuscripts.

[NYP]
Aug 10—1916

H. L.

I forgot to add that Lane's lawyer discovered just 3 danger spots. Since you did the same if you will suggest this it will cheer Doctor Jones and lift you high as a prophet.

Th.D.

[UPL]

H. L. Mencken
1524 Hollins St.
Baltimore.

Aug. 11, 1916.

Dear Dreiser:

I am writing to Jones by this mail and shall see him on Tuesday or Wednesday. Why not let us dine together on Wednesday evening? Let me have a note at the Smart Set Monday telling me whether this is all right. I have already written to Huneker and to Harry Leon Wilson,[1] and I am trying to stir up the Authors' League of America.[2] The only book of stories by Harris Merton Lyon that I know was printed by William Marion Reedy of the St. Louis Mirror, about three years ago. The rest of Lyon's work is scattered through the magazines or in manuscript. His widow, Mrs. Belle Lyon, lives at N. Colebrook, Conn. When he died, I had in my hands part of the manuscript of a novel on which he was working. He wanted me to do a chapter in it for him. (The chief character was a musician and Lyon knew very little about music). After his death I returned this manuscript to Mrs. Lyon. It was a rather poor story and not at all in his usual style.

I have sent a set of the clippings to the Tatum.[3] She came in to see me in New York some time ago and I assumed from her talk that you and she were on good terms.

I shall send news of the case in all directions and try to stir up the animals near and far. It would be well if Jones would get up a statement of the facts, including the list of specifications, for such use. I am suggesting it to him.

Curiously enough, that Boston fellow who has been hammering you, Wright, Huneker and me in the Transcript, sent me a very friendly letter the other day.[4] He said that my articles on you had pleased him very much and that he hoped what he had written about me in the past had not hurt my feelings. In my reply, I told him that all good men should stand together in your defense.

Yours,

M

1. Harry Leon Wilson (1867–1939), humorist, novelist, playwright, editor.
2. The Authors' League of America, which included the Authors' Guild and the Dramatists' Guild, was founded in 1911 to safeguard the rights of authors. Dreiser had refused to join the Authors' League in 1913, considering it a refuge for second-rate talent—a snub he probably regretted at this point, since it was the only organized group of writers at hand. Mencken did manage to get the League to back Dreiser in this case.

3. Anna P. Tatum.
4. Probably a reference to Edwin Francis Edgett, who only slowly came to admire Dreiser's work.

SMART SET
A Magazine of Cleverness
452 Fifth Avenue, New York

Sunday. [13 August 1916]

Dear Dreiser:-
I am out of sets of the articles. If you have any more will you please send sets (corrected) to:
Harry Leon Wilson, Ocean Home, Monterey, Calif.
Current Opinion.
The Listener, c/o Boston Transcript
The Bellman, Minneapolis
Some publicity may be got out of this.[1]
The proof-readers made my own errors worse. I'll read proof myself on any future articles.

Yours in Xt.,
M

Also, please send Gloom[2] a set.[3]

1. Mencken's practice was to send letters and his articles on Dreiser to influential journals and individuals, in hopes of organizing support for his cause.
2. Gloom is the nickname of Estelle Bloom Kubitz, the sister of Marion Bloom.
3. The postscript is handwritten.

H. L. Mencken
1524 Hollins St.
Baltimore.

Aug. 14, 1916.

Dear Dreiser:
Within is a carbon copy of my review of "A Hoosier Holiday."[1] It is scheduled for the October Smart Set, out September 15th. I have sent another copy to Jones. I'll see you Wednesday.

Yours in Xt.,
M

1. In this review ("The Creed of a Novelist," *Smart Set* 50[October 1916], 138–43), Mencken compares Dreiser to Conrad at length, and declares *A Hoosier Holiday* to be "Save for passages in 'The Titan' . . . the high tide of Dreiser's writing—that is, as sheer writing" (see Appendix 2, pp. 760–67).

[UPL]

H. L. Mencken
1524 Hollins St.
Baltimore.

Aug. 19, 1916.

Dear Dreiser:

I inclose proposed drafts of two protests. Copies have gone forward to Jones today. I assume, of course, that they will be considerably re-written before they are sent out for signatures. Perhaps it would be well to take advice before settling on the actual text. The Authors' League pundits may suggest changes. I am sending copies to Hersey by this mail.[1]

Yours in Xt.,
M

1. Harold Hersey (1893–1956), editor, poet. As an officer of the Authors' League, Hersey played a large part during this period in organizing support for *The "Genius."*

[UPL]

H. L. Mencken
1524 Hollins St.
Baltimore.

Aug. 22, 1916.

Dear Dreiser:

Jones writes that the executive committee of the Authors' League is to sit on the case next Thursday. What these pundits will do remains to be seen. My belief is that they will decide to lend a hand.

I have read the Tribune and Times articles. Why did you deliver such a crack at Jones in the Tribune article?[1] Surely this is a bad way to keep him on the track.

Your talk about injunctions is absurd. If the book is ever barred from the mails, Jones' obligation to print it will cease at once, all contracts to the contrary notwithstanding. It is impossible to enforce a contract which involves the performance of an unlawful act. This is one of the primary axioms of law.

In case you decide upon getting signatures to the protest I sent up the other day, I think the best way to go about it will be to have Jones print a hundred or so copies and then put them into the hands of four or five men who will personally beseige the leading authors of the country. By leading authors, of course, I mean those best known to the public. The signature of such an old ass as Brander Matthews[2] would be worth a great deal.

Sincerely yours,

M

1. Dreiser had been interviewed, and in a 20 August 1916 news account he threatened to deliver an injunction against John Lane if it acceded in the demands for the destruction of the book plates of *The "Genius."*
2. Brander Matthews (1852–1929), teacher, critic, editor, novelist. Matthews was well known as a professor at Columbia University and as a prolific writer of fiction and essays. Though he did not favorably impress Mencken, he was a liberalizing force in his time.

[UPL]

H. L Mencken
1524 Hollins St.
Baltimore.

Aug. 23, 1916.

Dear Dreiser:

I am sending you today, all the copies of the three Dreiser articles that exist. The stock of the Sun is now reduced to two or three copies of each issue. If I get a chance during the week, I'll write one or two more articles.

Please let me know the result of the conference with the Authors' League tomorrow. Tell Jones that if he wants to use any parts of my review of "A Hoosier Holiday", he is free to take whatever he desires. All I ask is that he spells my name correctly and gives me the title of Mr. I am tired of going through life without any title whatever.

Yours in Xt.,

M

[NYP]

165

Aug 25—1916

Henry L—
  Fairest of His Sex:
  The Authors League went on record yesterday in some words a copy of which I have not as yet by me.[1] They were fairly adequate words it seemed to me and bore directly on The "Genius" Next week there is to be a fuller meeting of the Executive Committee in which (I trust) a whack at puritanism is to be taken. Whether The "Genius" will again be connected with it I dont know. I doubt it
  At this moment I have a fine young thought for you which would do a power of good if you would act on it. In order to clinch this business—to keep the League from blacksliding or backsliding—(which the h—— is it?) an editorial should be written—anywhere will do—the Eve. Sun as well as any headed say—"Changing Aspect of American Lit" or something like that in which the curiosity (first time in Am. History Stuff) of a League of American Authors coming to the rescue of an American fictioner is commented on. This published and sent at once to executive sec'y would tend to cause the dear league to stand pat.
  Do you get me?
  It would be a strong move in my judgement.
  Outside that, nothing. I am getting quite a number of letters urging me to stand pat and fight which of course goes without saying The trouble is, some of the letters have to be answered. I hope your fit again and that you think of me kindly Say at least five hail marys for me, every morning. Between us the plates of The "Genius" are now outside the state. I once thought of shipping them to you—and may yet. I am determined to prevent their being attacked and destroyed (possibly)
  Don't worry over the Tribune interview. Business of rough stuff between author & publisher not at all important. I've threatened Jones to his face & mean it, but theres no ill feeling. He knows that I've done many a turn of him & he owes me one, now.

Th.D

Write Schuler[2] & praise him. It will strengthen his stand
You might write Vance too.[3] It would keep him up.
Do you still want to meet Powys when you come again? What night?[4]

  1. The resolution reads as follows: "It was the sense of the meeting in discussing the proposition involved in the proceeding pending against the John Lane Co. and Theodore Dreiser in re the suppression of *The "Genius"*, that the book complained of

by the Society for the Prevention of Vice is not subject to condemnation by it and that the same is not lewd, licentious or obscene, and it is further the sense of the meeting that the test ordinarily applied in such cases is too narrow and unfair, and that it may, if not modified, prevent the sale of many classics and of much of the serious work which is now being offered, and it is further the sense of the meeting that the League take such action as may be possible to prevent the suppression of the work complained of" (quoted in Elias, *Letters*, 1:226, n.26).

2. Eric Schuler, secretary of the executive committee of the Authors' League.

3. Louis Joseph Vance, a member of the League's executive committee who was ambivalent about defending *The "Genius."*

4. The postscript was placed at the top of the letter. Like Mencken, John Cowper Powys was drafting a protest.

[UPL]

H. L. Mencken
1524 Hollins St.
Baltimore.

Aug. 28, 1916.

Dear Dreiser:

Hay fever has fallen on me like a ton of bricks and I am quite knocked out. My plan is to go to New York this afternoon and if I can't find relief at Long Beach, to go to New Hampshire at once. I can neither sleep nor do any work, and reading is almost impossible. If I am still in New York tomorrow, I'll call you up. Even during my absence, the plates of "The 'Genius'" might be shipped to me here, though if the moralists got wind of it, they could trace them and seize them. I am writing to Hersey by this mail. More anon.

Yours in Xt.,
M

[UPL-H]

SMART SET
A Magazine of Cleverness
George Jean Nathan
and   } Editors
H. L. Mencken

[30 August 1916]

Dear Dreiser:

I tried to get hold of you by phone yesterday afternoon @ last night, but failed. Hay fever has me by the ear and I am forced to go back to Baltimore. I am taking a lot of the protests, @ shall get them into circulation.

Yours in Xt.,
M

[NYP]

Sept 4—1916

Here is a sample of the sort of thing that my friendly publishers see that I get by special delivery.[1] Let me have it back.

Th D

A man by the name of M. A. Giffen—612 W. 137th St. N.Y. phones just now & wanted me to get you, Powys and one or two others—names not given—to speak on Vice Commisions, Puritans, etc. at the Liberal Club any Saturday evening. He has just phoned to suggest Max Eastman & Prof. Giddings[2] as additional names.

1. John Lane sent Dreiser a negative notice of *The "Genius"* printed in a Canadian newspaper.
2. Franklin H. Giddings (1855–1931), author and teacher at Columbia University who was a pioneer in sociology.

[UPL]

H. L. Mencken
1524 Hollins St.
Baltimore.

Sept. 5, 1916.

Dear Dreiser:

This Canadian notice is typical. As I have told you before, the moralists are enormously more active and powerful in Canada than in the United States. Many American moral organizations, for example, the Lord's Day Alliance, are of Canadian origin. In more than one part of the Dominion, street cars are forbidden to run on Sunday. Canada, indeed, offers a perfect picture of Puritanism and Democracy. It is a commonwealth of cads.

For God's sake, don't start making speeches at the Liberal Club.[1] This organization consists of all the tinpot revolutionaries and sophomoric advanced thinkers in New York. It is of the first importance that you steer clear of such bands of comedians. As for me, I should refuse any invitation with the utmost indignation. These jitney liberals are forever trying to get advertising by hooking on to better men. If they announced me as a lecturer, I should certainly sue them for libel.

Yours in Xt.,
M

1. The Liberal Club, located at 137 MacDougal Street, was a famous Greenwich Village institution organized in the early teens as "A Meeting Place for Those Interested in New Ideas."

[UPL]

H. L. Mencken
1524 Hollins St.
Baltimore.

Sept. 18, 1916.

Dear Dreiser:

By all means let me see the English cablegram.[1] As for the newspaper notices, they are in exact accordance with my expectations. The newspapers in America are run by cads and it goes without saying that they are Puritanical. Once the case actually comes to trial, you will find all of them, with perhaps one or two exceptions, against you.[2] I shall get great delight reading their reviews of my Book of Epigrams—perhaps the most thoroughly immoral book ever printed in America.[3] I believe, however, that I have managed to evade the law. It will be interesting to find out. I don't know of a single thing that virtuous Americans hold in respect that is not denounced in these seventy-five pages. I'll send you a copy as soon as I get some from Jones.

Yours in Xt.,
M

1. On 16 September 1916, Dreiser wrote Mencken saying that he had gotten a cable in support of *The "Genius"* from the British authors H. G. Wells, Arnold Bennett, W. J. Locke, Hugh Walpole, and E. Temple Thurston. The cable read: "We regard The Genius as a work of high literary merit and sympathize with the Authors League of America in their protest against its suppression." [UPL]
2. In fact, a number of important newspapers and popular journals had already come to Dreiser's defense, including the New York *Tribune*, the *Des Moines Register*, and even the *Saturday Evening Post*.
3. *A Little Book in C Major* (*Opus 11*) (New York, 1916) is a collection of 226 epigrams taken from *Smart Set*.

<u>165 W. 10</u>

Sept 21—1916

Dear Mencken:

Would it be possible to arrange to secure three hundred or even five hundred copies of the particular form containing your article on "A Hoosier Holiday". I dont want to buy the S.S. whole and I dont want to wait for return copies. If 500 proofs could be pulled from the plates of those pages & sold to me separately I could use them to great advantage—particularly at this time. Let me know and if there is any chance don't let them destroy the plates before the proofs are pulled.

Th.D.

Your book of epigrams has just arrived.¹ I shall examine it prayerfully. Thanks.

1. Mencken's inscription in *A Little Book in C Major (Opus 11)* reads, "To Theodore Dreiser, with archepiscopal blessings."

H. L. Mencken
1524 Hollins St.
Baltimore.

Sept. 22, 1916.

Dear Dreiser:

Unfortunately the plates of the Smart Set are destroyed immediately an edition is run off. Moreover, it would be impossible to sell you 300 copies, even of returns, at a low enough price. My suggestion is that you have the article, or such parts of it as you want to distribute, set up by a job printer, and 500 copies run off. This should cost you no more than $10.00, which is scarcely more than it would cost to pull 300 proofs. In addition, it would allow you to make whatever changes you desired. I agree, of course, to any such changes, and this letter is sufficient authority for you to reprint the article. You will, of course, give credit to the Smart Set and put the magazine's copyright line at the bottom. As for the inclosed open letter,¹ I am full of doubts that it should be printed in its present form. For one thing, you make too general an attack upon the American. For another thing, you drag in a gratuitous fling at religion. Such a double-headed attack would do you vastly more harm than good. The time to tell the truth about the American is not while you have a law case pending with a possible jury ahead, but after you are safely out of it. So with religion. As you yourself say, it is quite impossible to trust any American. Scratch him and you will find a Puritan. I make no exceptions whatever. The only genuine anti-Puritans to be found in this country are men who are not Anglo-Saxons. Even Wright, who bears an Anglo-Saxon name, is actually Dutch and French in ancestry. The name of Wright, in fact, was assumed by his grandfather. The family name is something quite different.

If you decide to send anything out to the newspapers, I'll be glad to have it published in Baltimore. But the inclosed leaves me in very serious doubts. It would do you no good whatever and it might conceivably do you much harm. On the whole, I think it better for you to keep quite still the result of the fight before the Post Office is determined.

What have you done in the direction of getting signatures to the protest? You once mentioned several well-known men who would probably sign at your request. Have they been approached? I have sent out many letters and got a number of signatures, but it is necessary that there be concerted action. Moreover, it must be done quickly. Has Howells been approached?[2]

Yours,
M

1. Dreiser had sent Mencken an open letter to be published in the newspapers.
2. William Dean Howells did not sign the protest.

[NYP]

165 W. 10

Sept 23—1916

My Dear Mencken:

Through one effort & another my own included Hersey now has about 150 names. He will send them to you, or show you them when you come. Masters, Tarkington, Gertrude Atherton, Meredith Nicholson, Ida Tarbell, Harold McGrath, Ernest Poole, Samuel Hopkins Adams, Montague Glass, Wm Marion Reedy, Zoe Akins, Ethel Watts Mumford, Charles Hanson Towne, etc. etc. etc have signed. Do you know anything about Rupert Hughes, Harry Leon Wilson, Jack London & George Ade or Finley Peter Dunne? I sent Ade a protest, without comment, but no signature has come yet. What of Nathan's list of playwrights? There ought to be a supplementary list to contain Locke, Powys, Wilkinson, Wells, Bennett, Thurston, Adachi Kinnosuke, Elias Tobenkin etc.[1] I make the suggestion that when the list is fairly full and strong it be taken to Howells, Brander Matthews, Wm Lyon Phelps etc. & their signatures requested   I can't see why Rex Beach, Geo. Barr McCutheon, Owen Johnson, Sam Blythe,

Robert W. Chambers, Hamlin Garland & Wm Allen White wouldn't sign. I will write Owen Johnson personally if no one else can land him.

Thanks for the opinion as to the letter to the newspaper. I'll let it rest for the present anyhow

Th.D

1. Dreiser's idea is to separate the foreign authors from the Americans.

[UPL]

SMART SET
A Magazine of Cleverness
452 Fifth Avenue, New York

Monday. [25 September 1916]

Dear Dreiser:-

I'll be in New York on Thursday and call you up. The names of Rubert Hughes and Harry Leon Wilson are quite safe. Both have agreed to sign. Wilson is in California and hard to reach. Hughes has been on the border with the militia. I am after both. I don't know London, or Ade, or Dunne. Hersey should be able to fetch them on Authors' league stationary. I am after Phelps. I'll tackle Blythe through Bob Davis. Why not write to Johnson yourself? The plan of tackling Howells with a full list is a good one. The playwrights are being approached. Let us trust in God.

In Xt.,
M.

[UPL]

SMART SET
A Magazine of Cleverness
452 Fifth Avenue, New York

[before 28 September 1916]

Dear Dreiser:-

I'll be in New York Thursday. I think it would be well to hold a meeting and take stock. Why not let me come to your house Friday evening, say at 8.15, and call in Hersey with his list of names? The thing is going a bit too slowly. William Lyon Phelps[1] has refused to sign—the first refusal I have encountered.

M.

Let me know at the office.

1. William Lyon Phelps (1865–1943), critic and teacher at Yale University.

[UPL]

SMART SET
A Magazine of Cleverness
452 Fifth Avenue, New York

Friday. [6 October 1916]

Dear Dreiser:-

This afternoon a Baltimore second-hand book-seller handed me a copy of the Authors' League protest,[1] just received from Lane. I note that, despite our talk of last week, you have inserted the names of four or five tenth-rate Greenwich geniuses, including two wholly unknown women, and left out such men as Churchill and Ade. Let me say once more that I think this a damnably silly, perverse and dangerous policy. You are making it very hard for Hersey, who has already imperilled his job in your behalf,[2] and spitting into the eyes of the rest of us. Just what satisfaction you get out of this course I'll be damned if I can see. Why start a fight in the trench while a bombardment is going on? All of these jitney geniuses are playing you for a sucker. They can't advance your reputation an inch, but you make a very fine (and willing) stalking horse for them.

Yours,
M

1. For *The "Genius"* Protest and a list of signers, see Appendix 2, pp. 802–4.
2. In his correspondence with Dreiser, Harold Hersey gives no indication that Dreiser's actions impeded the League's progress in any way. During this period, Dreiser loaned money to Hersey, who was in tight straits financially.

[NYP]

165 W. 10th

Monday. Oct 9—1916

Dear Mencken:

I do not get the reason for the unnecessarily harsh & dictatorial tone of this letter but for various reasons I am going to explain anyhow—once. I suppose Harvey, Dell, Mrs. Duncan, Abbott, Eastman & Mrs. Stokes are the tenth rate village geniuses referred to.[1] As compared with some of the other names approved by you and never heard of by me they may be tenth-rate. I do not know, and I do not particularly care. They are not friends of mine.

The move which calls forth your ire concerns 238 or 40 letters sent by me—with the aid and consent of Jones—to old book store dealers throughout the United States. The reason for this was obviously not to obtain signatures—(that is too silly for consideration)—but with the special intention of getting this & my other books displayed in these stores, solely with the purpose of breaking down the prejudice which exists in most of the new books stores to either carrying or displaying them. I need not tell you that right here in New York City a number of the larger stores refuse to display them at all—ever. If the old book store dealer, by a series of cards which I had planned could be induced to make a separate display, regardless of what prices might be charged a considerable selling wedge would have been driven in. That & no other was the sole reason for sending out this particular letter.

Regardless of that however the list of names you complain of was made up by me before we or Hersey or anybody else discussed whether such a list was ever to be sent out to anybody—even before the list had attained to more than a fraction of its present proportions. As you may or may not know my original idea when I first considered your proposition was to get a number of preliminary signers with the sole idea of drawing others & this I suggested to Hersey, Schuler & others the night the protest was discussed. It was not a bad idea, and despite your feeling it was this much despised list, put in the hands of several of my intimates, (as personal & private of course) which secured a few of the best signatures in the list. When it came to reaching these old book men, seeing that they were miles removed from any connection with editors, publishers, literary editors and authors, I thought it advisable to use it, as making out a case for the display and backing of this particular book. It is possible that this was an error. Personally, all conditions considered, I cannot even now see it as one. I cannot see how it can possibly affect either you or Hersey or the Authors League or indeed anyone connected with this movement. It was not and will not be sent to any editor, literary editor, publisher or author other than those referred to. In sending it to the old book men, as you possibly saw, it was tied up with the original vice report, the several statements of the Authors League, the English Cable, a card adv of The "Genius" etc. No comment, (at least none that I have seen) has appeared anywhere in any paper, save one,—in the N.Y. Sun and that a mere mention of the fact that such a protest was being circulated. Since Don Marquis received a copy to sign it is not unreasonable to suppose that he may have inspired the notice.

Aside from my letter however and this list, your letter seems to me to be curiously animated by something which does not appear on the surface and is not likely to have been inspired by this particular move. Recently, on several occasions you have gone out of your way to comment (and before others) on my supposed relationship to this band of "jitney radicals and tenth-rate village geniuses" to whom you seem to think I am wedded—or with whom I hold some relationship not compatible with my standing etc:—and that in spite of the fact that I have frequently told you and as everyone who knows anything about my private life really knows that the reverse is true. I am <u>not</u> in touch with the life of this section. I do not go out with or receive here any radicals of any sort—or village characters—not any. Although I have privately said to myself and here and now state to you that it is really none of your business, any more than your private or public friendships or relationships are to me, still you persist. Have I tried to supervise your private life or comment on any of your friends or deeds? Whats eating you, anyhow? Who are these people who are friends of mine? Dell? I have not seen him in nine months and here he is looked upon as one who really dislikes me very much. Who are the others? Who, to be exact, is using me. Name me the people—or one, even   But beyond that I still seem to sense something in this letter which is not on the surface by any means and which I resent, being unspoken, if it is unspoken. Whose knocking, and to what end? I owe you too much to turn on this or any occasion and say the few ugly things we all can say when hurt. I have had my share in this fight & have done very much more than appears on the surface. Be that as it may. Your letter smacks of something I do not like & if you have any real downright grievance come accross. More than likely there an ample explanation at hand. If not why lug in a sledge to kill a fly? And why bother with my private or public life unless you have definite corrective facts to go on.

Dreiser

I feel sorry to have to answer your letter in this way at all

1. All the names Dreiser mentions are writers and editors who were associated with radical or leftist politics: Alexander Harvey, Floyd Dell, Margherita Sargent Duncan, Leonard D. Abbott, Max Eastman, Rose Pastor Stokes.

[UPL]

The
SMART SET
A Magazine of Cleverness
452 Fifth Avenue, New York

Tuesday. [10 October 1916]

Dear Dreiser:-
    Whatever the origin of that list, I still think it was wretchedly bad policy to circulate one bearing the names of such professional revolutionists as Abbott and Eastman and such nobodies as the two women. On the one hand it hooks up your cause with causes that are definitely unpopular, and on the other hand it greatly embarrasses Hersey, to whom the support of

the Authors' League is chiefly due, and who has been imperilled already by the suspicions and opposition of the respectables. I was wholly unaware that this list was made up before our talk. The presence of Rupert Hughes' name on it made me think, and quite naturally, that it postdated our talk. What was my surprise then to encounter what appeared to be a gratuitous crack in the nose for the only men who have devoted any honest effort to the case, and done it any appreciable service!

I haven't the slightest right or desire to question your private doings. They are, I am informed, of a generally immoral nature, and hence abhorrent to a right-thinking man. But I would be a false friend if I stood idly by and let you do things certain to injure you, and some of your most faithful partisans with you. I have opposed the publication of the list, at least at this stage, for plain and simple reasons. If it were printed in full the names of the birth controllers, jitney Socialists and other such vermin would give the moralists the very chance they are looking for. And if a selected list were printed, then you would bring down upon yourself the bitter enmity of all the signers omitted, and some of them are in a position to do you serious injury. This is sound politics, and I stick to it. Once the case is decided I withdraw all objections. In fact, I am already planning to print a pamphlet about it myself, giving a full list of the signers (perhaps with a few such lice as Hirshberg omitted) and exposing the pecksniffery of those who have refused to sign. To this end Hersey and I are carefully preserving all material.

I am coming to New York this afternoon, and shall call you up tomorrow or next day. Thanks very much for the Booth pictures.[1] They are excellent.

Yours,
M

There is, in fact, no secret grievance. You surely know me well enough to know that I never have <u>secret</u> grievances.

1. A set of Franklin Booth's illustrations sent by Dreiser.

[UPL]

SMART SET
A Magazine of Cleverness
452 Fifth Avenue, New York

St. Luke's Day. [18 October 1916]

Dear Dreiser:-

The N.Y. Sun stuff is capital. Evidently a few decent men are still left on that sinking ship.

As for the circular to college professors, I doubt that it will do much good. On the contrary, I believe that it will only provoke the Methodists among them—about 80%—to take a hack at you. The whole professorial corps is stupid and poltroonish. Not long ago a professor of English at the Johns Hopkins admitted to Boyd that he was afraid to utter his honest opinion about books. William Lyon Phelps I now write down as an ass. His last book, just out, is unimaginably bad. I shall lay him out in due course.

Forward the Zeppelins! I am tired waiting.

> Yours in Xt.,
> M

[UPL]

H. L. Mencken
1524 Hollins St.
Baltimore.

Oct. 25, 1916.

Dear Dreiser:

I have your letter of October 21st on my return.[1] I have nothing from Huebsch and doubt that much could be accomplished by sending him notes for his debate with Sumner. Unless he is sure of the subject and has all the arguments against Puritanism at his fingers' ends, he will inevitably make a bad showing against a man who is constantly arguing for the other side. I think that Wright will do much better. He is an alert and effective debater and he will tackle Sumner with ridicule and abuse. These thing always go well with an audience. Its vote is invariably given to the most cruel and boisterous man. It wants to see somebody beaten up.

When it comes to getting together money for your own case, I need not remind you that I want to be counted in. Harry Wilson is also eager to make a contribution.[2]

> Yours,
> M

1. On 21 October, Dreiser sent Mencken a letter asking him to send "a short argument of some kind" to the publisher Benjamin W. Huebsch, who planned to debate the issue of censorship with John Sumner before the Twilight Club in New York. [NYP]
2. In the 21 October letter, Dreiser said he would go to court if he could get financial support for a case.

[UPL]

H. L. Mencken
1524 Hollins St.
Baltimore.

Nov. 1, 1916.

Dear Dreiser:

The book is here and an excellent job Lane has made of it.[1] The only objections to it are two in number. One is that it is somewhat too heavy to read comfortably and the other is that the gray-green cover is very easily marked by the fingers. But it certainly makes a distinguished appearance and the illustrations by Booth are very fine. I shall be glad to read it again for $25.00 cash in hand.

The Saturday Evening Post editorial was a bolt from the blue.[2] I suspect that Sam Blythe did it.[3] What is going on in the case? I have heard nothing for a week past save the news from James Hay, Jr.,[4] that Lamar, solicitor of the Post Office Department, told him that the case was not officially before the Department. Lamar asked for a copy of the book and agreed to read it privately and to prepare his decision in advance of any possible offical action. The advantage of this scheme will be that Hay will have a chance to get at him and beat him into line before anything is done. Lamar is a Maryland politician of an extremely dubious type, and if the worst comes to the worst, I think I can bring some pressure to bear on him here. In such matters it is always much better to deal with a professional politician than with an ass who is full of the uplift and believes that he is a modern Jesus.

Yours,
M

1. *A Hoosier Holiday.*
2. The editorial attacked literary censorship and deplored the attack on *The "Genius."*
3. Samuel Blythe (1868–1947), journalist, memoirist who was associated with the *Saturday Evening Post* in these years.
4. James Hay, Jr., a writer based in Washington, D.C.

[NYP]
Nov 4—1916

My Dear H. L. M.

Thanks for your cheery letter and the news from James Hay, Jr. Mr. Hay was in here yesterday and told me that he had seen Judge Lamar & that

Lamar said that in so far as he knew no action (no proper action anyhow) had been begun and that he doubted if any would be. He had never heard of the book. Hay said he (Lamar) was going to read it and that when he (Lamar) had done so that Hay would get his opinion privately and that if it proved unfavorable, which he doubted, he would bring considerable pressure on him to make him change his mind. He told me Lamar had said to him that it would have to be a mighty tough book before he would condemn it. What's more Lamar suggested to Hay that in case his opinion was favorable that I or someone get somebody to make a fierce attack on the book to the postmaster general so that it would come officially before him   In that case he would write a favorable opinion which could be given out to the press generally and used as an adv.!!

At this end things are going exceedingly well. Stanchfield and Levy[1] are my attorneys—and they are heartily interested in the proposition. Already they have secured a written opinion from the U.S. Federal District Attorney for this district in which he says that he has read the book and that it is one such against which the government will not act—that no reasonable complaint can be found. Again an ex-assistant district attorney of this city now in the employ of Stanchfield & Levy states that he talked to an assistant District Attorney who is close to Swann[2] and that Swann had told this man that Sumner was an ass and that he would have nothing to do with the case. Stanchfield and Levy propose very quickly now to go into the State court here and ask for an injunction restraining Sumner & his society from interferring with the sale of the book. After this is won they will bring an action for damages against him and his directors and patrons.

In regard to Jones—my estimate of him is now so low that I can scarcely bring myself to talk to the man anymore. He has broken his word in every matter concerning which we had a specific agreement. He told me among other things that in case the government did not act inside two months that he would sell the book and stand trial and defend it, also that in case the Authors League or Hersey was successful in getting a list of important names that he would take the protest and names and publish in at least a dozen leading American newspaper etc. etc. A week ago I demanded to know where he stood. He wilted, hedged and mumbled. I finally asked him if in case Stanchfield & Levy took the case without a cent of expense to him whether (since they desired it) he would sell the book so Sumner could bring an action and so that S & L could defend it. Will you believe it when I tell that he began to spring the directorship stuff on me and tell me he couldn't say. I gave twenty-four hours in which to write me a letter saying he would do exactly as S & L requested in this matter & S & L now have that letter. Later, when I asked about the protest he hedged by saying he would print any copies required by Hersey for distribution. He has lied to me about the cost of "A Hoosier Holiday"—its size weight & everything in connection with it. He has done one other thing—made me a proposition of which I will not speak of now—which is distinctly wrong in my judgement—the first thing of the kind (financial) that I definitely know of. Personally I'm through. He's a bag of mush and I want to quit. I really think the man has no real publishing acumen and at the first real chance I am going to leave.

I am grateful to you for this Hay man. He is very kind and earnest and will do about as he says I think. Luck and health & length of days. When you come again see me. I have a scheme to help American letters in general.[3]

Th. D

1. John B. Stanchfield and Louis Levy.
2. The district attorney, Edward Swann.
3. Dreiser's idea was to form an organization to help needy authors and to fight literary censorship.

[UPL]

H. L. Mencken
1524 Hollins St.
Baltimore.

Nov. 7, 1916.

Dear Dreiser:

I'll be in New York on Thursday, and Hersey writes that he has arranged for us to meet on Saturday night. The campaign outlined by Stanchfield looks very appetizing.

Yours,
HLM.

[NYP]

165 W. 10

[after 7 November 1916]

Your on—only why not take dinner with me & then we'll recieve Hersey afterwards? No?

Th.D

[UPL]

H. L. Mencken
1524 Hollins St.
Baltimore.

Nov. 14, 1916.

Dear Dreiser:

I am planning a general offensive against the lice who have refused to sign the protest and shall send out a hundred or more letters this week. Will you please let me have about a hundred copies of the printed protest? I'll inclose it with some of the letters and can use it in other directions to profit.

Yours in Xt.,
M

[NYP]

P.O. Box 282

Nov. 20—1916

My Dear Mencken:

Thanks for your letter. I mailed you an inscribed copy so you can send that Jones copy to me.[1] I need it. By the by—give the devil (the fair sex) his due. Kirah Markham made that book—design & all. Selected pages, size, did the lettering and arranged the type pages. And a sweet time she had getting them to obey.

The sun shines here[2] six days out of seven & more without a flaw. I am laying in a supply as against greyer days up north later. Success to all Hyphenates. I like the idea of the four star title. The real clever critics would insist that the right name of the book was Hennessey and that it drove them to drink.[3]

Verstehen sie[4]
Th.D.

I used to know an Irish barrel house alderman out in Chicago could, when drunk enough, occasionally get up this—
"Verstay do dass mine
liebes Lalla palooser"[5]

1. Dreiser's inscription in *A Hoosier Holiday* reads: "To Henry L.—from Dreiser. Thou scoundrel!——this night shalt thou be compelled to once more glance it through."
2. Dreiser was vacationing in Savannah, Georgia.
3. Mencken had suggested that the four stars used by the publisher as a substitute

for the yet unwritten volume of autobiography be used as the book's title. Dreiser here replies that it may be confused with the four-star Hennessey whiskey label.
4. Do you understand.
5. A macaronic verse: "Do you understand that my dear lallapalooser."

[UPL]

H. L. Mencken
1524 Hollins St.
Baltimore.

Nov. 24, 1916.

Dear Dreiser:

I am sending out about twenty-five letters a day, each carefully designed to fit the mental capacity of the recipient, and the response is becoming very gratifying. The number of positive refusals is strangely small, and in most cases I am still pursuing those who have refused, and hope to get their names in the end. This is true of such men as Leroy Scott. Scott objects to one phrase in the Protest, but swears by thirty-five saints that he is in favor of you and even volunteers to do any work assigned to him. Another one who refuses is Mary Austin, but her letter is so absurd that I have destroyed it in a reply and I believe that she will sign in the end. A good many authors of considerable prominence, are not only signing but sending in enthusiastic letters. One such is Josephine Peabody Marks, author of the Piper; another is Paul Kester. Yet another, curiously enough, is Gerald Stanley Lee, the platitudinarian. The most unlikely people are coming to the bat. One of them is Earl Derr Biggers, who was reported by Hersey as refusing to sign. He not only signs but sends me a thousand word letter, swearing war on the Comstocks and greasing me as a learned critic. Yet another signature comes from E. W. Howe, the Kansas philosopher. William Allen White has also yielded as has Charles Rann Kennedy, the dramatist. From Forrest Halsey comes a violent tirade against the Comstocks. All in all, the scheme seems to be working and I believe that the Protest, once it is completed, will quite startle Sumner.[1]

A week ago I wrote to Hacket[2] asking him to tackle certain men that I couldn't approach myself. He has not replied to my letter. Yesterday, I wrote to him again. I suspect that he is trying to evade doing anything. I shall, however, pursue him until he makes an open decision, and if, in the end, he refuses to help, I shall expose him in the pamphlet. This Hacket is an unpleasant fellow—an Irishman who flatters and cultivates the English. I know about him through Boyd.

Why don't you send out a few letters yourself? Your scheme of writing college professors seems to me a waste of energy. The average college professor is against you without even hearing your case. Can't you get the signatures of such men as Poultney Bigelow and Rex Beach? At all events, why not make the effort? We should practice a certain economy of enterprise and concentrate on possibilities. Hersey's experience shows that signatures are not to be got by simply sending out blank copies of the Protest. The thing must be done by personal solicitation and now and then pressure must be brought to bear upon recalcitrants.

Yours,

M

1. All the writers and editors that Mencken mentions in this letter, and more, did not impress Sumner, who wrote Alexander Harvey: "Authors taken as a whole may be very good judges of the . . . literary merits of any particular writing, but as judges of the tendency of that writing on the manners and morals of the people at large they are no more qualified than are an equal number of mechanics of ordinary education." (19 September 1916 [UPL])

2. Mencken means the critic and author Francis Hackett (1883–1962), who volunteered to distribute copies of the protest.

[NYP]

<u>165 W. 10</u>

Nov 26—1916

Dear H. L. M.

The results you are getting are interesting and illustrate nothing so well as how the average writer fears his critics. They cant stand the sharp point of searching comment. I would like to help with direct appeal if it were worthwhile in my case but it would do more harm than good. I went after Sam Blythe, George Ade and some others as a last resource—indirectly however—and their signatures came in. I would do the same in connection with Rex Beach except that I understand that at this moment he, Augustus Thomas, Hamlin Garland, Mary Austin, Mary Roberts Rinehart, Leroy Scott and several others are planning to issue a protest against the minutes in favor of the "Genius" or to have them rescinded at the next meeting which occurs after Thanksgiving. Jones called my attention to a request from the secretary of Thomas for a copy of the book and incidentally certain conversations over the phone one day when I was in Schulers office having him visé the contract for the Bulwark led me to the same conclusion. Hersey states that something to that end is on but that he is barred from all information.

I am seriously concerned to have them delay this if possible. My lawyers are just about ready to act and an action of this kind, if given to the papers would do my chances in court serious harm. Incidentally Levy & Auerbach[1] have been having a hard time with Swann who has been seen by Sumner and something done to set him by the ears   It is possible that a rump committee of malcontents has been to see Sumner and is aiding him. What do you suggest? I propose to call up Schuler in the morning and ask him what he knows & what he can do for me—assuming he is so disposed. Will write you later.

The Four act tragedy is all but done.[2] Will send you a copy, if I may, next week for your opinion.

Yours
Dreiser

Gloom is in Washington or New Windsor—I don't know which.
A charming letter from Basil King[3] & various others.

1. Joseph S. Auerbach, an attorney who pled the case for Dreiser in May 1918 and published the argument he delivered before the Appellate Division of the New York Supreme Court in *Essays and Miscellanies*, 3 vols. (New York, 1922), 3:130–65.
2. *The Hand of the Potter*.
3. A Canadian novelist.

[UPL]

THE SUN
Baltimore, Md.

[after 26 November 1916]

Dear Dreiser:-

I doubt that some of the men you mention have approached Swann, or will go far with their counter protest. I have letters from Leroy Scott and Mary Austin that denounce the moralists; their publication would make fools of both. Mary Roberts Rinehart has actually signed the protest. As for Augustus Thomas, I hear that he is a broken-hearted man, and in bad shape financially. His day has passed. There remains only Hamlin Garland. His opposition is already discounted.

Don't put any truth in Schuler. He is far more concerned about his job than he is about you. But he has signed the protest, and he knows that I am going to print a record of the case. Signatures continue to come in, and I have still nearly 100 letters to send out. My stenographer has been working day and night. The expected ones have refused: Agnes Repplier, Dr. Frank Crane, etc.[1] I shall attend to them in the pamphlet.

As for Swann, he is a swine. He takes orders, I hear, from Cardinal Farley.[2] However, he is not needed. A prosecution in the State courts needn't bother you; the main thing was to hold off the Postoffice. This, I believe, has been done; Marshall's letter cooks Sumner's goose in that direction. Let the dogs rescind their minute. We have the protest. Very few are refusing on the direct ground that they are against the book. Nearly all say they haven't read it. I can well believe them.

If the worst comes to the worst, I think Hersey can fix things, through Phelps, so that no news of the rescinding of the minute will reach the newspapers. Don't quarrel with Schuler yet. Give him a chance to work this.

I'll be in New York on Friday and shall call you up.

Yours,

M

1. Agnes Repplier (1855–1950), novelist, poet, historian whose writing showed the lasting influence of her early Christian convent education; Frank Crane (1861–1928), clergyman, columnist.
2. Cardinal John Farley (1842–1918), archbishop of New York.

[UPL]

SMART SET
A Magazine of Cleverness
George Jean Nathan
and   } Editors
H. L. Mencken

December 4, 1916

Dear Dreiser:

I had a talk with Schuler this morning and I gathered from him the impression that Hersey is an alarmist. Schuler says that there is not the slightest chance of the Executive Committee rescinding its action and that the agitation against you is confined to a few persons and is very weak. He promises absolutely to let me know in case any of these dogs attempt anything and to do so in plenty of time for me to get into action against them. He says that the Executive Committee will stick to its minute and that you have nothing to fear. I believe that Hersey has probably jumped to unwise inferences.

Yours,

M

[UPL]

H. L. Mencken
1524 Hollins St.
Baltimore.

Dec. 6, 1916.

Dear Dreiser:

Please be careful of any hint that you are thinking of jumping the John Lane Company and getting another publisher. I have heard whispers to that effect in New York and they may reach Jones. If they do, he will simply throw up the case and leave you in a hole. Better let all such things remain in status quo until after the battle is over.

It may interest you to know that Joyce Kilmer, the eminent critic of the New York Times, has refused to sign the Protest. May the good God help Joyce.

Yours,
M

[UPL]

H. L. Mencken
1524 Hollins St.
Baltimore.

Dec. 8, 1916.

Dear Dreiser:

If you receive the manuscript of an article against the moralists from a woman named Lida Calvert Obenchain, Bowling Green, Ky., please be polite to her. This Obenchain writes novels under the name of Eliza Calvert Hall, and they are enormously successful. Moreover, they are of a high moral nature. Nevertheless, she is one of your hottest partisans and was an early signer of the Protest. Her article, though it deals with books of fifteen years ago, contains some excellent stuff, and I think you might induce her to write another one in your favor.[1]

Yours,
M

1. On 8 December Mencken wrote to Mrs. Obenchain saying that *Smart Set* could not accept her article, since most of the books she deals with are "now almost forgotten." [UPL] But he suggested that she write Dreiser her opinion of him. On 11 December, she wrote Dreiser and sent him the article with a request that he return it: "It will form one chapter in a book of essays I am writing." [UPL] The book was never published.

[NYP]

<u>165 W. 10</u>

Dec. 13—1916

My H. L. M:

Under separate cover tonight I am mailing you the play.[1] I hope among the many things you are compelled to do before "getting off" you will find time to examine this leisurely.[2] The one thing I am concerned about is to have little inaccuracies of dialect corrected. In the case of Daubenspeck, act III I would be grateful if you would look after his broken German.

Greeting. All goes well. The trial activities start Monday I believe. Details too long to relate here. Have recieved various copies of letters, for which thanks. Stanchfield & Levy desire Jones, at time of trial—(beginning)—to publish the protest with all signatures in several N.Y. papers. Can the signatures you have obtained be used without further correspondence for this purpose. There are to be two actions. One before U.S. Commissioner—one before Appellate Court here—and almost simultaneously

Am now returning to The Bulwark

Th.D.

May spend Jan to May in Nevada
May be arrested here to accomodate S&L.

1. *The Hand of the Potter.*
2. Mencken was leaving for Denmark and Germany in late December as war correspondent for the *Sun.*

[UPL]

H. L. Mencken
1524 Hollins St.
Baltimore.

Dec. 14, 1916.

Dear Dreiser:

Let me have the manuscript of the play by all means. I think I'll be able to read it carefully before I go, but whether there will be time for a meeting remains to be seen. I'll be in New York on Tuesday next, but with a very heavy burden of business on my hands. I'll return on December 27th and sail on the 28th. I inclose a complete list of the signers to date, alphabetically arranged. You will note that the name of Bob Davis is included.[1] My impression is that Bob has since withdrawn his name. Be careful about this. I can't understand the proceedings engineered by Stanchfield, but I haven't the slightest doubt that they are prudent. If they involve a few days in jail for you, I shall shed no vain tears over you. Six months would do you good.

Please note that in the case of the copies of letters that I am sending you, they are to be held in the utmost confidence, and not used in any manner save for plain information. If the lawyers produced them in court, it would lead me into endless embarrassments. Give this your personal attention.

Please have Gloom keep me informed of developments from time to time.

Regarding your proposed Nevada visit, I can offer no advice or comment. Every man to his own poison.

Yours in Xt.,
M

1. Robert Davis (1869–1942), writer who at this time was Sunday editor of the New York *World*.

[UPL]

SMART SET

A Magazine of Cleverness

Saturday. [16 December 1916]

Dear Dreiser:-

Frankly, the play seems to me to be hopeless, not only because the subject is impossible on the stage, but also and more especially because the treatment is lacking in every sort of dramatic effectiveness. After the first act it is nothing but a series of speeches. The scene in the grand jury room would bore an audience stiff; the long soliloquys of Isadore would make it think of "Hazel Kirke".[1] Nor does it seem to me that you illuminate the central matter in the slightest. You merely state certain commonplace facts, and then follow with a commonplace theory to account for them. The whole thing is loose, elephantine and devoid of sting. It has no more dramatic structure than a jelly-fish.

I say the subject is forbidden on the stage, and mean it. It is all very well enough to talk of artistic freedom, but it must be plain that there must be a limit in the theatre, as in books. You and I, if we are lucky, visit the bowel-pot daily; as for me, I often have to leave a high-class social gathering to go out and piss; you, at least, have been known to roll a work-

ing girl on the couch. But such things, however natural, however interesting, are not for the stage. The very mention of them is banned by that
convention on which the whole of civilized order depends. In no country
of the world is such a thing as sexual perversion dealt with in the theatre.
Even in Germany and Russia, where Wedekind's "Fruehlingserwachen" is
played regularly, a touch of Krafft-Ebing would bring up the polizei.[2] I
once encountered a Danish play in which one of the characters mentioned
his bowel movements to his physician, but even in Denmark that was regarded as beyond the limit, and the passage was cut out. Nothing is more
abhorrent to the average man than sexual perversion. He would roar
against it in the theatre.

I see you getting into an understandable but nevertheless unfortunate
mental attitude. Resisting with justice the imbecilities of the Comstocks,
you unconsciously fly to an extreme, and demand a degree of freedom
that is obviously impossible. I have no patience with impossibilities. No
man in the world is hotter for artistic freedom than I am, nor more willing
to fight for it, but I know that there are certain rules that can't be broken,
and I am disinclined to waste time trying to break them when there is so
much work to do in places where actual progress can be made. The real
cause of the Comstockian attack upon "The 'Genius'", I have always
thought, is not that Witla works his wicked will upon the girls, but that
you make him insert his thumb into Angela's (as yet) virgin person. Copulation may go down, but the decencies must be observed. You and I, I
hope, are good friends. I would not hesitate to tell you that I had fallen
from virtue. But I would surely not recite for you the precise details of
the act.

This is a distinction to be remembered.

In the present case, I daresay you will accuse me of a lingering pru-
dishness. Accuse all you please; it is not so. If the thing were possible, I'd
advocate absolutely unlimited freedom in speech, written and spoken. I
think the world would be better off if I could tell a strange woman, met at
a church social, that I have diarrhoea—if the stage could be used to set up
a more humane attitude toward sexual perverts, who are helpless and un-
happy folks—if novels and other books could describe the precise process
of reproduction, beginning with the hand-shake and ending with lacta-
tion, and so show the young what a bore it is. But these things are forbidden. The overwhelming weight of opinion is against them. The man who
fights for them is as absurd as the man who fights for the right to walk
down Broadway naked, and with his gospel pipe in his hand. Both waste
themselves upon futile things while sound and valuable things remain to
be done.

For these reasons—setting aside its badness as a play—I am against

"The Hand of the Potter". It is empty of significance and gratuitously offensive. You can do infinitely better work—and work that every civilized man will stand behind. Surely you don't want to get into the position of a mere bad boy of letters—shocking the numskulls for the mere sake of shocking them. Consider the politics of the situation. Imagine the play printed tomorrow. The moralists would pounce upon it with cheers. And remember that not only your own artistic freedom, but also the freedom of many other men depends upon the issue.

The mss. will reach you in a day or two.

M

1. *Hazel Kirke* (1908), a popular play written by Steele MacKaye.
2. The German dramatist Frank Wedekind (1864–1918) whose *Fruehlingserwachen* (1906) shocked the public at its opening because it dealt frankly with the sex urge of the adolescent. Wedekind's expressionistic play indicts the school system and the ineptitude of parents as it dramatizes the tragedy of the central character, Wendla Bergmann, a girl of fourteen whose seduction leads to her death as the victim of abortives.

Baron Richard von Krafft-Ebing (1840–1902), the German psychiatrist whose *Psychopathia Sexualis* is a modern classic in the study of sexual deviation.

[NYP]

165 W. 10

Dec. 18—1916

My Dear H. L. M:

For the life of me I cannot discover what there is in the subject matter of this play to have evoked this tirade—all this denunciation and elucidation of the limits of the stage. Admittedly the idea may be badly worked out—a botch. But the subject! A poor weak pervert, defended or tolerated and half concealed by a family for social reasons commits a sex crime—not shown on the stage—and thereby entails a chain of disaster which destroys the home and breaks the spirit of the father and mother. What pray is there about this that is so low and vulgar? You proceed to recite a litany of vulgarities which cannot be practised in the open. List me the impossible vulgarities or obscenities in this. I have attempted a tragedy. To you it is not tragic—technically a botch. Now what else.

Actually I reread your letter and I cannot get at the kernel of all this excitement. Smilingly I can accept your denunciation of the play as a hopeless botch. That is the first function of criticism   When you go further and tell me what I can or cannot put on the stage, what the artistic or moral limitations of the stage are and what the American people will stand for you may be well within your critical rights but my answer is that I have more respect for my own judgement in this matter than I have for yours. In other words your limitations are not mine and this thing which you deem so offensive is in my eyes anything but that.

I wonder sometime whether you are allowing preconceived notions of what I can or cannot do to influence you? You speak of the text failing to illuminate the central matter. I wonder really what you assume the central matter of this play to be. You write as if you thought I were entering on a defense of perversion—trying to make it plausible or customary. If you would look at the title page you would see it is labeled a tragedy. What has a tragedy ever illuminated—unless it is the inscrutability of life and its forces and its accidents   What has one ever sought to teach or inculcate.

However I do not care to argue this further, now or in the future. To you, technically and artistically the thing is a botch. I have one request to make. The thing was submitted to you in advance and privately as it were. Do not, please, speak of it to Jones. Do not precede other reviewers, in case I decide to publish it, with a condemnatory blast. Say what you please along with the others (or nothing) at the time the play appears, but don't lead the procession. If you should you would more or less guide a sycophantic chorus which hangs on your word and drown the voices of a number of unprejudiced minds   You may rake me all you please once the thing is on the table, but with preknowledge you are in a position to do the work serious harm. I know you will not want to do that believing, as you do, that it will fall of its own weight

Greeting. The fireman's prayer book & the wall plaque labelled "Jesus" have already been consigned to the ash can where I trust some reverent slop collector will find them. If I don't see you before you leave—a happy voyage to you—all the best of Germany and Austria.

Dreiser

[UPL]
[20 December 1916]

Dear Dreiser:-

Despite all your honeyed eloquence, I still think it rotten politics to come out with a play on sexual perversion at such a time. Think how the moral reviewers will fall upon it, and bellow "I told you so". Really, the enterprise is quite insane. You are making it impossible for your lawyers to do anything. Worse, your play is a very bad one. The sexual perversion will appear to be dragged in by the heels—a mere effort to be nasty. Such strikes for liberty of discussion do not interest me. If you had anything to say on the subject, I'd be for saying it. But you actually say nothing. Cut out the scandalous interest, and there is no interest left. Fully half of the signers of the Protest, painfully seduced into signing by all sorts of artifices, will demand that their names be taken off. You fill me with ire. I damn you in every European language. You have a positive genius for doing foolish things. Put the ms. behind the clock, and thank me and God for saving you from a mess. Also, avoid Reno as you would the great pox while the case is on.¹ Imagine the headlines when you come to trial. In brief, apply to this business the elementary reasoning powers of a streptococcus. Don't crab it so magnificently.

As for the review, my chaplain advises me to promise nothing. For such a disease as you show the most violent remedies are indicated by the pharmacopeia. A big dose, filling the patient to the gills—down, down she goes! St. Barnabus, what a taste! But it will do you good, my dear Mon Chair. Almost I grow moral.

Change your play into something else. Jack the Ripper is an old, old story—a shilling shocker these many years. Read it in cold blood. Take the advice of men with hair on their chests—not of women. Leave it to anyone you choose—Huneker, or Wilkinson, or Masters.² This is my sober, honest judgment: The play is a piece of pish—clumsy, banal, unnatural, almost idiotic. Its publication would lose you your case, forfeit the respect of all intelligent persons, and make every man who has labored on the protest look like an ass. This I verily believe. Call me an ass an thou wilt, but you can't get around my offer to submit it to arbitration. Show this letter to Wilkinson, and then let him read the play—or vice versa.

If you pull any stuff about the morals of Baltimore, I'll have you killed within ten days.

Yours in Xt.,
M

Don't forget that we meet on the 27th. The place: Lüchow's beer-rooms. The time: 7 P.M. Bring the fair Gloom.³ I sail on the 28th. Done by me, etc.

1. Dreiser was contemplating a divorce from Sara White Dreiser, a step he never took.
2. James Huneker, the British novelist Louis Wilkinson, and Edgar Lee Masters.
3. Estelle Bloom Kubitz, called Gloom, had by this time become Dreiser's secretary and mistress.

[NYP]
Dec. 21—1916

My Dear Mencken:

Really all this row about this so called impossible play—a botch, a failure,—is beyond belief. If it is so bad who will publish it? Who produce it?

After all managers and publishers are not lunatics and a wild, disruptive or trashy thing like this can get no countenance from any sane being. Is not that true? Why then does your hair stand on end? Why rage and roar? I have not published it yet. If what you say is true I cannot get either a publisher or a manager   So you and I and the moralists and conservative friends of letters are all safe. I'm damned before I begin.

Curiously, before you ever wrote me I had been doing some of things you suggest as tests. I outlined it exactly as it is to Edgar Lee Masters when he was here in the fall. He was feverish to have me do it—write it. Ditto Hutchins Hapgood, whom you may not know (author of "The Spirit of the Ghetto", "The Spirit of Labor", "Autobiography of a Thief" "An Anarchist Woman")   Same result: He liked it very much thought it a splendid idea. Then I tried it on Gloom—before writing. Same result. Mrs. Paul Armstrong.[1] Same result. I then decided to write it.

Having finished it I sent it to you. A Roar. Astonished I decided to try Messrs Stanchfield & Levy (overawed by what you said about its effect on my trial, the Am. Pub. etc). I even (pardon the discourtesy) submitted your letter. Levy, after passing it on to Stanchfield and a leading movie producer whose name slips me for the moment returned it with the statement that he thought it a great play, ditto Stanchfield, ditto the movie producer and that the latter "is crazy to produce it". I quote his words. Your letter, he states, is beyond him and he cannot get your point of view at all. As for any injury to my reputation he thinks (ditto Stanchfield) that it would help it.

At least there goes one of your suggestions

Having three copies one has gone to Powys and one to Lea.[2] A rougher draft went to Mrs. * * * * * * *[3] whose views I have always been compelled to respect   She reports "A fascinating piece of work",—"the best of your dramatic work so far". Gloom was and remains unalterably pro. No doubt her opinion in your judgement is worth nothing   If Powys & Masters agree—I suppose you will bellow louder than ever.

Really, Henry L—you and I must merely agree to disagree at times unless you want to become an out and out Eck, which seems to me pointless and unnecessary. Not all that I do needs to appeal to you surely to keep us companionable

Nevertheless I do not propose, as I say to rush madly into print with this thing. I propose to take judgement and in the end follow my ultimate conviction. If that remains as it is the play will be published willy-nilly— if I died the next day. What pains me is to hear you quoting "the moral reviewers" to me, talking of the individuals who signed the protest taking their names off—(What a horror); shouting that "the subject is forbidden on the stage" (by whom, please? Sumner?) that "there must be a limit in plays as in books". (Could Anthony[4] do better, I ask you?)

Look at these sentences

"Banned by that convention on which the whole of civilized order depends"

"In no country in the World is such a thing as sexual perversion dealt with in the theatre". (Jacob Gordin did it at Thomashefsky's theatre N.Y. for years)[5]

"There are certain rules that can't be broken"

"There is so much work to do in places where actual progress can be made". (Henry L! Henry L! This old cry from you. Why not have asked me to be safe and sane?)

"Witla works his wicked will upon girls" (!!!!) (!!!!)

"The overwhelming weight of opinion is against you". (Mass opinion.!!!!)

"Work that every civilized man will stand behind". (Alas! Alas!) (I haven't appealed to civilized man very much, so far, eh?)

However, I am doing just what you suggest—getting opinions. If I can reach Wilkinson so much the better. Mind you I am not saying the play is well done. It may be as bad as you say. Plainly it couldn't be worse. (No one else seems to agree with you as to that or any of your other contentions so far—but waive that for the time being.) It is your swift, dogmatic rulings as to the limits of the stage, the absolutely alien character of perversion, the reading into this play a plea for perversion or an excuse for my personal interest in such things. This is the limit. Gregory VIIIth[6] could do no worse.

I deny absolutely your right to say this. I deny your ruling in connection with perversion and its place on the stage. Tragedy is tragedy and I will go where I please for my subject. If I fail ridiculously in the execution let the public and the critics kick me out. They will anyhow. But so long as I have any adequate possession of my senses current convention will not dictate to me where I shall look for art—in tragedy or comedy. My inner instincts and passions and pities are going to instruct me—not a numbskull mass that believes one thing and does another.

So far, so good. I will see you on the 27th. Personally I am very doubtful of injecting George Jean Nathan into this. He is no doubt a very amiable and charming person. You seem to think highly of him. In a social way I haven't the slightest objection but if this play is coming up you are probably making me one more good enemy and without any particular reason for it. I rarely argue with anyone but yourself and when I do it results fatally—for me.

Yours
Dreiser

1. Rella Abell Armstrong, a writer and friend whose critical judgment Dreiser valued.

2. John Cowper Powys and, perhaps, Edgar Lee Masters.
3. This word is not distinguishable but appears to be either Martin or Matin.
4. Anthony Comstock.
5. Jacob Gordin (1853–1909), Russian-born writer whose plays brought new forms of realism to the Yiddish theater in the late nineteenth century.
6. Dreiser is referring to Pope Gregory VIII (1020–1085), one of the great reformers of the medieval church.

[UPL]

H. L. Mencken
1524 Hollins St.
Baltimore.

Dec. 21, 1916.

Dear Dreiser:

Pondering my letter of last night I become full of fears that I did not make its objections to the play strong enough. If you have any such feeling, please add 40% to every adjective and 100% to those that seem the weakest. I had rather see you sold into white slavery at once than have you print such a play at this juncture. The delight of the Comstocks would be wholly beyond expression. They would fix upon you forever the reputation of a man who dealt in the most unmentionable indecencies and your goose would be cooked. If the play must be printed, then for God's sake get Ella Wheeler Wilcox[1] or Dr. Frank Crane to sign it. You are the one man in America to-day who cannot afford to monkey with such dangerous buzz-saws. For all you and I can say to the contrary, this is still a great moral republic, and there is plainly such a thing as tempting its pious sentiment too far. Seriously, the only feasible course is to print the play under a nom de plume and then acknowledge it after the row is over. But you will never acknowledge it. Two years hence, reading it in cold blood, you will rank it with that early book of yours which now stands suppressed but is read with gloating by occasional visitors to the Congressional Library.

I inclose you a tract appropriate to the season.[2] The author is a very good friend of mine.

Yours,
M

1. Ella Wheeler Wilcox (1850–1919), poet, sentimental novelist.
2. The piece has disappeared.

[UPL]

H. L. Mencken
1524 Hollins St.
Baltimore.

Dec. 22, 1916.

Dear Dreiser:

I am still full of fears that I adopted a too suave and conciliatory tone in my letters about the play. Please destroy them forthwith. I shall give you my verdict through a megaphone when we meet. Whenever I take a pen in hand I immediately grow artificial and ineffective.

Yours,
Mencken

[UPL]

H. L. Mencken
1524 Hollins St.
Baltimore.

Dec. 23, 1916.

Dear Dreiser:

Your eloquent arguments in favor of the high artistic purpose and noble intent of your play do not convince me at all and neither do the encomiums of the critics you mention. Any man who gives unqualified praise to such a loose and shambling piece of work simply confesses that he is incompetent to express an opinion. I haven't the slightest fear that any intelligent publisher will publish it, but what I am afraid of is that you will fall into the hands of some petty publisher who is eager to capitalize your present predicament, and who will at once rank you, and forever, with the pornographic authors whose books are so beautifully advertised in The Masses. In other words, you stand in serious danger, through this play, of being definitely labeled as a mere shocker of boobs. If the piece showed any sound thought, if it contributed a single intelligent idea to the subject, if it were in any sense a work of art, I'd be hot for it and you well know it. But for the life of me I can see nothing in it save a boyish desire to manhandle a subject that is fit only for black headlines in yellow journals. Why you waste your time on such futile quasi-pathology when there are so many tempting things to be done, is more than I can make out. I have thought of various theories and one that survives is that you are addicted to some secret and terrible drug—perhaps, castor oil or bicarbonate of soda. Theoretically, to be sure, such subjects may be handled on the stage, and it is possible, as you say, that certain Yiddish dramatists may have actually tackled them. But no theory is worth a hoot in the face of an immovable fact, and here we have the immovable fact that the thing you treat would never be discussed intelligently and decently by those who saw and reviewed the play, but would be immediately seized on as pornography. I could write a parody on this play and perhaps make it a much better play at bottom, in which a surgical operation for haemorrhoids constituted the principal scene. This, too, might be art, but surely you do not argue that it would be suitable for Broadway or even for Christendom.

Your allegation that I am a moralist is as intelligent as your treatment of your subject in your play. No one knows better than you that I am nothing of the sort. I have written ten times as much against the moralists as you have and perhaps twice as much as any other American. What is more, I shall continue to do so. But there is nothing that enrages me more than an attempt to put over banal improprieties on the ground that they are profound and artistic. That is why I urged you to cut out a lot of stuff in "The 'Genius.'" Don't forget that there is just as much freedom of speech in "The Titan" and that I never made the slightest complaint against it. The difference lies in the fact that "The Titan" is a sincere and creditable work of art while "The 'Genius'" in large part seems to be mere drivel. I offer these opinions, not for their novelty or authority, but merely because you seem to invite them. If I believed, for instance, that you seriously regarded your play as a piece of work worthy of your reputation, I'd apply for your commitment to an insane asylum. You know at bottom that it is silly stuff, and no matter how much you denounce my view of it, you will have to admit in the end that I am right. Masters has not seen it as it stands and neither has Wilkinson. As for Powys, I can't understand his criteria of judgment and therefore have no interest in his opinion.

Once more 10,000 damns upon all such enterprises. You are the one man in America who can write novels fit for a civilized man to read and here you waste yourself upon enterprises not worth ten minutes of your time. After all, what do you say about your pervert? Nothing that every child doesn't know. And what do you show regarding the influence of his crime upon his family? Nothing that even a newspaper reporter couldn't imagine. The whole thing is a mass of platitudes, and if the crime at the bottom of it were simple larceny or piracy, not a soul would show any interest in it. One of the things you have got to realize is that a childish interest in such things as perversion is one of the most salient proofs of an essentially moral mind. One step more and you will be writing sex hygiene books for use in nunneries.

The dinner on Wednesday had better be called off. You may be sure that I would, under no circumstances, show the play to Nathan or even describe it to him accurately. He views you with a great deal of respect. Meanwhile, I surely hope you celebrate the birthday of our Redeemer in a truly Christian manner and that you do not commit the infamy of going to bed sober. If I don't see you before my departure, my chaplain will attend to the daily prayers for you. God knows when I'll get back; it may be a few weeks and it may not be for months.

Yours,
M

[NYP]

165 W. 10

Dec 25—1916

Fairest Mencken:

Can't we laid aside this argument for the time being anyhow   I propose to do nothing without taking considerable more testimony from various sources. Meanwhile let us meet Wednesday evening. I should like to see you before you sail. My objection in regard to Nathan is not personal. I was fearful lest the damn play come up at the dinner table. In the face of so much pro-British subterfuge how can you turn on a fellow Menschener[1] in this cruel fashion.

Von Dreiser

Merry, Merry Christmas—and, if I don't see you—may 1000 German subs see you there & back safely.

1. Man.

[UPL]

H. L. Mencken
1524 Hollins St.
Baltimore.

Dec. 26, 1916.

Dear Dreiser:

An armistice is declared and I surely hope you will keep its terms and not foully murder me when I am not looking. At the moment the proposed

Estelle Bloom Kubitz (H. L. Mencken Papers, New York Public Library)

dinner for Wednesday is off, but I'll try to fix it up again tomorrow (Wednesday) and shall call you up. I am leaving Baltimore at midnight tonight and shall reach New York early tomorrow morning. My papers are now in order and I expect to get through without difficulty.

I share your suspicions of the Bruno proposition.[1] The novelette he mentions is an intolerably idiotic piece of writing. It comes very close indeed to burlesque and it would be dangerous for you to hook up your name with it. Altogether, Bruno seems to me a bad man for you to have dealings with at this juncture. He has played the jitney genius to such an extent that he is a public comedian.

As I say, I'll call you up some time tomorrow. My last day is naturally crowded with work and even if we meet I doubt that it will be for more than an hour or so. I must go over the whole Smart Set situation with Nathan before I leave. Things are in a very serious state.

Yours,
M

1. Guido Bruno, editor who was devoted to the cause of literary freedom. At this time, he was moving from the short-lived *Bruno's Weekly* to a weekly called *Bruno's*. On 23 December 1916, he wrote Dreiser of John Sumner's objection to Alfred Kreymborg's novelette "Edna: The Girl of the Street" and asked for a contribution to his next issue that would reveal Dreiser's "viewpoint upon the Comstockian society in general and Mr. Sumner in special." [UPL]

[UPL-H]

SMART SET
A Magazine of Cleverness
George Jean Nathan
and
H. L. Mencken } Editors

[27 December 1916]

Imperial German Ship Service

Operator No 717, Theodor Herman von Dreiser, is to report at Lüchow's December 27 at 7 P.M. Fail not. (and bring Gloom).

(L.S.) The Oberkommandant:
H. L. Mencken
(L.S.) Amtlich:
von Nathan

P.S.—Marion will come with me, and N. will bring a lady.

von M.

Marion Bloom (H. L. Mencken Papers, New York Public Library)

[NYP-T]

A Shark, Esq.,[1]
   Atlantic Ocean.

[December, 1916]

Dear friend and brother:

The bearer, Mr. Henry Lolipop Mencken of Baltimore, U.S.A., lecturer, essayist, poet, raconteur, is now en route to his native land, and has prevailed upon me to permit him to meet you. Knowing your sympathetic interest in and partiality for men of Mr. Mencken's personal proclivities and outward physical pulchritude, as well as his inner and, as it were, spiritual content, I venture to accomodate him, as well as to forward by him a small package, the contents of which will, I am sure, prove of mutual satisfaction to both of you. The smaller, a bottle, is for external application only, and if properly applied should add to the interest and even zest you will take in Mr. Mencken, I am sure. The remainder of the package is for internal use or dressing. If my friend can be prevailed upon to take these, they will, I am sure, add to his pleasure in the first and yours in the last instance. I trust you will find Mr. Mencken not only diverting, but filling, to the last degree. His position in America, as connoiseur of the best entente cooking (Bratwurst, pigs' feet, sauer kraut, and beer) will, I am sure, tend to elevate him in your eyes as well as in other ways.

Greeting! I trust all is well with you in your watery realm and will remain so. Two such amiable and experienced souls should find <u>much</u> in each other.

I remain, dear sir, (where I very much prefer to be)

> Yours in Xt.
> Sanctus Maria Theodore de Ava
> Dreiser.

1. Mencken sailed on the *Oscar II*, and Dreiser sent him this letter along with a farewell "bottle."

[UPL]

1524 Hollins St.
Baltimore, Md. U.S.A.

[March or early April 1917][1]

Dear Dreiser:-

The portrait matter still rests upon my heart, but at the moment I can't fix any date for the operation, and it will probably have to lie over.[2] I am coming to New York this week if it is possible, but don't know how long I can stay. My mother and sister are here alone, and I don't want to leave them unprotected. Mobs are already afoot here and last night they raided a pacific meeting and raised hell. It is very likely that there will be some smashing of windows and other delicate heroics when war is declared. You know the Anglo-Saxon patriot. If things quiet a bit I'll probably come over Thursday. But I can't ask the artist to waste his time on such uncertainties.

Yours in Xt.,
M

1. Mencken returned in mid-March, and America entered the war on 6 April 1917. This letter was written sometime in this period.
2. Mencken was to sit for a portrait.

[NYP]
Mch 30—1917

Dear H. L. M.

I would be interested to know what if any stand the Authors' League is taking in connection with Susan Lenox.[1]

Contrast the attitude of D Appleton & Co with that of John Lane.[2]

D

1. See Mencken to Dreiser, 23 April 1911, n.2. When John Sumner attacked the novel, declaring it contained some one hundred obscene pages, the Authors' League took no stand. But Phillips's publisher, unlike John Lane, defended the book.
2. D. Appleton & Co. wanted to be Dreiser's publisher and suggested the firm might take over *The "Genius."*

[UPL]

1524 Hollins Street
Baltimore, Md., U.S.A.

[after 30 March 1917]

Dear Dreiser:-

I shall feel out Schuler on the Susan Lenox matter, and let you hear the result. Appleton is stalling too. I have tried to get a direct statement of his plans out of him, but he seems to be hedging a bit.

Another invention that would help the world would be a rifled condom.

Yours,
M

[UPL]

The
SMART SET
A Magazine of Cleverness
George Jean Nathan ⎫
and ⎬ Editors
H. L. Mencken ⎭

April 9, 1917

Dear Dreiser:

I am sorry I missed you last night and that I must return to Baltimore today without enjoying the enchantment of seeing you. Confidentially, I think it well to be near home at this moment. In consequence, I dare say that the proposed limning of my features must go over until the Autumn. I shall return on April 27th. Why not have lunch with me at Lüchow's on the 28th, Saturday? I am also inviting Huneker. The hour I suggest is one P.M. George Nathan will visit the dump in the interval and see that the appropriate victuals are on the fire and that enough kegs are tapped to keep Huneker well oiled.

                    Yours in Xt,
                    M

de Bloom just called up.[1]

   1. The postscript was handwritten. Mencken is referring to Marion Bloom.

[NYP]
April 14—1917

Dear H. L. M:

The proposed dinner appeals to me. At least I will get one meal this spring. I do not know about the portrait myself. If he is in trim & you have time and wish it I will see about it. I would like to see it done. But otherwise—I mean unless you would like to fool with it—don't bother.

Mr. Sunday's[1] sermon begins at 2:15 & I must run.

                    Dreiser

   1. Billy Sunday.

[UPL]

1524 Hollins Street
Baltimore, Md., U.S.A.

[April, 1917]

Dear Dreiser:-

I see by the papers that sufragettes are enlisting for the war. This will lead to immorality. I propose that you and I go in as midwives.

Yours In Xt.,
M

[UPL]

The
SMART SET
A Magazine of Cleverness
452 Fifth Avenue, New York

[before 28 April 1917]

Dear Dreiser:-

The way this ass admits your case is really too lovely.[1]

What of the slaughter of Michelob on April 28th? One P.M. is the time, and the place is Lüchow's.

When you go to Diamond Jim's funeral,[2] drop a tear for me. He, too, had bladder trouble.

Yours,
de M.

1. This has not been identified.
2. James "Diamond Jim" Brady (1856–1917), financier and philanthropist.

[UPL]

The
SMART SET
A Magazine of Cleverness
452 Fifth Avenue, New York

[before 28 April 1917]

Dear Dreiser:-

A number of the names on your list are those of persons who are not authors. I think it would be unwise to publish them, for the simple reason that it would give the moralists a chance to accuse you of padding the returns. Beside, so many wholly unknown names make the whole thing look thin and feeble. There are about 350 names of genuine authors—a very good showing. Hersey writes that Jones has the original signatures. I notice some errors on your list—for example, Frank Capin Bray instead of Frank Chapin Bray. Again, Leo-Rar Oxtell sounds fabulous. If that is the fellow's name, make him change it.

I will meet you at Lüchow's at one P.M. Saturday, and perchance before.

Yours in Xt.,
M

[NYP]

Blue Room
The White House
Washington D.C.

May 2nd 1917

Dear Sir and Honored Compatriot:

These touching lines to a worthy English soldier have just been called to my attention.[1] As a loyal fellow Briton I wish to most sincerely thank you

Arthur J. Balfour

1. Dreiser attached to this letter a copy of Mencken's early poem in the manner of Kipling, "The Orf'cer Boy," which had been published in *Ventures in Verse* (1903). See Appendix 2, pp. 804–5, for text of the poem.

[NYP]
May 5—1917

To H. L. M.

A bleak, cheesy day. Under separate cover I sent you the brief filed by Stanchfield & Levy with the Appellate division. Since it is necessary for me to return this speedily I registered it for safe keeping & would like to have it back as quickly after you glance through it as possible. The citation of other cases at the end may interest you.

Dreiser

I have just talked with Lord Revelstake who finds your poem perfect.

[UPL]

1524 Hollins Street
Baltimore, Md., U.S.A.

[after 5 May 1917]

Dear Dreiser:-

Thanks for the chance to see the proofs of the brief. It is a very able document. Please let me have a couple of copies of it as soon as it is printed. I am returning it posthaste.

Ben Hecht[1] is forming a company of Volunteer Woodchoppers to chop down German flagpoles. I have put you down for a commission as First Gravedigger. All day I write poetry.

Yours in Xt.,
M

1. Ben Hecht (1893–1964), journalist, novelist, playwright.

[UPL]

1524 Hollins Street
Baltimore, Md., U.S.A.

[May 1917]

Dear Dreiser:-

Please run your eye through this, and let me know it if there are any errors in fact. It is part of a chapter in my Prefaces book. Knopf, by the way, is to do it.

I get news from my agents in the Carroll county hinterland that you are scandalizing the Dunkards by going about in Chinese jeans, with your virile parts plainly outlined. This is regrettable.

Please let me have the enclosed as soon as you can. It is to go into type at once.

Yours in Xt.,
M

Once that the world is made safe for democracy, all that will remain will be to make democracy safe for the world.

[UPL]

The
SMART SET
A Magazine of Cleverness
452 Fifth Avenue, New York

[May 1917]

Dear Dreiser:-

I suspect that the aesthetic argument was written by Wright, though he has said nothing about it.[1] Whether it is likely to influence the learned judge is for the lawyers to decide. As for me, I confess that I can't make up my mind. Am I to keep the copy?

I finished my preface book last night. A week or so of polishing—i.e., of changing all intelligible English into fantastic and mystical balderdash—and it will be ready for Jones. It is my hope that he will gag at it. I have overtures from Little-Brown, Houghton-Mifflin and Knopf.

In Jesus' name,
M

1. Dreiser sent Mencken a copy of the brief to be presented in the case for *The "Genius."* Mencken suggests that Wright wrote the argument that Merton Yewdale presented.

[UPL]

The
SMART SET
A Magazine of Cleverness
452 Fifth Avenue, New York

[May 1917]

Dear Dreiser:-

Wright has taken the veil. Observe the enclosed list of volunteer officers.[1]

I have been rewriting my preface book from snout to tail—a fearful job. But there is now some very good stuff in it. I tell the truth about you, and discover to my astonishment that much of it is almost creditable to you.

By the way, an accurate bibliography of your books ought to be put together. I might use it as an appendix. Give it your powers of meditation.

My regards to Hersey, Sumner and Hopkins.[2]

Yours In Xt.,
M

1. Mencken included a list of military volunteers with one W. H. Wright on it.
2. Arthur Hopkins, a producer of avant-garde plays who wanted to stage Dreiser's *The Hand of the Potter*.

[NYP]
May 24—1917

Dear H. L. M:

You are on much better terms with Wright than I am so perhaps you can find occasion to do me a service. Persuade him to quit using my name to his advantage and my disadvantage. He is now saying—possibly to bolster up his own situation, I don't know—that Jones is going about town saying that he is delighted to be stint of Wright & Dreiser. The combination as you notice sounds a little better than just Wright alone. As a matter of fact I know that this is not true. He may have said he was glad to be rid of Wright—(I hold no brief for Jones) but he has made and is still making overtures to me, looking to my staying, and naturally would not say anything of the kind. Wright I hear is saying I owe the John Lane Company money. This is not true. The John Lane Co is willing to advance me money which I do not now need. My relations with Jones outside of two single literary points are of the friendliest. I have told him what I think of him but to him alone. My avoiding Wright—once and for all, is due to the conviction that he is a trouble maker—to go no further. I cannot quite stomach his methods, the while I am interested to applaud and further any serious work he may do. I have never asked for aid or support of any kind from him and I wish sincerely he would cut his sled loose from my somewhat wobbly wagon and let me go my way alone. It is difficult enough to put this thing over singly.

Yours
Dreiser

N.B. If someone hauled out one of those five sheet Wilson Campaign posters reading "he has kept us out of war" and pasted it up opposite the White House, would he be hung as a traitor or shot as a spy?

[UPL]

1524 Hollins Street
Baltimore, Md., U.S.A.

[after 14 June 1917]

Dear Dreiser:-

Poor old Reedy becomes pathetic.[1] The notion that you are headed toward Nietzscheism is really astounding. The Bourne article is the best thing ever written about you[2]—a very fine and just estimate.

In Xt.,
M

1. William Marion Reedy had been discussing Dreiser, in Nietzschean terms, as a "superman" (see "What I've Been Reading," *Reedy's Mirror* 25(15 December 1916), 839–40; repr. in Salzman, 289–91).
2. Randolph Bourne, "The Art of Theodore Dreiser," *Dial* 62(14 June 1917), 507–9; repr. in *The Stature of Theodore Dreiser*, eds. Alfred Kazin and Charles Shapiro (Bloomington, Ind., 1965), 92–95.

[NYP]

c/o Harry Bailie Smith
R.F.D. 10—
Westminster, Maryland

June 26—1917

Fairest M—

Do you know anything about all those islands in the Chesapeake—any mild deserted land near the water. I'm thinking of idling about down there a little later in the summer. And what about the Havre de Grace region. Is it attractive there? Dont trouble to investigate if you dont already know. Would have called you up Sunday but understood you were off fishing. Tried the Rennert for "hogs jowl and greens" on the recommendation of a well known gourmet-critic but was betrayed as usual.

Honorious XVIIth

[UPL]

1524 Hollins Street
Baltimore, Md., U.S.A.

[after 26 June 1917]

Dear Dreiser:-

Can't you get me a copy of the answer to the Jones brief? Jones sent me a copy of the brief itself, but I have only your copy of the answer. I want to have a complete record of the case. I'll return the answer when you get back to New York, or earlier if you say so.

Avoid the Chesapeake shore as you would the great pox. It is hell's kitchen. Western Maryland, however, is a beauteous demesne.

                    In Xt.,
                    M

                                                                    [UPL]

                    1524 Hollins Street
                    Baltimore, Md., U.S.A.

                                                        [after 26 June 1917]
Dear Dreiser:-
    Am I to keep the Sumner brief and answer? The answer to Sumner is the best document that the case has so far brought out. It demolishes the moral cause completely.
    Thank God, Jones bucked at my preface book. I think Knopf will print it. It was too anti-English for Jones. I made it so deliberately.

                    M.

                                                                    [UPL]
                                                        [before 28 June 1917]

[To Dreiser]
                    Challenge.
    I will shoot dice with you to determine which shall be the last volunteer.

                                                                    [UPL]

                    1524 Hollins Street
                    Baltimore, Md., U.S.A.

                                                        [before 28 June 1917]
Dear Dreiser:-
    What if I should motor to R.F.D. 10 <u>Tuesday</u> morning, bringing a case of malt?[1] Answer prepaid. Also, what is the route from Westminster?

                    Yours in Xt.,
                    M

1. Dreiser spent most of June and part of July at Westminster, Maryland, with Estelle Bloom Kubitz. They stayed on the farm of Harry Bailie Smith, a Bloom family relative.

[NYP]

c/o Harry Bailie Smith
R.F.D. 10—
Westminster, Md.

June 28—1917

Dog of a Hyphenate—

The route is intricate—a strangely complicated affair. Thou takest the main automobile road to Westminster Maryland and there inquirest for one H. Baile Smith who has a 60 or 70 acre farm just outside New Windsor. No one will be able to tell thee. Tis a dark secret. But for a little silver rubbed in the palm and the cabalistic words "Kaiseriscuss Armyrusque Belgianicus" seven times repeated—also "God save the King" you will be shown. A bottle of plain Bushnill awaits thee. Also apple dumplings and a religious or sacrificial offering known as <u>Cherry</u> <u>Dolly</u>. Do thou come at thy convenience

In the meantime peace and immediate enlistment for thee. I accept thy challenge. Also this day I have strung a hammock in a nearby grove, have hung up "The Orficer Boy" for a talisman and am now ready for any fate

As I write I can hear Berts[1] corona ticking busily below. Soon the farm dinner bell will ring—a clanging thing on a pole. Hail.

In writing your auto-b—have a care lest you tell the truth.

Josephus Daniels[2]

Seriously—why not come up Saturday & stay over Sunday   You needn't bring the car & you are heartily welcome   Mrs. S.[3] is one of your ardent admirers. Or failing that come Sunday—or plan anything yourself

In case you get as far as Westminster & cant find it Ring Westminster 802—F5

1. Bert is a nickname for Estelle Bloom Kubitz.
2. Josephus Daniels, secretary of the navy, waged a campaign to make the navy "dry."
3. Mrs. Harry Bailie Smith.

[UPL]

1524 Hollins Street
Baltimore, Md., U.S.A.

[after 28 June 1917]

Dear Dreiser:-

For the moment a trip to Westminster looks impossible. My brother's[1] wife and child are still here and he is returning on July 4th. Later in the week I must go to Phila. and New York. Will you still be on the farm week after next? If so, I'll be delighted. I'll bring a case of beer, and some red wine, gin, rum, vermouth, bitters, vodka, chartreuse and curacoa. Also, some free-smoking cigars.

I have an offer of $500 for the moving picture rights to "The Orf'cer Boy". Shall I sell?

Yours,
M

1. Charles Mencken (1882–1956). Of Mencken's three siblings—Charles, Gertrude, and August—Charles alone had a child. Mencken and Charles were the only two to marry, and Mencken had no children.

[NYP]

R.F.D. 10
c/o H. B. Smith
Westminster, Md.

June 29—1917

Ava, Caesar:

I think I can get a copy of Auerbachs reply. Will try anyhow. Do me a favor. Look up Admiral Perry in your Encyc. and give me the details of his visit to Japan—the year, what port, what the Japs said, whether he fired on the defenses before he was admitted—or not. I am making a reference to it. The Jim-Jam-Jems[1] containing the attack on Sumner is the June number now on the stands

Thomas Jefferson

1. The July *Jim-Jam-Jems* contained an exposé of John Sumner, accusing him of fraud in an early business transaction.

[UPL]

1524 Hollins Street
Baltimore, Md., U.S.A.

[after 29 June 1917]

Dear Dreiser:-

Commodore Matthew Perry arrived at Kurihama, on the Bay of Yedo, July 7, 1853, with 4 ships and 530 men. He delivered his demands to the representative of the Shogun on the 14th, to wit, that shipwrecked American sailors be returned and well treated, that Japan buy American goods, and that one American consul be permitted to take post in Japan. He then sailed for China to give the Japs time to digest the stuff. He returned in February, 1854, with 10 ships. The Japs then signed the treaty. It allowed American ships to enter Shimoda and Hakodate. The Brittanica says that Perry "was without authority to support his proposals by any recourse to violence." Not a shot was fired. Peary's report, in 3 vols., was printed in 1856, and may be seen in any public library. All this is true, as God is my judge. I would not lie to you.

In Xt.,
M

[UPL]

1524 Hollins Street
Baltimore, Md., U.S.A.

[after 30 June 1917]

Dear Dreiser:-

As the enclosed shows Wright has taken over the book page of the Mail and is trying to make something of it.[1] I got him the job. Needless to say, he will do whatever he can for you—and he can do a lot, for the New York field is virgin. The important thing is to get him started—and to make the Mail people realize that a book page can be a live thing. I have suggested to him that he encourage correspondence. It introduces controversy, and makes for interest. Why not write him a brief letter for publication, on anything or everything? Ten lines would be enough. The thing is to get real names into it, and make interest. Here is a chance to butter your own parsnips. Note his tendency, even in the first issue, necessarily experimental.

M.

1. Mencken sent Dreiser pages from the book page of the New York *Mail* of 30 June 1917. Among other things, they show Wright's anti-British bias in literature, his willingness to promote Dreiser and other realists, and his stand against literary censorship.

[UPL]

1524 Hollins Street
Baltimore, Md., U.S.A.

[before 5 July 1917]

Dear Dreiser:-

All I know about the whole Chesapeake littoral is that it is damnably hot in summer, and full of cheap trippers, and devoid of decent eating or drinking. Moreover, it is malarious and typhoidodaisical. In brief, a hell's hole. Stay where you are, in Goddes name. Invite me politely, and I'll run out some day to visit you. Send careful directions, with a map. I'll bring the alcohol. I'd have come out this week, but my house is full of relatives and I must act as chauffeur, also buying the gasoline.

I am at work upon my autobiography, and have just finished the chapter describing my baptism and seduction.

Yours in Xt.,
M

[NYP]

R.F.D. 10—etc

July 5—1917

Dear Senator:

You don't need any invitation to come up here. How silly. There's a spare room next to mine, and you'd be more welcome than I am—which isn't saying too much, now that I come to think of it—but you'd be vastly welcome. Do you want me to have Mrs. H. B. send you an invite—

I'll be here next week. I'll be in Baltimore Friday and will call you up, but don't let me interfere with your plans   Gloom wants to see a lawyer & I want to buy six or seven things which can't be had here. I'll take you to lunch or dinner if you want to come.

The enclosed¹ is being used in all the Scripp-McRay papers—50—I understand. Wright's book page is good. I'm willing to do anything I

can—but what specifically? The mysterious word was <u>chorus</u> (referring to
"On the Banks".)[2]
Peace—if I don't see you—and come whenever you want to

Thomas Aquinas

1. The item is missing.
2. "On the Banks of the Wabash," the Indiana state song composed by Dreiser's
brother, Paul Dresser.

[UPL]

Rev. Theodore Dreiser,
c/o H. B. Smith,
R.F.D. No. 10,
Westminster, Md.

July 10, 1917

Dear Sir:
    Mr. Mencken requests me to inform you that he is quite ignorant of
the matters to which you refer. He further instructs me to ask you to
kindly refrain from pestering him with a long and vain correspondence.
He is engaged at the moment upon patriotic work which takes his whole
time and he has no leisure to fool with the bughousery of the literati.
    Having no more to say, I will now close.

Very sincerely yours,
Ferdinand Balderdash
Captain, 16th U.S. Secret Service

[NYP]

<u>165 W. 10</u>

July 30—1917

Dear Major:
    I have just been assailed in this den by Messrs Boni & Liverwright
Inc. who suggest they take over all my works—consolidate the issue as it
were & contract for all future output. This is the proposition I was going
to make to some publisher myself soon. If I win the "Genius" case this
fall the situation should be considerably improved.
    What I want to say to you is that if you approach Lothrop or the other

firm you mentioned it should be with this idea of consolidation in mind. It is useless for me to put out a book here & a book there. It gives me no background. If you see anyone at all discuss the transfer from this point of view. I can get my various publishers to let go my books I think.

Greeting. I think of my days in Balto with great pleasure

Avicenna.

Naturally I did nothing about Boni & Liverwright. I know nothing about them as yet

[NYP]

165 W. 10th St.

Oct 25—1917

Dear M—

Bert was telling me of your proposition in regard to 50 copies of the "Genius"—fifty-fifty on the primary cost of the books and the profits.[1] Yesterday I took the matter up with Jones who wishes to refer it to his board of directors, lawyers etc. Should he ever act I will be glad to supply the books

Dreiser

He has shut me out of so many minor offers that I am not hopeful. As I understand it there are 400 copies of the book bound & on hand

1. Mencken offered to purchase, with Dreiser, fifty copies of the book to sell privately. Because of the Sumner case, the book's sales were frozen and Dreiser was not earning money on the novel.

[UPL]

The
SMART SET
A Magazine of Cleverness
George Jean Nathan
and ⎱ Editors
H. L. Mencken ⎰

[December 1917]

Dear Dreiser:-

My best thanks for the noble necktie. I shall wear it to church on Sunday, and mayhap prevail upon the soprani with it. I enclose an illustration for your work "The American Mind".¹ My chaplain bombs the ears of Omnipotence with your virtues.

Gott mit uns!

Yours,
M.

1. Mencken enclosed a photograph of "The St. Paul Street Champion Bowling Team," on which he wrote, "The Master Mind Complex."

[NYP]

<u>165 W. 10th</u>

May 10—1918

My Dear Mencken:

This is submitted to S.S. because I can think of no publication which would either use it or to which it would be so well suited.¹

Th.D.

1. Dreiser is referring to his play *Phantasmagoria*.

[UPL]

1524 Hollins Street
Baltimore, Md.

May 13th [1918]

Dear Dreiser:-

"Phantasmagoria" has just reached me, forwarded from the office. It is fine stuff. My one doubt is whether it fits into our present scheme of popularization—a scheme we were forced into by the heavy tread of bankruptcy, audible in the ante-chamber. I am sending it to Nathan at once for his opinion.¹ Have you anything else? We have six or eight novelettes in type, but are eternally short of short stories. Running a magazine, in these days, is a constant going over the top.

Yours in Xt.,
Mencken

1. *Smart Set* did not publish the play.

[NYP]

Havre de Grace
Md.

June 27—1918

My Dear Mencken:

I do not know whether you publish essays any more or not. If not send this back without examination.[1] If so see if it is anything you can use.

Th.D.

Return it to 165 W. 10th St. as I am leaving here Saturday.

1. Dreiser's essay "Hey Rub-a-Dub-Dub."

[UPL]

1524 Hollins Street
Baltimore, Md.

June 28th [1918]

Dear Dreiser:-

If I still had the same hopes and plans for The Smart Set that I had when I started, I'd take this without a moment's hesitation, and Nathan would agree. But the thing has got into such a state that a serious article would appear in it like a flash of common decency in a Methodist. Our names have not appeared as editors (on the contents page) for nearly a year. We are frankly holding our heads under water.

In fiction it is still possible, now and then, to slip in something not downright idiotic, but even in that field the chances seem to lessen. The truth is simply this: that a civilized magazine is quite impossible, at least to us.

The article in the Brooklyn Eagle, following your interview, did not surprise me.[1] The Catholics grow quite as bad as the Presbyterians. We once had a very rough bout with them.

If we ever get $2,000 to fool with, I am going to print <u>one</u> issue of a genuine magazine, and then decamp to Haiti.

Yours in Xt.,
M

1. Berenice C. Skidelsky, "Theodore Dreiser Deplores Suppression of His Novel 'The Genius' by Vice Agent," Brooklyn *Daily Eagle*, 26 May, sec. 3, 2, 5.

[NYP]

<u>165 W. 10</u>

July 16—1918

My Dear H. L. M:

I think you ought to see this.[1] It may be out of your line these days—again it may not. Sorry to note that the Mail blew up.[2] Hope it does not affect your finances too much. You noticed of course how gracefully the court has dodged the issue.[3]

Dreiser

1. Dreiser sent Mencken his satiric fantasy, the closet drama entitled, "The Court of Progress."
2. Mencken had been working for the New York *Evening Mail.* In July 1918 the publisher, Edward A. Rumsly, was charged with taking money from the Wilhelmstrasse. The new publisher broke Mencken's contract, although there was no evidence that he was involved. Mencken resolved the issue by settling for $250 of the $450 owed him under the contract.
3. After Dreiser's lawyer, Joseph Auerbach, presented a lengthy argument for *The "Genius"* before the Appellate Division Court in New York, the judges dismissed the case on a technicality. This left Dreiser with something less than a victory, since the case established no precedent for future cases.

[UPL]

1524 Hollins Street
Baltimore, Md.

July 16th [1918]

Dear Dreiser:-

You and I snort over it, and wallow generally in such florid fancies, but a fat woman with diabetes—the normal magazine reader—would stop her subscription. Hence my regrets. If I had a gift of prayer I'd have you put to a novel with a Methodist as the central character: suave, sneaking stuff, turning him inside out. What has become of "The Bulwark?" Done as you can do it, it would be worth 100 burlesques. The attack must be made by indirection.

At least eight kind friends supplied me with prompt reports of the juridic evasion. After all, it didn't surprise me. The courts are simply afraid to be decent; the time has long passed for that sort of thing. What is the next move? If I understand the law of contract, "The 'Genius'" now reverts to you. Who is to do "The Bulwark"?

These are lovely days for a man with a taste for the ironical. The bond-holders of the Mail, taking the paper back but NOT returning the money they got for it, now ban me on the ground that my stuff is immoral. My contract, running to Sept. 11th, is probably not worth a cent. They already hold up my money, honestly earned. I stand to lose about $500. It would cost twice as much to resist. My pastor counsels prayer.

In Xt.,

M

[NYP]

Aug 20—1918

Dear HL.M:

Gloom was telling me the other day that you were looking for a copy of The "Genius". Under separate cover I sent you one Monday last

Dreiser

My compliments

[UPL]

1524 Hollins Street
Baltimore, Md.

Thursday [after 20 August 1918]

Dear Dreiser:-

My best thanks for the copy of "Free".[1] I tried to get hold of you in New York Tuesday night, but couldn't raise you. Next morning hay-fever had me by the ear, and since then I have been almost all in. The trip down by train today was a terrible experience. I marvel that M.[2] could sit in a car with a man so hideous and in such a state of nerves. Today I am very wobbly.

Yours in Xt.,

M

1. *Free and Other Stories* (1918). Dreiser's inscription reads simply, "For Henry L. Mencken, from Theodore Dreiser. Aug. 20–1918. N.Y.C."
2. Marion Bloom.

[UPL]

1524 Hollins Street
Baltimore, Md.

August 21st [1918]

Dear Dreiser:-

My best thanks. But my conscious speaks up raucously: I intended the book for a fellow who is not worth so much trouble. I may decide against him, and return it. You must be very short of them. But it was a Christian act to send it. (It is not yet here)

Who in hell was your medical consultant in "Free"? Some 3rd ave. abortionist, I do suspect. Know ye that blood transfusion is not done for leaky heart valves, that the blood cannot be brought in a bottle, that the person giving it up must go to bed beside the patient (often a charming business, and responsible for most public offers), that horse blood is not thicker than human blood, that horse blood would poison the patient, etc., etc. Come to the old reliable Dr. Mencken when you want pathology. Forty years uninterrupted practise in private diseases. I cured your grandpa and I can cure you. No publicity. All medicines free. An office arranged like a pawnship. No patient can see another patient.

I hear that you are about to enter upon a military life. As for me, I am actually invited, and by the Government itself. This compliment bemuses me.

Yours in Sso. Corde Jesu,
M

[UPL]

1524 Hollins Street
Baltimore, Md.

August 24th [1918]

Dear Dreiser:-

My best thanks for "The 'Genius'". Now that it is here I incline to circulate it among the intelligentsia. They are otherwise unable to get it. Let it be at your order. That is, if you ever want it back, temporarily or permanently, a note to me will bring it instanter. I bucked at circulating my own autographed copy. You know the accidents that may happen when a lady takes a book to bed to read, and maybe some friend comes in, and she has to fight either for or against her honor. It was thus that I lost my first edition of "In His Steps".[1]

> Yours in Sso. Corde Jesu,
> M

1. *In His Steps; What Would Jesus Do?*, a best-seller by Charles Monroe Sheldon.

<u>165</u> <u>W.</u> <u>10</u>

Sept 3—1918

Dear Mencken:

Learned the other day of an easing process for hay-fever—bits of dry medicated cotton stuffed in the nose to keep out irritating germs. A victim of 20 years standing assures me it is the only thing and he has paid out money for all sorts of cures. Says it reduces the symptoms by 1/2 and even 3/4ths. I offer it for what it is worth. Glad to know the books came safely. Luck in the face of the many impending difficulties of this next year.

> Dreiser

> 1524 Hollins Street
> Baltimore, Md.

September 4th [1918]

Dear Dreiser:-

The cure has merit, but you apply it to the wrong malaise. It helps hay-fever very little, but is excellent for piles. Seriously, it gives some relief to the nose, but at the expense of the throat. Mouth-breathing, its necessary consequence, promotes laryngitis, bronchitis and asthma. I am reasonably comfortable this year. One day may be bad, but the next day is apt to be good. At all events I manage to get through some work.

My agents tell me that you begin to yearn for trench-life. Perhaps it may be God's will that we meet at the front, and jointly horn the abhorrent Hun. I grow more patriotic every day. After all, as Lieut. Hersey said, this is Our Country.

> Yours in Sso. Corde Jesu,
> Mencken

[NYP]
Oct 10—1918

[To Mencken]
Your noblest of works is before me.[1] In due season and prayerfully the same shall be considered.

Philip the Fair (HXM)

1. Probably *In Defense of Women* (1918).

[UPL]

1524 Hollins Street
Baltimore, Md.

October 25th [1918]

Dear Dreiser:-
Your "Life, Art and America" is being printed serially in The Continental Times, a Berlin paper, printed in English. Part II is in the issue for September 4th. I get the Times irregularly—it has to pass through four censorships. Part I is missing. A couple of months ago the Times printed a full page review of my Prefaces book—the best published anywhere. I mean by "best" the most exhaustive and judicious: it was often unfavorable.

I'll try to get you a full set but it will probably be impossible until after the war.

Yours in Xt.,
M

[NYP]
Oct. 27—1918

HLM
Thanks. If that thing is much copied in Germany & Austria it will do me a lot of good over here I don't think.

D

[UPL]

1524 Hollins street
Baltimore

November 25th [1918]

Dear Dreiser:-

The copy of "The 'Genius'", borrowed from you several months ago, goes back to you by this mail. My best thanks. The cognoscenti who read it were much impressed. I hesitated to lend my autographed copy, fearing that they would thumb it, but as it turns out they bathed before reading, and so the copy I am returning is as good as new. They will do some useful gabbling.

Last week, being in New York, I succumbed to alcohol—the first time in many months. I was with John Williams, and now he says that we got into a discussion of your virtues and finally decided to call and pay our respects to you, and that we found you out and left our cards. If this is true, then I must have been very drunk indeed, for I have no recollection of it whatsoever. Let this episode teach you a lesson: rum is a serpent. I am too far gone but from the depths of a drunkard's grave I beseech you to take warning by my folly. My one excuse is that I am a widower, and lonesome. This is another thing to avoid: the passion of romantic love.

I enclose the cast of a play I think of doing.[1]

Yours in Xt.,
H. L. M.

1. This is missing.

[NYP]
Dec. 4—1918

My Dear Mencken:

I have given strict orders to the janitor to sound "lights out" whenever editors, publishers, critics and managers appear in this vicinity. Actors are stopped at the confines of the village by the police. Only suitable credentials and a safe conduct will gain you admission here. I learn on good authority that you are to be awarded a distinguished service medal by our beloved English Premier, Lloyd George, for your poetic effusions intended to hearten the British Army during its darkest hours

I am sir, with renewed assurances of my distinguished private comments

Dreiser X.Y.

[UPL]

H. L. Mencken
1524 Hollins St.
Baltimore.

December 6th [1918]

Dear Dreiser:-

Why not simplify all that guard by employing a one-legged soldier to stand at the door? He is welcome to my medals. Beside, he will be in the fashion. Pretty soon the whole country will be flooded with damaged veterans. When I was a boy there were still 7,000,000 remaining from the Civil War.

Nevertheless, the real objection to the Jews is that, with the lynching started, they let the other two members of the Trinity go.

Dei et Apostolicae Sedis Gratia,
Mencken

[NYP]
[December 1918]

To Henry L. Mencken:
Critic, Poet, Editor, Essayist, Raconteur and gourmet—
To the continued and careful perusal of whose searching and illuminating criticisms I acknowledge my debt for style and much of my most popular subject matter.

Gratefully and with reverence
Charles Garvice[1]

Regents 9K. London. Christmas 1918

1. Dreiser sent along with this the book jacket of *Violet,* by the popular British novelist Charles Garvice.

[NYP]
[December 1918]

To my kind critic and friend—Henry L. Mencken from his sincere admirer—

Bertha M. Clay
Christmas, 1918

A rare first edition which I have just recovered.[1]

1. Dreiser wrote this on the cover of the 1908 edition of Bertha M. Clay's *When Love Lures: Or, No Thought of Danger.*

[UPL]

H. L. Mencken
1524 Hollins St.
Baltimore.

December 25th [1918]

Dear Bertha:-

What angel whispered to you to send me your lovely book? Last night, anticipating a heavy strain upon the liver and lights today, I took a dose of castor oil. Unluckily, my mind was upon other things, and so I swallowed a whole seidel of the damned stuff. Today I have been a prisoner within white-tiled walls, but my long vigil has been made happy by your incomparable tale of true love. It is sweet. It is touching. It is lovely.

No, I have not heard from Theo lately. I doubt that he loves you any more. The last news I had of him was that he had been converted to the patriot cause by the noble work of the Y.M.C.A. The man is rough externally, but he has virtue in him at bottom. I hear that he will take to the stump for the League of Nations.

May God bless you in 1919, say I!

Yours in Sso. Corde Jesu,
Henri

[NYP]
Dec.25 1918

Dear Friend Henry:

Will you be good enough to accept this inscribed copy of my latest and best work[1] with my deepest acknowledgements of your sincere and unselfish help and criticism during many trying hours—

—and all my best wishes for your dearest happiness throughout the coming year   May heaven protect and prosper you, Henry dear,

Laura

The Brambles—Flatbush, Brooklyn
Xmas 1918

1. Dreiser wrote this on the inside cover of *Kidnapped at the Altar*, by Laura Jean Libbey.

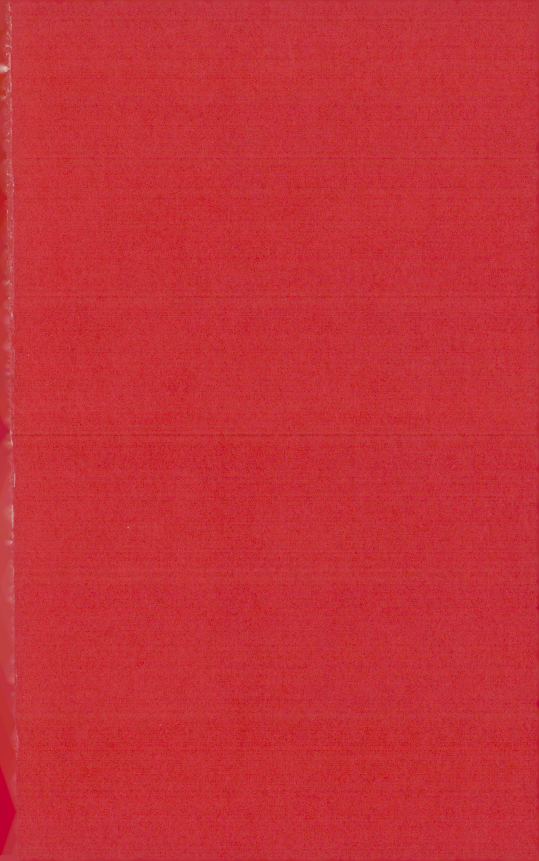